A Sephardi Sea

SEPHARDI AND MIZRAHI STUDIES
Harvey E. Goldberg and Matthias Lehmann, editors

A Sephardi Sea

JEWISH MEMORIES
ACROSS THE
MODERN MEDITERRANEAN

Dario Miccoli

INDIANA UNIVERSITY PRESS

This book is a publication of

Indiana University Press
Office of Scholarly Publishing
Herman B Wells Library 350
1320 East 10th Street
Bloomington, Indiana 47405 USA

iupress.org

© 2022 by Dario Miccoli

All rights reserved
No part of this book may be reproduced or utilized in any form or by any means, electronic or mechanical, including photocopying and recording, or by any information storage and retrieval system, without permission in writing from the publisher. The paper used in this publication meets the minimum requirements of the American National Standard for Information Sciences—Permanence of Paper for Printed Library Materials, ANSI Z39.48–1992.

Manufactured in the United States of America
First printing 2022

Library of Congress Cataloging-in-Publication Data

Names: Miccoli, Dario, author.
Title: A Sephardi Sea : Jewish memories across the modern Mediterranean / Dario Miccoli.
Description: Bloomington : Indiana University Press, 2022. | Series: Sephardi and Mizrahi studies | Includes bibliographical references and index.
Identifiers: LCCN 2022010016 (print) | LCCN 2022010017 (ebook) | ISBN 9780253062925 (hardback) | ISBN 9780253062932 (paperback) | ISBN 9780253062949 (ebook)
Subjects: LCSH: Jews—Mediterranean Region—Identity. | Jews—Foreign countries—Identity. | Jews—Foreign countries—Social life and customs. | Jewish diaspora—History. | Jews—Migrations—History. | Mizrahim. | Collective memory.
Classification: LCC DS135.M43 M537 2022 (print) | LCC DS135.M43 (ebook) | DDC 909/.04924—dc23/eng/20220427
LC record available at https://lccn.loc.gov/2022010016
LC ebook record available at https://lccn.loc.gov/2022010017

CONTENTS

Acknowledgments vii

Note on Transliteration ix

Introduction: Being Jewish in the Mediterranean   1

1. Writing Exile: Sephardi and *Mizrahi* Literary Memories   23
2. (In)tangible Heritages: Migrant Associations, Museums, and the Internet   64
3. An Unfinished Present: Migrations of Sephardi and *Mizrahi* Memory   120

Conclusion: Afterlives of Exile   176

References 185

Index 215

ACKNOWLEDGMENTS

THIS BOOK IS THE RESULT of years of research and writing, during which I came to meet and talk to many people in places as different as Venice, Florence, Rome, Jerusalem, Tel Aviv, Paris, and New York. It was made possible thanks to the generous funding of the Rothschild Foundation Hanadiv Europe, the Department of Asian and North African Studies of Ca' Foscari University, the Erasmus+ Programme of the European Commission, the Memorial Foundation for Jewish Culture, and the Fondazione Vigevani—Associazione Italiana Amici dell'Università Ebraica di Gerusalemme.

Having now reached the end of this journey, I wish to thank all the friends with whom I discussed parts of my research, and particularly Michèle Baussant, who hosted me more than once in her Jerusalem home and read earlier versions of the manuscript, Giorgia Foscarini, Piera Rossetto, Emanuela Trevisan Semi, and lastly the colleagues of the Centre de recherche français à Jérusalem. Parts of the book were presented in conferences and seminars, where I could profit from the comments and knowledge of colleagues. I want to mention the GDRI research group Socio-anthropologie des judaïsmes, coordinated by Chantal Bordes-Benayoun, the friends of SeSaMO—Italian Society for Middle East Studies, Aviad Moreno, Yaron Tsur, and the participants in the conference New Directions: Sephardi and Mizrahi Migrations in Global Contexts (Bar-Ilan University and Ben-Gurion University of the Negev), and the research group Defeated Memories, hosted at the French Research Centre in Humanities and Social Sciences, Prague. Ketzia Alon, David Guedj, Silvina Schammah Gesser, the late Esther Schely-Newman, and many others shared with me their knowledge of Sephardi and *Mizrahi* studies and of Israel more generally.

Among my interviewees, I owe special gratitude to Ada Aharoni, the members of the Florentine association Donne per la pace, *rav* Joseph Levi, and Levana Zamir. I am most grateful to all the other people mentioned in the book and those who—in Israel, France, Italy, and the US—answered my questions and shared their memories of the Sephardi Mediterranean. Douglas Feiden kindly allowed me to reproduce a photograph of his late wife Lucette Lagnado. David Lellouche gave me permission to use as the book cover a painting of his father, Jules, that portrays the promenade of La Marsa, near Tunis. Finally, I want to thank the archivists and librarians who helped me in the pursuit of my research at the Ben-Tzvi Institute of Jerusalem, the National Library of Israel, the Jewish Museum of Rome, and Ca' Foscari University Library. The series editors, Harvey Goldberg and Matthias B. Lehmann, supported this project with enthusiasm and gave very important suggestions. This, together with the valuable feedback of the anonymous readers, helped me rethink many aspects of the book and hopefully improve it. At Indiana University Press, Gary Dunham and his team—particularly Ashante Thomas—assisted me with kindness from the very beginning. Carol McGillivray managed the copyediting, and Beverley Winkler attentively indexed the manuscript.

The first section of chapter 1 was previously published as "An Old-New Land: Tunisia, France and Israel in Two Novels of Chochana Boukhobza," in *Contemporary Sephardic and Mizrahi Literature: A Diaspora*, ed. Dario Miccoli (London: Routledge, 2017), 31–42. Chapter 2 re-elaborates subjects I have already discussed in the following essays: "Sephardic Jewish Heritage across the Mediterranean: Migration, Memory and New Diasporas," in *Cultural Heritage: Scenarios 2015–2017*, ed. Simona Pinton and Lauso Zagato (Venice: Edizioni Ca' Foscari, 2018), 485–505; "Les Juifs du Maroc, Internet et la construction d'une diaspora numérique," *Expressions Maghrébines* 13, no. 1 (2014): 75–94; and "Digital Museums: Narrating and Preserving the History of Egyptian Jews on the Internet," in *Memory and Ethnicity: Ethnic Museums in Israel and the Diaspora*, ed. Emanuela Trevisan Semi, Dario Miccoli, and Tudor Parfitt (Newcastle: Cambridge Scholars, 2013), 195–222.

NOTE ON TRANSLITERATION

THE TRANSLITERATION FROM HEBREW TO English follows a simplified system based on the *Encyclopaedia Judaica* general transliteration rules: ' stands for *'ayin*, ' for *'alef*, v for *vav*, h for both *heh* and *ḥet*, kh/k for *kaf*, q for *qof*, tz for *tzade* and the sign — between two or more words indicates the construct case.

With regard to Arabic words, ' stands for *'ayin*, ' for *'alif*, h for both *hā'* and *ḥā'*, kh for *khā'*, q for *qaf*, k for *kaf*. The emphatic letters (e.g., *ṣād, ḍād*) are not distinguished from the nonemphatic ones.

A Sephardi Sea

INTRODUCTION

Being Jewish in the Mediterranean

A SHIP CALLED *MASSALIA* DEPARTED from the quay of Alexandria in March 1963. Among the passengers were the members of a Jewish family that, until then, had lived in an apartment in Malaka Nazli Street, in central Cairo. They were going to Marseille with twenty-six suitcases, and clearly, they were not embarking on a holiday to France but on a much longer and more painful kind of voyage: they were leaving Egypt, never to return. A photograph (fig. I.1) remains of the long, extraordinary days spent on the ship that took this family from one side of the Mediterranean to the other. It portrays Loulou and Léon—the daughter and the father—holding on to each other while sitting on a canvas chair. "Past and future looked as vague and out of focus as the lone photograph that survives of my father and me aboard the *Massalia*. There we are, huddled on the upper desk, while behind us, dozens of people sit silently watching the sea. It is," Lucette Lagnado, born in Cairo in 1956 and the author of these moving autobiographical lines, wrote, "like a scene from a cruise ship ad gone awry: none of the passengers seem happy, least of all my father. In his dark felt hat, jacket, and tie, he is dressed far too formally for a sea crossing. He stares ahead at the camera, looking sullen and worn and, for the first time, old. I share his melancholy. My head is lowered, my eyes are downcast, and if it is possible for a six-year-old girl to feel defeated, then I look as if I, too, have lost my purpose."[1]

This book tells the story of Loulou, Léon, and of hundreds of thousands of Jews from the southern shore of the Mediterranean who, between the late 1940s and the mid-1960s, migrated or—in most cases—were forced to leave their country of birth for Europe, Israel, the Americas, or even Australia and

Figure I.1. Lucette Lagnado and her father, Léon, 1963.
Source: Douglas Feiden/Lagnado family archive.

South Africa. Theirs is a story of contrasted feelings for a vanished world whose echoes many can still hear, as if it were a phantasmic absence and the shadow of a past that becomes also present and future. Certainly, if one were to search for the exact year, day, or event that caused the end of this world and therefore the departure of the Jews from North Africa and Egypt, one would not find it. However, one could hear or read dozens, if not hundreds, of stories similar to that cited above in Lagnado's memoir *The Man in the White Sharkskin Suit*.

These stories took place in cities as distant as Tangiers and Alexandria, in different years—around 1948, in 1952, 1956, or even 1967—and were the result of a series of events that determined the departure and migration of these Jewish diasporas, as well as the beginning of a new kind of postcolonial existence. That said, in the cases of both the North African and Egyptian Jews who migrated to Israel and those who instead settled in a country in Europe, the migration took place within a Mediterranean world that they knew well. However, with reference to Israel and the so-called *Mizrahim* (lit. "Easterners, Oriental [Jews]"), the literary scholar Hannan Hever has written that when the Jews of the Middle East and North Africa started to migrate to this country after 1948 and especially in the 1950s, they did not arrive *from the sea*; they did not have to face a long boat trip from Europe to an unknown East—as that which the great Hebrew writer Shmuel Yosef Agnon narrated in his novel *Only Yesterday* (1945). Rather, they came from neighboring areas that always had been in more direct contact with Palestine.[2] As for the Jews who migrated from the southern Mediterranean shore to Europe, they too landed in a continent that was not entirely foreign: many already knew the language of the country of immigration, and some—from the time of colonialism or even earlier than that—had had significant cultural and economic ties with the West.[3] But then why was the act of leaving so painful, and why, more than half a century afterward, is its memory still so tangible?

To answer these questions, one should remember that by the 1950s the Mediterranean region—both its northern and southern shore—was starting to look very different from that in which these Jews and their forebears had been born. The uprooting of the Jews from the Arab world took place at a time of rapid political and social changes that brought about profound shiftings in the identity of these migrants and in their cultural attachment to the homeland: both to the old country of birth and to the new country of immigration. *A Sephardi Sea* will look at the memories that emerged in the aftermath of the migrations that occurred in the 1950s and 1960s, when most of the Middle Eastern and North African Jews left their countries of birth, following the establishment of the State of Israel, the outbreak of the Arab-Israeli conflict, and the process of decolonization. At the core of the book is the remembrance of a Sephardi Jewish world born along the southern shore of the Mediterranean Sea, which—with affection, sadness, nostalgia, and sometimes anger—nowadays is perceived as vanished forever.

More precisely, my aim is to see how the centuries-old history and cultural heritage of the Jews who lived in the countries of the southern Mediterranean shore is remembered and transmitted at a time when Jews and (Muslim) Arabs, Europe, Israel, and North Africa are often envisioned as irreconcilable ethno-religious groups or cultural/national spaces. In the following chapters, I will argue that after the mass migrations, this diverse and sometimes divergent Sephardi Mediterranean world—rooted in a physical/real space and in a long history of Arab-Jewish coexistence that, in different and not always linear ways, had gone on for centuries—reconsolidated in the shape of a shared cultural imaginary and a connecting memory that created new diasporas. Over the decades, this brought the Jews of places as different as Casablanca, Djerba, and Cairo closer to one another, while separating them from their former (Arab) neighbors and also underlining their otherness from the European Jews or the Ashkenazi Israelis. The migration consolidated the emergence of a constellation of identities that, one next to the other, have produced a new, and relatively unified, memory. In this context, the Mediterranean stands as a metaphor for a life that disappeared and, at the same time, becomes a frontier that sanctions the increased distance between past and present: it is a site of loss, where a vanished Jewish past is being looked at nostalgically or, in some cases, reinvented through artistic creativity. Therefore, in a way that resembles what occurred to the European Jewish worlds destroyed during the Holocaust, places like Meknès, Alexandria, Benghazi, Constantine—and others that will not be included in this book, such as Baghdad or Aleppo—"[have] become accessible to pilgrimages real and imagined, ritual and literary, as unredeemable and *indestructible ruin*," in an ongoing history of exile that "territorializes those lands as an (already lost) home."[4]

The fact of having crossed the Mediterranean to migrate and start a new life in Europe or Israel binds together the rather different Jewish diasporas that once thrived in North Africa and in the Middle East. But the Mediterranean is also the sea along whose shores many of them still live and dream: a space, writes the historian David Abulafia, bearing many stories and names, from the Latin *mare nostrum* and the German *Mittelmeer*, to the Arabic *bahr al-Rum* ("the sea of the Greeks") and *al-bahr al-abyad* ("the white sea"), and finally the Hebrew traditional expression *yam ha-gadol* ("Great Sea").[5] That said, in the last few decades, the Mediterranean undoubtedly lost much of its historic evocative power as a sea of encounter and dialogue, to become a divisive space where both old and new ethno-religious and national struggles have developed. It is true that if one looks at the Mediterranean from the point of view of classical Judaism, connectivity and the existence of social, cultural, and commercial bonds between different people—one of its alleged key features—never seems to have been prominent, since a kind of particularistic identity already dominated ancient Jewish culture. But nonetheless, early modern and modern Mediterranean Jewish societies can be said to have taken a more ambivalent path: one of proximity and reciprocity, exchange and confrontation.[6] Taking this into consideration, *A Sephardi Sea* goes back to the memories of a bygone Sephardi Mediterranean to see how this world, and the memories that come with it, are preserved in three national contexts—Israel, France, and Italy—where the Jews of the Middle East and North Africa and their descendants migrated and nowadays live.

As said, *A Sephardi Sea* looks at the migration of the Jews of the Arab world as a historical event that encompasses, on the one hand, Jewish and Israeli history, and, on the other, that of the Mediterranean and of decolonization. This is why it is crucial to look at the *'aliyah* (lit. "ascent [to Zion], migration") to Israel—where the majority of the Jews of the Arab world ended up resettling— and at the Jewish migratory flows toward countries of the Western world in a comparative manner, as they are part of the same, albeit diversified, population movement. If the choice of focusing on Israel may seem self-evident because of ethno-national and demographic reasons, and because it was there that most of the approximately 800,000–850,000 Middle Eastern and North African Jews settled, paying attention to the case of France is equally unavoidable. In fact, about 200,000 Jews from the southern shore of the Mediterranean migrated to this country, which until the 1950s and 1960s had been the major colonial power in North Africa.[7] Italy, on the other hand, saw the arrival of around 4,000–5,000 Jews mainly from its only North African colony, Libya, especially in the late 1960s, and of others of Egyptian origin, as well as from Tunisia, the Dodecanese islands, and later on Lebanon and Iran.[8] So, whereas France hosts a Jewish population that nowadays is largely made of North African—particularly Algerian—Jews, in Italy the memory of the Sephardi Mediterranean only concerns a minority of the country's Jewish population and still remains on the margins. Taken together, these three spaces offer a broad spectrum of the Sephardi migrations, of what triggered them, and most of all of how the Jews adjusted to three different social and national contexts, which in turn produced alternative yet complementary memorial approaches and postmigratory identities. The cases of Italy and France, because of their colonial past as well as the characteristics of their respective (and preexisting) Jewish diasporas, also permit one to grasp the differences present inside Europe concerning the place of migrants and of a minority group like the Jews in the society.

Furthermore, these countries have very different migration histories: if, especially after 1948, Israel has seen the arrival of Jews from all over the world, France from the 1960s has hosted a large number of North African and colonial migrants.[9] On the other hand, despite the fact that Italy too saw the return of colonial settlers from Libya, the Dodecanese islands, and Italian East Africa (Eritrea, Ethiopia, Somalia), until more or less the 1970s it has been essentially a country of emigration—even internal emigration from the south to the north—more than immigration from abroad. Only in the last three decades has the presence of immigrants from the Middle East and North Africa become numerically more relevant.[10] In selecting these three cases, I am of course aware that other spaces—such as Great Britain, Canada, the US, or Latin America— could have been chosen or added to the picture.[11] The comparative focus on Israel, France, and Italy—and, consequently, on the North African and Egyptian

Jewish communities that migrated in larger numbers to all three countries—is a point of departure that hopefully will open the way for other research and future voyages to continue tracking the manifold itineraries of the Sephardi and *Mizrahi* migrant memory.

Aside from the postmigratory differences that the country of immigration has determined and that in some ways continue to exist, it should be noted that there was also great heterogeneity in the premigratory history and identity of the Jewish communities of North Africa and Egypt. Therefore, both the *'aliyah* to Israel and the migration or so-called repatriation to the colonial metropole did not make these events less problematic: on the contrary, many perceived them as—and actually, in most cases they were—the beginning of a (postcolonial) exile in which the identity of the migrant was lost and then had to be slowly reconstructed. But although the migration caused a rift between *before* and *after*, between Jews and Arabs, in the course of the years that identity vacuum has been filled by practices of memory and heritage making. By intersecting parallel histories and identities and assembling both ancient and new mnemonic, imaginative frameworks—from the Bible and *Sefarad* to Zionism and the Holocaust—these Jewish migrants were able to construct a more shared Sephardi and *Mizrahi* past and transmit it to the next generations.

SEPHARDIS, MIZRAHIM, ARAB JEWS

This book takes its cue, of course, from the history of Jewish-Arab relations—a field of study that has developed greatly in recent years and that, since its beginnings, has proposed divergent readings of a past perceived as very controversial. For instance, in *Jews and Arabs*, published in 1955, the renowned historian of the Cairo *genizah*, Shlomo Dov Goitein, asserts that "the history of Jewish Arab relations is so rich in examples of significant contacts and cultural cooperation. . . . It reveals an amazing picture of close affinities between the two peoples."[12] On the other hand, the Tunisian Jewish writer Albert Memmi contends that "the famous idyllic life of the Jews in the Arab countries is a myth! The truth is, and I am obliged to go back to it, that we were first of all a minority in an hostile setting."[13] While the two surely stem from different ideological and biographical positioning, their approaches also exemplify the difficulty of historicizing the Jews of the Arab Muslim world in a univocal manner. This is because especially since the advent of Zionism and even more so of the State of Israel—as I will later explain in more detail—the categories of Jew and Arab have been seen increasingly in opposition to each other.

Even in recent years, Sephardi and *Mizrahi* history has continued to be an intellectual battlefield of sorts, in which the proponents of either an idyllic or very negative and conflictual vision of Jewish-Arab relations confront each other. Whereas for some historians the relations between Jews and Arabs have more or less always been excellent and worsened only in the aftermath of the birth of the State of Israel and because of the Arab-Israeli conflict, for others, the mass migrations of the 1950s were the final step in a much longer history of Jewish subalternity to the Muslim majority, exemplified by the Islamic juridical category of *dhimma*.[14] Despite the fact that in the Ottoman Empire the former was abolished in the mid-nineteenth century, the migrations and expulsion of the Jews from the Arab world for some scholars "can only be understood by accepting that it is the culmination of the long practice of the *dhimma*."[15] However, if in a case like Yemen this probably is valid, in others—like Egypt, Tunisia, or cities like Istanbul, Baghdad, and Smyrna—the Jews were an integral component of the late Ottoman and post-Ottoman society and took part in politics both at local and at national levels and in the 1940s and 1950s also contributed to the formation of Middle Eastern leftist and anticolonial movements together with their compatriots. This suggests that it is possible to adopt a more nuanced approach that sees the Jewish past in the Arab lands as made of moments both of interaction and of conflict.

A Sephardi Sea follows this assumption and sees the modern history of the Jews of the Middle East and North Africa—or, as concerns the book more precisely, of those living in the area that goes from Morocco to Egypt—as characterized by progress and harmony, as well as clashes and occasional violence. For this reason, that history's decline and end cannot be understood in a single manner or by recurring to monocausal explanations.[16] In saying so, I do not intend to abstain from taking a position in the intellectual debate surrounding the Jews of this region but to acknowledge the necessity of having more than one answer to the question of why they left their countries of birth and what kind of historical trajectories this determined for them.

It is undoubted that the mass migrations from the Middle East and North Africa represent a foundational, and in many ways still underestimated, moment in modern Jewish history. This is not just because, as I said, it has led to the formation of new diasporas and identities but because—were we to look at these migrations carefully—it contributed to a reshaping of the cultural, social, and political connections between the Jewish Diaspora, Europe, and the Arab world and the meaning of Arabness and Jewishness. By looking at the memorial itineraries along which these Jews—"*Sépharades sans patrie* but always patriots of their mythology"[17]—have been preserving and transmitting their past *in* and *as* the present, this book aims to discuss more generally the impact of migration and exile on processes of identity and heritage making. From this perspective, exploring the complexities of Sephardi memory and the contexts in which it is still developing helps to elucidate phenomena that go beyond Jewish history, and invest the modern world at an age of increased globalization and mobility.

At this point, a few words on definitions are due. First, with the expression Sephardi and *Mizrahi* Jews, the book only refers to the Jews born in Middle Eastern and North African countries and their descendants. The term Sephardi is not used to indicate the whole of the Sephardi Diaspora—which exists also outside the Arab Muslim world in places as different as the Netherlands, Italy, Bulgaria, and Greece[18]—but to signify the Jews, some of whom are actual descendants of Iberian exiles, who lived in Arab Muslim countries. More precisely, in the absence of a similarly encompassing term and following the contemporary French and English usage of the word, with Sephardi I refer to the Jews of the Middle East and North Africa who now live in the Diaspora.

Mizrahi ("Easterner"), on the other hand, designates a Jew of Middle Eastern or North African ancestry who lives in Israel. This category gained usage in the State of Israel especially since the 1980s, first in academic circles, and became standard during the 1990s. Before then, more common terms were either *'edot ha-mizrah* ("Eastern ethnicities") or, especially in official documents and for statistical purposes, classifications that referred to the continent or region of origin—for example, the expression *yehudei 'Afriqah ve-'Asiah* ("Jews from Africa and Asia"). Whereas *'edot ha-mizrah* resonated with continuing traditions from abroad, *Mizrahim* underlines the discriminatory practices suffered by newcomers from the Middle East and North Africa.[19] By opting for the term *Mizrahi*, I do not mean to underscore the internal diversity of Israelis of Middle Eastern and North African ancestry—something that numerous scholars, from Ella Shohat to Yehudah Shenhav, Yaron Tsur, and Sami Shalom-Chetrit, have demonstrated—but to acknowledge the centrality the term acquired over the last decades in Israel and in the public debate more generally. The term has even been politically reclaimed by some *Mizrahi* scholars and activists, countering its initial derogatoriness.

Unless when explicitly used by my informants or already present in the sources that I quote, I will refrain from adopting the definition of Arab Jew. This category, which had been used at least since the early twentieth century by Jews, especially Jewish intellectuals, living in places such as Palestine, Egypt, and Iraq—and which is still sometimes used, in its Spanish translation *judío arabe*, in Latin America to indicate the descendants of Jews from the Middle East and North Africa—has been reassessed recently as a category that would highlight the historical bonds that existed among Jews, Muslims, and Christians of the Ottoman and post-Ottoman world as regards language, culture, and in some cases even national identity. At the same time, if it probably fits very well in the case of the Jews of Iraq or Yemen, it is dubious that it can be applied as easily to diasporas like the Algerian or Egyptian—whose members from the late nineteenth century were not exclusively, or not mainly, Arabic speaking and did not necessarily identify as Arabs. Additionally, the category of Arab Jew sometimes seems to have to do more with today's intellectual discussions and preoccupations—as a tool of rapprochement between Jews and Arabs, Israelis and Palestinians—than with the historical reality and identities it wishes to represent.[20]

What all these definitions have in common is that they construct new collective identities for different Jewish diasporas, which share an only partially similar geographic and cultural origin. In other words, they contribute to the creation of contemporary diasporas that have slowly substituted—or, I should rather say, been superimposed over—those that existed before the birth of Israel and the migratory waves of the 1950s and 1960s. Moreover, they provoke new feelings of belonging that do not merely grow on top of previous urban/regional/national labels—like "Moroccan Jews" or "Jews of Alexandria"—but also of the new, postcolonial frameworks and national ideologies, such as Zionism, that these Jews encountered more directly after the migration.

A HISTORY OF THE JEWS IN THE MEDITERRANEAN

As already mentioned, up until the mid-twentieth century, the southern shore of the Mediterranean hosted a thriving Jewish population, which throughout the centuries played a significant role in the economic as well as social and cultural history of the region. On the eve of the 1948 war, around 285,000 Jews lived in Morocco; 140,000 in Algeria; 110,000 in Tunisia; 38,000 in Libya; 75,000 in Egypt; 20,000 in Lebanon; and finally around 80,000 in Turkey.[21] They belonged to different Jewish groups—Sephardi, Ashkenazi, Italian, Romaniot, and those that followed the many eastern *minhagim* ("rites")—and shared a variety of geographical origins. Some had been living in a country, for instance Morocco, since very ancient times; others had settled in North Africa or in cities of the Ottoman Empire, like Salonika, Smyrna, and Istanbul, after the 1492 expulsion from the Iberian Peninsula. Finally, still others had moved from southern or even eastern Europe to port cities like Alexandria and Beirut mainly for economic reasons in the course of the nineteenth and early twentieth centuries.

First the Napoleonic expedition to Egypt in 1798 and then, in the following century, colonialism—think of Algeria, which in 1830 became a French colony—stimulated new ties between the Jews of the two shores of the sea. Even before then, however, Jews living all over the eastern Mediterranean and in North Africa had been in contact with those of southern Europe in particular.[22] Some worked as tradesmen and entrepreneurs, often acting as mediators between the local authorities and foreign powers, and for this reason they obtained a European nationality. A different case is that of the Jews of Algeria, who in 1870 were granted en masse French nationality with the Crémieux Decree.[23] These Jewries experienced the passage from a more traditional societal model still connected to the Ottoman *millet* to a modern one, at the top of which stood a Westernized and well-off elite. On the whole, whereas some communities—like those of rural Marocco or the Saharan M'zab—remained more at the margins of processes of socioeconomic modernization, others, based in larger urban centers, experienced evident changes in their life: think of the Jews of Tunis or Marrakech (Tunisia and Morocco becoming French protectorates in 1881 and 1912, respectively).[24]

That said, one should remember that Jewish life in the region was not always easy, and some anti-Jewish incidents did happen. For example, in 1840 an infamous case of blood libel accusation—the Damascus affair—took place in Syria. Similar cases also occurred in Alexandria (1881) and Corfu (1891), although these were mainly due to the socioeconomic rivalries that opposed the Jews to local Greek-Orthodox communities, and in some cases to the spreading of originally European antisemitic stereotypes.[25] In France, the 1894 Dreyfus affair and the virulent campaign that it engendered are nowadays remembered as one of the most infamous episodes of antisemitism in nineteenth-century Europe. The affair also affected the French colonial empire, particularly Algeria— as evident from the *crise anti-juive* of Oran (1895–1905), when an anti-Jewish municipal council supported by the local settler population was installed and subsequently put in place a number of discriminatory measures. Then, with the spreading of Zionism, as well as with the advent of Fascist regimes in Europe and their ramifications on the southern shore of the Mediterranean, the situation for the Jews worsened. The antisemitic legislation enacted by Fascist Italy in 1938 and then by Vichy France in 1941 was in fact applied to Jews living in the colonies of Libya—under Italian colonial rule since 1912—and in French North Africa.[26]

Zionism, officially founded in 1896 when Theodore Herzl published his manifesto *Der Judenstaat*, at first had a limited impact on the Jews of the Arab world. Throughout the Middle East and North Africa, Zionist activities only interested a very small number of people—in part because of the influence of the assimilationist ideology promoted by the French Jewish philanthropic and educational institution Alliance Israélite Universelle.[27] With the fall of the Ottoman Empire (1918), the Jews were however no longer part of an interethnic entity but of nation-states increasingly built around an Arab Muslim identity. Whereas many preferred not to be directly involved in national politics, some, especially from the 1920s and 1930s, turned to nationalist movements or to the local Communist parties. From the late 1920s, as the migration of Jews to British Palestine increased, so worsened the relations between Jews and Arabs. The radicalization of the Middle Eastern political arena in the 1930s, and the growing relevance of Islamic movements like the Muslim Brotherhood, founded in Egypt in 1929, led to an increased sociopolitical marginalization of the Jews. From the 1940s, Zionism therefore started to attract more people, and the migration to the Land of Israel grew.[28]

Concerning the cultural and religious realms, from the mid-nineteenth century more secular models of instruction replaced the traditional religious ones, the Talmud Torah or, in Ladino, *meldar*. Important changes occurred in the field of welfare, where a better-organized philanthropy started to coexist aside the traditional communal *tzedaqah* ("charity"). Numerous philanthropic associations, literary societies, and women's circles were founded throughout the region. Also, the Bnei Brit—the Jewish freemasonry founded in New York in 1843—left a mark, especially in big urban centers like Cairo and Beirut. As a consequence of all that, the Jews started to found modern-style newspapers and to write secular literature, as well as history books influenced by the European historiography. In Salonika and Istanbul, and then in North Africa and the Middle East, a flourishing literature and press written in Ladino, French, Arabic, or Hebrew began around the second half of the nineteenth century. That said, while acknowledging that modernization was triggered by external factors like colonialism and European influence, one should not overlook the impact of the Ottoman reformism of the mid-nineteenth century.[29] Moving to the analysis of the rabbinic worlds, one should mention that the Maghrebine and Ottoman religious culture had always been characterized by a relatively high degree of flexibility, at least compared to Ashkenazi Europe, for example when it came to accommodating the Jewish law to the changes faced by the region's communities.[30]

On the other hand, the family maintained quite a traditional structure. That said, even though polygamy was permitted in several North African and Middle Eastern communities, from the late nineteenth century it became uncommon or disappeared in those most touched by processes of sociocultural modernization. Moreover, women acquired greater—if still limited—visibility in the public sphere, working, for instance, as teachers and collaborating to philanthropic and Zionist associations.[31] The influence of modern habits and gender models grew, leading to the birth of a Westernized elite increasingly afar both from the Jewish lower strata and in some cases from the Arab Muslim majority—especially in urban centers of North Africa and the eastern Mediterranean. On the other hand, the conversion to other religious faiths remained on the whole quite a rare event.[32]

The Second World War and the Holocaust determined the end of entire Sephardi communities in the eastern Mediterranean region that dated back to the early modern era, for instance those of Salonika and of the island of Rhodes. As for North Africa and Egypt, some Jews living in areas in which the Nazi armies arrived, like Libya and Tunisia, were deported to Nazi concentration camps or were interned and died in labor and prison camps located in the Maghreb itself.[33] However, in most cases it was only with the birth of the State of Israel in 1948, the rise of pan-Arabism in the 1950s, and the worsening of the Arab-Israeli conflict, that the condition truly deteriorated. Then, a difficult period—which resulted in expulsions and migrations from the countries of birth—started for all the Jews from North Africa and the Middle East. Those who moved to Israel faced very harsh years before adjusting to the new homeland, and they long remained at the margins of the Jewish state. For reasons ranging from the possession of a European passport to one's professional future or political positioning, others preferred or found it easier to migrate to Europe—especially France, Britain, and to a certain extent Italy—or the US, Australia, Canada, and Latin America. Nowadays, in North Africa, only Morocco and Tunisia continue to host a relatively significant Jewish community of around 2,000–2,500 and less than 2,000 people, respectively. On the other hand, only a few dozen Jews are still living in Egypt, Algeria, and Libya.

EXILIC HOMECOMINGS

By taking this historical background in context, the book aims to understand how the North African and Middle Eastern past is remembered and transmitted in the aftermath of the mass migrations and what Sephardi and *Mizrahi* Jews are doing to include it in the national history of the countries in which they now live, and in the public sphere more generally. The book does not focus explicitly on private spaces, like the family or the home, but on public ones, such as migrant associations, museums, the internet, and the political realm. Great importance is assigned to the analysis of the transmission of memory through the arts, particularly literature and self-writing, but also cinema. For this reason, one needs to start by asking what memory is and to what extent it depends on a variety of social and cultural contexts. Our knowledge of the past is in fact inextricably connected to the outside world and to that of the places and nations we inhabit(ed), as well as to our individual and collective perceptions of it. For Maurice Halbwachs, even though memory always functions within a collective context, it is "made of notions that are singular and historic," which "resemble those of the general society" but "are nevertheless distinct."[34] The passage of memory—which in *La mémoire, l'histoire, l'oubli* Paul Ricoeur interprets as the only resource to gain knowledge of the past—from the individual to the collective level thus becomes one of the foundational links between memory and history.[35] For the Jewish people, their history, perhaps more than other ethno-religious and national groups, since the very beginning and even more so with the advent of the diaspora in 70 AD, was based on an imperative to remember.[36] However, this does not mean that all Jewish memories were granted the same importance in the historical construction of the past. Indeed, the case of the Jews from the Arab world is less known than the European Jewish one, which, especially in the aftermath of the Holocaust, has been at the forefront of both scholarly research and public debates.

I already have explained that the Jews of the Arab world—similarly to the Jews of Europe—never formed a coherent or homogeneous diaspora. As regards this term, I follow the definition provided by Daniel Boyarin, who, looking at the history of the Babylonian Talmud, revised the notion of diaspora as a fundamentally cultural/discursive experience in which "there is no center" and which is not necessarily "a record of trauma."[37] This interpretative framework is of great relevance for the Sephardi and *Mizrahi* case, in which the movement of ideas, goods, and of course people across the Mediterranean highlights the absence of a clear center and, even after 1948, the persistence of physical and imaginative *allers* and *retours* between overlapping homelands and diasporas. One may even talk of the Sephardi and *Mizrahi* Diaspora as being anchored not in a single territory but in "a reticular territory *à l'échelle de la Méditerranée*."[38] For these reasons, the migrations of the 1950s and 1960s in most cases were an exile that, in the course of the years—because of personal reasons, due to the passing of time, or under the influence of national ideologies that conceived it as such, like Zionism—became *also* a homecoming or repatriation, although to a place in which many had never set foot. Perhaps they should be understood as *exilic homecomings* that took place along the shores of the Mediterranean Sea: a migration that cannot come to an end, since its protagonists—while they have indeed become attached to the country of immigration—still bring with them feelings of nostalgia for a time that is lost and a place that, despite everything, continues to be perceived as their truest homeland.[39] These migrations should be read against the background of earlier cases of Jewish exile and displacement in the region, first and foremost the expulsion from Spain that culminated in the royal edict of 1492. Although in different ways, all tell the history "less [of] a singular event than [of] a long and serpentine process followed by decades of Jewish migration throughout the Mediterranean," which stimulated the birth of new imagined communities of exiles that blur previous regional and national differentiations.[40]

A Sephardi Sea is based on a variety of sources, including archival documents, oral histories, literary texts, movies, newspapers, and ethnographic data that I collected while talking to people and visiting—and taking part in the activities of—museums, cultural centers, and heritage associations in Israel, France, and Italy and on the internet mainly over the last six years. My voyage across the two shores of the Mediterranean was not driven by a desire to rediscover a family heritage that was lost and see how it continues, or not, in the present. Nonetheless, it was born of a conviction that this region is a place where many of today's tensions and hopes are concealed. Europe, North Africa, and their ramifications across the Mediterranean can metonymically represent a world in fragments, inhabited by ancient and new diasporas that all inherit memories that are not easily transmitted but that nonetheless appear to be everywhere around us. The case of the Sephardi and *Mizrahi* Jews therefore is an example of how the past can be appropriated and utilized by the members of an ethno-religious group who reconstruct their own history in parallel with and beyond what professional historians are doing.

Leaving aside the tools of historiography, and almost like the people that we will encounter, I have myself crossed boundaries and languages, in the hope of writing a book that succeeds in combining the field of history—particularly the history of ideas and of the social imaginary that emerges from the analysis of the individual and collective past—with those of literary and memory studies. In the first chapter, I read literary texts published during the last three decades by North African and Egyptian Jewish migrants or by their descendants as an itinerary that, even though based on singular experiences and voices, eventually gives a broader insight into a shared Jewish past and into the loss of an Arab *and* Jewish world that nowadays is remembered with nostalgia and sorrow. This reflects the vision of the Mediterranean region as a neighborhood of ruptures and continuities, of moving histories that can be reconstructed only in a diachronic manner. For this reason, I focus on different spaces and times: Tunisia, France, and Israel in the postmigration period, as depicted by a Franco-Tunisian Jewish novelist, Chochana Boukhobza; the memory of colonial and early postcolonial Libya and its relations to Italy and the Mediterranean, as shown in the works of two authors, Victor Magiar and Raphael Luzon, who moved to Rome with their families after 1967; and finally the surreal and highly evocative ways in which Orly Castel-Bloom—a renowned Israeli-born writer of Egyptian descent—elaborates on her family's history from *Sefarad* to Egypt and Israel.

The second chapter shifts the gaze to a set of European and Israeli cultural settings where the Sephardi and *Mizrahi* Jewish heritage is being preserved. Acknowledging the increased importance—especially when it comes to minority or hitherto marginalized groups[41]—of processes of heritagization, and therefore the need to analyze the spaces where these take place, I begin by focusing on migrant associations founded by Israeli Egyptians and the activities they have undertaken since the 1960s. Then, the Jews of Algeria who migrated to France in the same years are presented as a community characterized by a *difficult heritage*, which reveals the legacies of colonialism and the obstacles encountered to gain space in the French (Jewish) memorial arena. To do so, I look again at migrant associations, and then at exhibitions, museums, and monuments in contemporary France that deal with the historical legacy of the Algerian and North African Jews. Lastly, I move to the digital diasporas that in the last years have come about on the internet: a space where, for instance, Jews of Moroccan and Egyptian origin open websites dedicated to their heritage and interact on social networks, exchanging photographs, memories, and various kinds of information. This chapter then looks at Sephardi and *Mizrahi* heritage as an (in)tangible construct and explains how, on the basis of the traumatic experience of exile and the complex *homecoming* to Israel, the migration—or *repatriation*—to Europe, new Jewish identities have been imagined.

The third and last chapter looks at migrations of the Middle Eastern and North African Jewish history. In other words, I consider events—and the memories that they evoke—characterized by their location on the border between the history of the Jews of North Africa and Egypt and that of the European Jews or of other ethno-national or religious groups, such as today's (Muslim) migrants to Europe. I begin analyzing the Holocaust as an *absent past*, which, even without being part of the history of all the Jews of the Arab world, nonetheless acquires a central role in their current postmigratory identity and imaginary, and in cultural media such as cinema and literature. This goes hand in hand with a second process: the representation of Sephardi and *Mizrahi* Jews as refugees and their contemporary history as almost equivalent to that of the Jews of Europe, or, in other cases, of the Palestinians, in the twentieth century.

The Jews from Arab Lands and Iran Day—established by the Israeli parliament in 2014—will be viewed as an interesting example of the interplay between memory, politics, and history. As a counterpoint to that, the last section of the chapter looks for interstices where novel possibilities of dialogue among these Jewish diasporas and other cases of migration and displacement can be found. Therefore, I discuss the work of Jewish-Muslim mixed associations in Italy and France and contextualize it vis-à-vis debates on Europeanness and the place assigned to migrants in the future of Europe. This last part of the book reflects the presentist attitude of the Sephardi and *Mizrahi* memory and heritage and asks in which ways their past and future are constrained by the contingencies of today and to what extent this prevents the consolidation of a more objective and less evocative history.

Literature, cinema, the internet, associations, museums, memorial days: these are the main spaces—real and virtual, national, transnational, and diasporic—that I will discuss in *A Sephardi Sea*. Certainly, they form a composite landscape that cannot result in a uniform and homogeneous picture of the Sephardi and *Mizrahi* Jews, of their history, and of the ways in which it is transmitted. Nonetheless, they share some characteristics that together help us to better understand how and why this landscape has emerged. In spite of the divergent historical experience of these Jewish diasporas, nowadays a similar memorial itinerary seems to arise, in reference to shared patterns and ideas about a past that was actually much more diverse. This points to North Africa, Europe, and their Mediterranean overlapping as sites where contrasting and ever-changing—yet connected—memories can be found and recuperated.[42] Looking at issues of memory and heritage from the perspective of these Jewish migrants, exiles, and refugees, thus means looking at them from the point of view of "the vanguard of their peoples"[43]: men and women who can act as emblems of diasporism, mobility, and displacement but also, in some cases, of social and cultural integration. Moreover, it means valuing both the national and transnational dimension and underlining the resilience of a Jewish diasporic imaginary that continues even after the migration.

This book—which is neither an exercise in oral history nor an ethnographic study of these Jewish communities, and yet is a bit of both—should be read as an attempt to reconstruct the memories that, nowadays and from the perspective of the world and countries in which they live, the Jews of North Africa and Egypt, and their descendants, have of the past. Its aim is to shed light on the ways in which this past and the heritage that it symbolizes are being evoked and preserved in the present. My hope is that *A Sephardi Sea* will show the centrality of migration and exile in Sephardi and *Mizrahi* identity and help to revise the binary opposition between Israel and the Diaspora, 'aliyah or repatriation, on the one hand, and migration, on the other. In fact, even though these categories all play a role in the history of these Jewries and mirror different individual and communal histories, their comparative analysis reveals the existence of an interconnected memory rooted in feelings of diasporic belonging that bind together Jewish milieus dispersed across the Mediterranean, Israel, and Europe, and even beyond these spaces. In turn, this region reveals itself as a foundational site of modern Jewish history, whose legacy still populates the imagination of people who—like many others before and after them—left their homeland to start a new life on the other shore of the Mediterranean Sea.

NOTES

1. Lucette Lagnado, *The Man in the White Sharkskin Suit* (New York: HarperCollins, 2007), 163–64.

2. Hannan Hever, "We Have Not Arrived from the Sea: A Mizrahi Literary Geography," *Social Identities* 10, no. 1 (2004): 31–51; Hever, *'El-ha-hof ha-mequveh* [To the yearned shore] (Jerusalem: Ha-kibbutz ha-meuhad, 2007).

3. Daniel Schroeter, "A Different Road to Modernity: Jewish Identity in the Arab World," in *Diaporas and Exiles: Varieties of Jewish Identity*, ed. Howard Wettstein (Berkeley: University of California Press, 2002), 150–63. On the existence of Sephardi cross-cultural networks across the early modern Mediterranean, see, for instance, Francesca Trivellato, *The Familiarity of Strangers: The Sephardic Diaspora, Livorno, and Cross-Cultural Trade in the Early Modern Period* (New Haven, CT: Yale University Press, 2009); Francesca Bregoli, *Mediterranean Enlightenment: Livornese Jews, Tuscan Culture, and Eighteenth-Century Reform* (Stanford, CA: Stanford University Press, 2014); Anthony Molho, "Ebrei e marrani fra Italia e Levante ottomano," in *Storia d'Italia, Annali* 11, ed. Corrado Vivanti (Turin: Einaudi, 1997), 1011–43; Jessica M. Marglin, "Mediterranean Modernity through Jewish Eyes: The Transimperial Life of Abraham Ankawa," *Jewish Social Studies* 20, no. 2 (2014): 34–68.

4. Sidra Dekoven Ezrahi, *Booking Passage: Exile and Homecoming in the Modern Jewish Imagination* (Berkeley: University of California Press, 2000), 139.

5. David Abulafia, *The Great Sea: A Human History of the Mediterranean* (Oxford: Oxford University Press, 2011), XXIII. See also Fernand Braudel, "Méditerranée," in *La Méditerranée: L'espace et l'histoire*, ed. Fernand Braudel (Paris: Flammarion, 1985).

6. Seth Schwartz, *Were the Jews a Mediterranean Society? Reciprocity and Solidarity in Ancient Judaism* (Princeton, NJ: Princeton University Press, 2010), esp. 21–44. Consider also the five-volume work by Shlomo D. Goitein, *A*

Mediterranean Society: The Jewish Communities of the Arab World as Portrayed in the Cairo Geniza (Berkeley: University of California Press, 1967–88).

7. Colette Zytnicki, "Du rapatrié au séfarade. L'intégration des Juifs d'Afrique du Nord dans la société française: essai de bilan," *Archives Juives* 38, no. 2 (2005): 84–102; Ethan Katz, *The Burdens of Brotherhood: Jews and Muslims from North Africa to France* (Cambridge, MA: Harvard University Press, 2015).

8. I thank Piera Rossetto for providing me with this figure, which is based on various sources, but especially Sergio Della Pergola, *Anatomia dell'ebraismo italiano* (Rome: Carucci, 1976), 55–56. On the Jews of Libya in Italy, see Piera Rossetto, "Mémoires de diaspora, diaspora de mémoires: Juifs de Libye entre Israël et l'Italie, de 1948 à nos jours" (PhD diss., EHESS Toulouse/Ca' Foscari University, 2015).

9. Gérard Noiriel, *Le creuset français: Histoire de l'immigration (XIXe–XXe siècle)* (Paris: Seuil, 1988); Todd Shepard, *The Invention of Decolonization: The Algerian War and the Remaking of France* (Ithaca, NY: Cornell University Press, 2006). For a broader perspective, see Patricia M. E. Lorcin and Todd Shepard, eds., *French Mediterraneans: Transnational and Imperial Histories* (Lincoln: University of Nebraska Press, 2016); Jean-Louis Miège and Colette Dubois, eds., *L'Europe retrouvée: Les migrations de la décolonisation* (Paris: L'Harmattan, 1994); Elizabeth Buettner, *Europe after Empire: Decolonization, Society, and Culture* (Cambridge: Cambridge University Press, 2016).

10. See at least Donna Gabaccia, *Italy's Many Diasporas* (Seattle: University of Washington Press, 2000); Mark Choate, *Emigrant Nation: The Making of Italy Abroad* (Cambridge, MA: Harvard University Press, 2008); Piero Bevilacqua, Andreina Clementi, and Emilio Franzina, eds., *Storia dell'emigrazione italiana* (Rome: Donzelli, 2001). The history of Italian colonial migrants is increasingly attracting the interest of scholars, and quite a complete overview is provided in Patrizia Audenino, ed., *Fuggitivi e rimpatriati: L'Italia dei profughi tra guerra e decolonizzazione* (Viterbo: Archivio Storico dell'emigrazione italiana, 2018); Pamela Ballinger, *The World Refugees Made: Decolonization and the Foundation of Postwar Italy* (Ithaca, NY: Cornell University Press, 2020).

11. Consider, for example, Aviva Ben-Ur, *Sephardi Jews in America* (New York: New York University Press, 2009); Davide Aliberti, *Sefarad: Una comunidad imaginada (1924–2015)* (Madrid: Marcial Pons, 2018). In some cases, the migrations dated back to the late nineteenth and early twentieth century. See Devin A. Naar, "From the 'Jerusalem of the Balkans' to the Goldene Medina: Jewish Immigration from Salonika to the United States," *American Jewish History* 93, no. 4 (2007): 435–73. For the case of Latin America, with particular reference to Moroccan Jews, I refer to Aviad Moreno, "Moroccan Jewish Emigration to Latin America: The State of Research and New Directions," *Hésperis-Tamuda*, no. 2 (2016): 123–40; Devi Mays, *Forging Ties, Forging Passports: Migration and*

the Modern Sephardi Diaspora (Stanford, CA: Stanford University Press, 2020); Adriana Brodsky, *Sephardi, Jewish, Argentine: Community and National Identity (1880–1960)* (Bloomington: Indiana University Press, 2016).

12. Shlomo D. Goitein, *Jews and Arabs* (New York: Shocken, 1955), XII. For a short introduction to the premodern history of Jews in the Islamic world, see Jane S. Gerber, "History of the Jews in the Middle East and North Africa from the Rise of Islam until 1700," in *The Jews of the Middle East and North Africa in Modern Times*, ed. Reeva Spector Simon, Michael Laskier, and Sara Reguer (New York: Columbia University Press, 2002), 3–18; Bernard Lewis, *The Jews of Islam* (Princeton, NJ: Princeton University Press, 1978).

13. Albert Memmi, *Juifs et arabes* (Paris: Gallimard, 1974), 50.

14. The *dhimma* is an Islamic juridical category to denote and regulate the status of non-Muslim minorities (Jews, Christians, and Zoroastrians). See Claude Cahen, "Dhimma," in *Encylopédie de l'Islam*, ed. Bernard Lewis, Charles Pellat, Joseph Schacht, and Charles E. Bosworth (Leiden: Brill, 1977), 2:234–38; Heather Sharkey, *A History of Muslims, Christians, and Jews in the Middle East* (Cambridge: Cambridge University Press, 2017). For a critical overview, let me refer to Dario Miccoli, "The Jews of the Middle East and North Africa: A Historiographic Debate," *Middle Eastern Studies* 56, no. 3 (2020): 511–20.

15. Georges Bensoussan, *Jews in Arab Countries: The Great Uprooting* (Bloomington: Indiana University Press, 2019), 5.

16. Sarah A. Stein, "Black Holes, Dark Matter, and Buried Troves: Decolonization and the Multi-sited Archives of Algerian Jewish History," *American Historical Review* 120, no. 3 (2015): 915.

17. Esther Benbassa, preface to *Itinéraires sépharades: Complexité et diversité des identités*, ed. Esther Benbassa (Paris: PUPS, 2010), 9.

18. Esther Benbassa and Aron Rodrigue, *Sephardi Jewry: A History of the Judeo-Spanish Communities 14th–20th Centuries* (Berkeley: University of California Press, 2000).

19. See Anat Leibler, "Disciplining Ethnicity: Social Sorting Intersects with Political Demography in Israel's Pre-state Period," *Social Studies of Science* 44, no. 2 (2014): 271–92; Harvey Goldberg, "From Sephardi to Mizrahi and Back Again: Changing Meanings of 'Sephardi' in Its Social Environment," *Jewish Social Studies* 15, no. 1 (2008): 165–88.

20. Ella Shohat, "The Invention of the Mizrahim," *Journal of Palestine Studies* 29, no. 1 (1999): 5–20; Shohat, "Rupture and Return: Zionist Discourse and the Study of Arab Jews," *Social Text* 21, no. 2 (2003): 49–74; Yehudah Shenhav, *The Arab Jews: A Postcolonial Reading of Nationalism, Religion, and Ethnicity* (Stanford, CA: Stanford University Press, 2006); Sami Shalom-Chetrit, *Intra-Jewish Conflict in Israel: White Jews, Black Jews* (London: Routledge, 2010). On earlier usage of the category of Arab Jew, see Jonathan M. Gribetz, *Defining*

Neighbors: Religion, Race and the Early Arab-Zionist Encounter (Princeton, NJ: Princeton University Press, 2014); Orit Bashkin, *New Babylonians: A History of Jews in Modern Iraq* (Stanford, CA: Stanford University Press, 2012); Lital Levy, "Mihu yehudi-'aravi? 'Iyun meshaveh be-toldot ha-she'elah, 1880–2010" [Who is an Arab Jew? A comparative historical analysis of the question, 1880–2010], *Te'oriah u-viqoret*, no. 38–39 (2011): 101–35; Emily Gottreich, "Historicizing the Concept of Arab Jew in the Maghrib," *Jewish Quarterly Review* 98, no. 4 (2008): 433–51; Re'uven Snir, "'A Carbon Copy of Ibn al-Balad'? The Participation of Egyptian Jews in Modern Arab Culture," *Archiv Orientální*, no. 74 (2006): 37–64; Snir, *Who Needs Arab-Jewish Identity? Interpellation, Exclusion, and Inessential Solidarities* (Leiden: Brill, 2015).

21. Simon, Laskier, and Reguer, *Jews of the Middle East and North Africa*.

22. Aron Rodrigue, "L'exportation du paradigme révolutionnaire. Son influence sur le judaïsme sépharade et oriental," in *Histoire politique des Juifs de France*, ed. Pierre Birnbaum (Paris: Presses de Sciences Po, 1990), 221–43. See also Matthias B. Lehmann, "A Livornese 'Port Jew' and the Sephardim of the Ottoman Empire," *Jewish Social Studies* 11, no. 2 (2005): 51–76; Francesca Bregoli, "Hebrew Printing and Communication Networks between Livorno and North Africa, 1740–1789," in *Report of the Oxford Centre for Hebrew and Jewish Studies 2007–2008* (Oxford: Oxford University Press, 2009), 51–59.

23. Denis Charbit, "L'historiographie du décret Crémieux: le retour du refoulé," in *Les Juifs d'Algérie, une histoire de ruptures*, ed. Joëlle Allouche-Benayoun and Geneviève Dermenjian (Aix-en-Provence: Presses Universitaires de Provence, 2015), 43–61.

24. This was part of a larger process of modernization that encompassed the late Ottoman world as a whole, as explained in Keith D. Watenpaugh, *Being Modern in the Middle East: Revolution, Nationalism, Colonialism, and the Arab Middle Class* (Princeton, NJ: Princeton University Press, 2006).

25. Jonathan Fraenkel, *The Damascus Affaire, "Ritual Murder," Politics, and the Jews in 1840* (Cambridge: Cambridge University Press, 1997). On Egypt, see Jacob Landau, "Ritual Murder Accusations in Nineteenth-Century Egypt," in *Middle Eastern Themes: Papers in History and Politics*, ed. Jacob Landau (London: Frank Cass, 1973), 99–142; Dario Miccoli, *Histories of the Jews of Egypt: An Imagined Bourgeoisie, 1880s–1950s* (London: Routledge, 2015), esp. 54–61.

26. Michael Laskier, *North African Jewry in the Twentieth Century: The Jews of Morocco, Tunisia, and Algeria* (New York: New York University Press, 1994); Geneviève Dermenjian, *La crise anti-juive oranaise 1895–1905: L'anti-sémitisme dans l'Algérie coloniale* (Paris: L'Harmattan, 1986).

27. On the history of Zionism, consider Walter Laqueur, *The History of Zionism* (London: IB Tauris, 2003). For an overview of the history of the Alliance, see Michael Laskier, "Aspects of the Activities of the Alliance Israélite

Universelle in the Jewish Communities of the Middle East and North Africa: 1860–1918," *Modern Judaism* 3, no. 2 (1983): 147–71; Aron Rodrigue, *Images of Sephardi and Eastern Jewries in Transition: The Teachers of the Alliance Israélite Universelle* (Portland: University of Washington Press, 2003); André Kaspi, ed., *Histoire de l'Alliance Israélite Universelle de 1860 à nos jours* (Paris: Armand Colin, 2010).

28. On the Jews implicated in North African and Middle Eastern Communist and anticolonial movements, see Robert Watson, "Between Liberation(s) and Occupation(s): Reconsidering the Emergence of Maghrebi Jewish Communism, 1942–1945," *Journal of Modern Jewish Studies* 13, no. 3 (2014): 381–98; Pierre-Jean Le Foll Luciani, *Les juifs algériens dans la lutte anticoloniale: Trajectoires dissidentes (1934–1965)* (Rennes: Presses universitaires de Rennes, 2016); Rami Ginat, *A History of Egyptian Communism: Jews and Their Compatriots in Quest of Revolution* (Boulder: Lynne Rienner, 2011); Joel Beinin, *The Dispersion of Egyptian Jewry: Culture, Politics and the Formation of a Modern Diaspora* (Berkeley: University of California Press, 1998), 143–78; Bashkin, *New Babylonians*, 141–82. On Zionism, see Michael Laskier, "The Evolution of Zionist Activity in the Jewish Communities of Morocco, Tunisia and Algeria: 1897–1947," *Studies in Zionism* 4, no. 2 (1983): 205–36.

29. Robert Mantran, *Histoire de l'empire ottoman* (Paris: Fayard, 1989); Carter Vaughn Findley, "The Tanzimat," in *The Cambridge History of Turkey*, ed. Resat Kasaba (Cambridge: Cambridge University Press, 2008), 4:11–37; Selim Deringil, *The Well-Protected Domains: Ideology and the Legitimation of Power in the Ottoman Empire* (London: IB Tauris, 1998).

30. On Jews and colonialism, see Ethan Katz, Lisa Leff, and Maud Mandel, eds., *Colonialism and the Jews* (Bloomington: Indiana University Press, 2017).

31. Rachel Simon, "Between the Family and the Outside World: Jewish Girls in the Modern Middle East and North Africa," *Jewish Social Studies* 7, no. 1 (2000): 81–108.

32. Reeva Spector Simon, "Europe in the Middle East," in *The Jews of the Middle East and North Africa*, ed. Reeva Spector Simon, Michael Laskier, and Sara Reguer (New York: Columbia University Press, 2003), 19–28; Schroeter, "Different Road." For the case of Egypt, see Miccoli, *Histories*.

33. See "Les Juifs d'Orient face au nazisme et à la Shoah," special issue, *Revue d'histoire de la Shoah* 205, no. 2 (2016); Sarah A. Stein and Aomar Boum, eds., *The Holocaust and North Africa* (Stanford, CA: Stanford University Press, 2018). On Morocco, see Yaron Tsur, *Qehillah qru'ah: Yehudei-Maroqo ve-ha-le'umiyut 1943–1954* [A torn community: The Jews of Morocco and nationalism 1943–1954] (Tel Aviv: Am Oved, 2001), esp. 15–74.

34. Maurice Halbwachs, *On Collective Memory* (Chicago: University of Chicago Press, 1992), 83.

35. Paul Ricoeur, *Memory, History, Forgetting* (Chicago: University of Chicago Press, 2004).

36. Yosef Haim Yerushalmi, *Zakhor: Jewish History and Jewish Memory* (Seattle: University of Washington Press, 1992).

37. Daniel Boyarin, *A Traveling Homeland: The Babylonian Talmud as Diaspora* (Philadelphia: University of Pennsylvania Press, 2015), 17.

38. Nicole Abravanel, "L'historicité en milieu sépharade ou le primat de la spatialité," *Vingtième siècle* 117, no. 1 (2013): 184.

39. I refer to Sidra DeKoven Ezrahi, *Booking Passage: Exile and Homecoming in the Modern Jewish Imagination* (Berkeley: University of California Press, 2000).

40. Jonathan Ray, *After Expulsion: 1492 and the Making of Sephardic Jewry* (New York: New York University Press, 2013), 8. See also Mahir Saul and José Ignacio Hualde, eds., *Sepharad as Imagined Community: Language, History and Religion from the Early Modern Period to the 21st Century* (New York: Peter Lang, 2017).

41. Serge Noiret, "'Public History' e 'Storia pubblica' nella rete," *Ricerche storiche* 39, no. 2–3 (2009): 275–327. Let me refer also to Emanuela Trevisan Semi, Dario Miccoli, and Tudor Parfitt, eds., *Memory and Ethnicity: Ethnic Museums in Israel and the Diaspora* (Newcastle: Cambridge Scholars, 2013).

42. Maurizio Isabella and Konstantina Zanou, eds., *Mediterranean Diasporas: Politics and Ideas in the Long 19th Century* (London: Bloomsbury, 2015).

43. Hannah Arendt, "We Refugees," in *The Jewish Writings* (New York: Shocken, 2008), 274.

ONE

WRITING EXILE

Sephardi and *Mizrahi* Literary Memories

"THE SEPHARDI MEDITERRANEAN FROM WHICH I come is a world of many languages and no borders"—the Egyptian-born Gini Alhadeff wrote in 1997 in the memoir *The Sun at Midday*, thinking about her family, half of which comes from Alexandria via Leghorn and Spain, half of which comes from the island of Rhodes, and which now is scattered across Italy, New York, Britain, and other places.[1] As I mentioned in the introduction, it is true that in the course of the centuries the Mediterranean has often been a connecting sea, with a frequent cross-cultural exchange between its two shores. Yet, in other instances, it was a divisive and *corrupting* space, a frontier between Christianity and Islam, colonizer and colonized.[2] Today, the Mediterranean has become a sea tormented by ethno-religious conflict and characterized by economic and social discrepancies and, literally, the cemetery of thousands of migrants who try to escape from war and poverty in Africa, the Middle East, and elsewhere. However, it is perhaps still possible to conceive of it also as a neighborhood and a positive space in which to develop social, cultural, and political cooperation between Europe and the North African countries.

Taking all this into account, in the first chapter of *A Sephardi Sea*, I look at the Mediterranean region as a site of exile and memory through the eyes of Jewish authors who left Tunisia and Libya to migrate to Europe (France and Italy), or who were born in Israel from parents of Egyptian Jewish origin. The country of birth—as seen in the works of the Franco-Tunisian-Israeli Chochana Boukhobza, the Israeli of Egyptian origin Orly Castel-Bloom, and the Italo-Libyan Jews Raphael Luzon and Victor Magiar—can be considered as a spatial and temporal elsewhere, located in a bygone world that is remembered after the trauma of exile and from the place where these migrants resettled. In their works, the Mediterranean is both a friendly neighborhood *and* a divisive zone, which one hopes to trespass with the help of the imagination and of writing.³ That said, even if the act of writing the past from the point of view of the country of immigration allows writers to go back in time and space with their fantasy, it never erases the difficulties of exile and the quasi impossibility of truly going back. The Sephardi and *Mizrahi* memories and stories disseminated in the Mediterranean highlight, in fact, the existence of new diasporic milieus in Europe and Israel. This is why the Mediterranean can be taken as a laboratory of memory where identity is reimagined so as to find a way out of binary oppositions and sometimes to foster a rapprochement between contrasting ethno-religious and national groups.⁴

Thus, by interrogating Jewish postcolonial processes of literary memorialization, I will not only investigate how the migration from North Africa and the Middle East has been told in narrative form but unravel how memory travels across the spaces that these migrants encountered in the process of identity (re) making. As I will explain, from the 1950s and 1960s, Jewish men and women—and their memory—migrated, principally from the southern to the northern shore of the Mediterranean. In some cases, they embarked on multiple voyages: for example, from Tunisia to France and then to Israel. This leads to the conceptualization of Mediterranean Jewish memory as a set of *noeuds de mémoire* ("knots of memory"), with which Michael Rothberg understands "rhizomatic networks of temporality and cultural reference that exceed attempts at territorialisation (whether at the local or national level) and identitarian reduction," as opposed to Pierre Nora's strictly national *lieux de mémoire*.⁵ The next pages will introduce some of the knots scattered along the migratory itinerary of the Jews of the Mediterranean region, insofar as they emerge in the form of literary writing.⁶

In fact, literature always plays a crucial role in the memorialization of the past, even more so for communities and diasporas—like the Jews of the Middle East and North Africa—that long remained on the margins of historical research. This marginality depends on many factors, of which the most important one is the greater weight and impact that European/Western paradigms of Jewish identity and history have had both in Europe and in Israel, especially but not only in the aftermath of the Holocaust. As people who in most cases did not directly experience the Holocaust, the Jews of the Arab world did not well fit the predominant Jewish historical canon, and therefore their past has long been put aside. As Albert Memmi eloquently wrote in 1974, "so far, Jewish history has been written by Western Jews only... as a result, we only know the Western aspects of the *malheur juif*."[7] Even in the field of colonial studies, the history of the Jews has been difficult to handle since it complicates the opposition between colonizer and colonized and often disrupts any linear understanding of the relations between Europe and the Arab world: think, for example, of the Jews of Algeria who, even though they were French citizens from the time of the promulgation of the Crémieux Decree, also remained attached to Algerian Arab-Berber society.[8]

Literature, then, functions as an individual and collective tool capable of filling the gaps of historiography, of maintaining imaginative links with the motherland, and of transmitting an identity and heritage from one generation to another. Certainly, literary writing entails a historical value, but at the same time, it is different from history tout court and, generally speaking, does not require one to distinguish in a clear manner between different temporalities or articulate them in a coherent discourse. It can rejoice in uncertainties and emotions that would be deemed inappropriate in a work of history. It can talk about what is left behind us, on the basis of fragments of memory that "involve a past of loss and a longing for a world that perhaps never was."[9] Furthermore, literary writing has the potential of transmitting the past in a very intimate and immediate way, recording details and stories that do not always feature prominently in institutional archives. It is true that historians too write narratives that—even though grounded in facts and sources—are always acts of personal creation.[10] Nevertheless, "reality ('the thing in themselves')," Carlo Ginzburg noted, "exists," and that is why literature can help us get a mediated approach that goes beyond both "'positive' historical inquiry based on a literal reading of the evidence, on the one hand, and 'historical narratives' based on figurative, uncomparable and unrefutable interpretations on the other."[11]

In this chapter, I will read literary texts by Jewish migrants and their descendants as an itinerary that, while rooted in individual experiences and voices, brings them together to provide new insights on a wider Jewish past and on its reverberations in the present. This leads me to conceive Sephardi and *Mizrahi* identity as a polyphonic construct based in a Mediterranean (Jewish) history of ruptures and continuities that only can be reconstructed in a diachronic manner.[12] Finally, from a more explicitly literary perspective, these texts highlight the need to look at Jewish and Israeli literature in a comparative manner— paying attention to the existence of a multilingual Sephardi Diaspora of writers and intellectuals—that mirrors the complexity of these Jewish communities and their migrant identity.[13]

DISPLACED FEELINGS: CHOCHANA BOUKHOBZA BETWEEN TUNISIA, FRANCE, AND ISRAEL

Chochana Boukhobza has frequently defined herself as an exile: having been born in Sfax, Tunisia, in 1959 and grown up in Paris, she moved to Israel at seventeen years old but after a few years went back to France, where she now lives. Since her debut in 1986, she has published a number of novels, among which are *Bel Canto* (1991), *Le troisième jour* (2010), and *Métal* (2013), and also has written scripts and codirected two documentaries. Here, I discuss *Un été à Jérusalem* (1986) and *Pour l'amour du père* (1996), the two novels by Boukhobza that more explicitly discuss her Tunisian Jewish background and the peregrinations of a family across the Mediterranean, from Tunisia to France and Israel.

The migration of Tunisian Jews began around the mid-1940s and continued up until the early 1960s, reaching a peak of 15,000 migrants in 1956—the year of Tunisian independence. Another 25,000 left between 1956 and 1960. In the end, most of the approximately 110,000 Tunisian Jews resettled in France, but part of the community reconstituted in Israel and in other countries as well. As in the case of many other North African and Middle Eastern Jewries, the Tunisian Diaspora was formed of different subgroups, of which the largest were the so-called *twansa*, followed by the *grana* and the Jews of Djerba. Whereas the *twansa* resided in Tunisia since at least the late antiquity, the *grana* descended from Sephardi Jews who arrived from the Tuscan port city of Leghorn at the end of the seventeenth century. Lastly, Djerba hosted a small yet ancient Jewish community that constituted an integral component of the island's *mosaïque communautaire*. The life and sociocultural status of Tunisian Jews greatly improved during the French protectorate, established in 1881, at a time when many Jews also underwent a gradual process of Frenchification— even though, as opposed to the Algerians, the Tunisians never obtained French citizenship en masse. The profound impact that France had on their identity certainly influenced their life trajectories when the French protectorate ended in 1956, and many Jews, who in the meantime had become Tunisian citizens, decided to migrate to France rather than to Israel.[14] It should be noted, however, that in the last years a growing number of French Jews—many of whom are of Maghrebine ancestry—have started to make *'aliyah*, in some cases out of fear of the increase of (Muslim) antisemitism in France. Even though the effects of this migration on the future of French Jewry remains to be seen, it is already interesting to see how this and preceding processes of multiple diasporization, in which more than one past and memory intersect, can be narrated—for example, in two novels by Boukhobza published in the 1980s and 1990s, respectively.[15]

Boukhobza's novels are part of a vast corpus of texts—from novels, poems, and short stories to memoirs and autobiographies—published especially since the 1980s by Jews of North African and to some extent Egyptian Jewish origin that nowadays live in France. I am referring to authors such as Pol-Serge Kakon, Nine Moati, and Jean-Luc Lellouche that in their works all describe the family's past and the migration from North Africa to France.[16] *Un été à Jérusalem*, which came out in 1986, was Chochana Boukhobza's debut novel. It tells the story of Sarah, a French-born girl of Tunisian Jewish origin traveling to Jerusalem during the Lebanon War (1982) to visit her family, which had moved to Israel from Paris a few years earlier. In reality, it was the girl who had pushed for the migration to Israel, but she changed her mind and went back to France on her own after some time. This led to her estrangement from the family, especially from her religious parents, who accused her of misbehaving and dishonoring their good name. Whereas back in Paris the girl had a relationship with a Jew of Ashkenazi origin, in Jerusalem she goes out with a man who has a North African Jewish background. Thus, the father, who wishes his daughter would behave according to Tunisian Jewish traditions and religious obligations, harshly reprehends her conduct. On top of all this is the war between Israel and Lebanon and its impact at a familial—the protagonist's two brothers are both drafted in the army—and national level.

Awarded with the Prix Méditerranée, a French literary prize that "celebrates ... the cultural space between different countries of which the Mediterranean is the crucible,"[17] *Un été à Jérusalem* is the painful elegy for a Tunisian and Mediterranean world that struggles to continue in Paris and Jerusalem but is destined to die in front of the protagonist's eyes. At the center of the novel is Jerusalem, a city "out of the limits of my logic. It dances inside me with meaningless and deeply banal details.... Jerusalem is cumbersome. You think it is frail but it oppresses you."[18] Jerusalem figures as an oppressive space, which is represented neither by the vestiges of the Old City and monuments like the Western Wall or by the modern cafés of Jaffa Street. It is a no man's land made of stones "that do not say anything," of contrasting neighborhoods that go from the ultra-Orthodox Meah Shearim to the surroundings of Abu Tor, with its "Arab children, floating in their djellabas," up to "the road that, after Talpiot, leads to Bethlehem and then to Hebron."[19] Under the sky of Jerusalem, which "on certain mornings, becomes a sea,"[20] the protagonist meets strange people like Mavrika, a Maghrebi Jewish prostitute with whose uprooted and cursed existence she likes to identify.²¹ Boukhobza guides the reader along a complex Jerusalemite itinerary constellated by silence and oblivion and by a lack of emotions between the members of the family, who all live in their own little corner without really listening to what the others have to tell.²² The idea of Jerusalem as meaningless certainly contrasts with the Zionist view of the city and of the Land of Israel as Jewish spaces par excellence. But, at the same time, it also extremizes traditional Jewish depictions of the city as a ruined and desolated shrine—think of Karaite narratives from the Middle Ages or, to mention a very different example, the description in the 1925 short story *Tehillah*, by the Israeli novelist Shmuel Yosef Agnon: "Stark are the hills of Jerusalem, they have no sanctuaries and no castles. Since the time of our exile, the nations came here and brought destruction and ruin."²³ Whereas for Agnon the Gentile nations have caused harm to Jerusalem, Boukhobza seems to believe that the city itself is an oppressive space, burdened under the weight of the past. Thus, it is in Tunisia—actually, in the memory of this lost space and the time that it represents—that her Jewish identity struggles to reside.

It is not only Jerusalem but Israel at large that is described as a space of desolation. Particularly, this is how the south of the country and the city of Beer-Sheva—where the protagonist's grandmother lives—are presented. The choice of Beer-Sheva is not a coincidence, since from the 1960s many Middle Eastern and North African Jewish migrants settled in that area, following ad hoc Israeli policies of urban planning and development.²⁴ Beer-Sheva is "the door to the desert," a city populated by "doddery elders, gutless and lazy Georgian immigrants, dangerous Moroccans who speak with the knife more than with the mouth."²⁵ From their exile in Beer-Sheva, the migrants transformed the Maghrebi past into "a mythical paradise, a North African *Shangrila*, where Jews lived in great happiness."²⁶ Yet for the protagonist it is not like that: she perceives Tunisian Jewish life as a dead body, just like that of her grandmother Rachel, or as something that only survives in traditional dishes and clothing. Israel is not the space that put an end to the Diaspora and where celebrating the Jewish return to the ancestral homeland but, on the contrary, a momentary step in a diasporic existence that never comes to an end: "The voyage has been long.... First awakening: North Africa. Then the exile to Paris, Lyon, Marseille with sneezings of nostalgia, tinglings of the chest, poisoned *tête-à-têtes* with the 'paradise.' In front of a crowded compass, they repacked their suitcases, a fantasy. Jerusalem. An expensive caprice."²⁷

The migration to France and then the *'aliyah* to Israel made the protagonist's entire family feel like victims of history: none of them migrated out of individual will but because of historical contingencies or "a caprice." This is even more evident when it comes to the elders of the family, for whom Israel "only represents ... that most holy land where they came to die and that will bury them under a tombstone."[28] Far is the joyful depiction of this land as *mizug galuyiot* ("ingathering of exiles"), the place where Jews would finally build a state for themselves and forge a new, shared national identity.[29] In *Un été à Jérusalem*, every character is a nomad who is unable to find a place to stay and for whom the past is gone irremediably, surviving only in the objects that were brought from Tunisia.[30]

The death of the grandmother, which occurs shortly after the opening of the story, symbolizes the beginning of the loss of an entire world, which cannot be transmitted to the younger generation: "One by one, our elders are dying, and Tunisia, Morocco, Yemen will die with them."[31] Even those who are not dead are like ghosts resurrecting from an unknown past who suddenly make their appearance in Jerusalem for the shivah—the traditional Jewish seven days of mourning—of the grandmother: "They came from the North, from the *kibbutz* of the coast or from Dimona the White, sensing in this death their imminent disappearance. They still wear the traditional clothes of Gabès or Souss[e], the baggy trousers and the *kabouch*. ... They are beyond everything. When they walk, their body trembles, imprisoned under their weight."[32] Marianne Hirsch, in a deeply personal work on the Jews of Czernowitz (in today's Ukraine) tellingly entitled *Ghosts of Home*, argues that "objects and places can function as triggers of remembrance that connect us, bodily and thus also emotionally, with the physical world we inhabit."[33] But if this process is quite obvious for those who actually used those objects or lived in those places, what happens to subsequent generations? How can they relate to objects that for them only have an indirect memorial connotation?

In Boukhobza's case, the Tunisian elders wander in a world that is no longer theirs, but they nonetheless still carry with them—or rather on them, by wearing Tunisian traditional clothing—the little that remains of the past. On the other hand, the generation to which the protagonist belongs does not seem to have a past of its own. On discovering that her aunt Aliza had given the grandmother's traditional clothes to some ragman in Beer-Sheva, Sarah gets very angry, as if her past could only exist in these clothes: "'You are crazy! You destroyed the past because of your jealousy! We already have so few memories because of the exile. How will I explain to my children that I come from North Africa if you throw our history in the dustbin?' 'Invent, embellish, imagine. ... You know enough to fill in the gaps.'"[34] But does this young girl really know enough? Will she ever be able to reconstruct her past and fill in the gaps, or will everything always remain uncertain in an era of postmemory characterized by the decline of—or the unwillingness to cultivate—what Pierre Nora called *milieux de mémoire*?

The conflict that opposes the young Sarah to the previous generations, those of her parents and grandparents, is a cliché that can be found in many other novels by Sephardi and *Mizrahi* writers. It relates to the traumas that these families had to go through upon leaving, in this case, first North Africa and then France, but also to more universal generational divides. As said, Sarah's family is like a remnant of the dying Tunisian world to which the girl feels attached but that she wishes to delete so she can conduct a normal life in France. The trauma of exile also is mirrored in that of the wars that Israel fights, particularly the 1982 Lebanon War. During this conflict, all sorts of misfortunes happen, from the death of *Safta* to that—because of a stray bullet—of the protagonist's lover, who had gone to Beirut as a reporter. The friend who brings the news tries to console her by saying, "*Mektoub! C'était son heure,*" but the girl angrily accuses him: "It is your fault. You killed him. You! Not the Arab in front [of him]! You! You!" Jerusalem is not a holy city inhabited by God, as the prostitute Mavrika indicates: "I think God has cursed you, Jerusalem! Let all your sons die! One day, you will come back to your ruins!"[35]

The setting of the novel in 1982 is due to the timing of the publication, which came out a few years later in 1986. However, it also has to do with the great impact that this conflict had on Jews in the Diaspora and clearly on Israel. It was a turning point that made many rethink the role of the army in Israeli society and the future meanings of Zionism at a moment when this ideology seemed to enter into crisis.[36] The war and events such as the killing of Palestinians by the Lebanese Christian *Phalangistes* in the refugee camp of Sabra and Shatila—which the Israeli army failed to prevent—also triggered a change in the perception that sectors of the European public opinion had of Israel: no longer a small state that wanted to defend itself from the enemies but one that could act in questionable or even immoral ways.[37]

As if to further elaborate upon this critical juncture in Jewish and Israeli history, the other in *Un été à Jérusalem* is not so much the Arab but an internal Jewish other that haunts the present and the future: Jewish Tunisia, the migration and *rue du Chemin-Vert* in Paris, the dead grandmother, the protagonist's (Ashkenazi and North African) lovers. New diasporic spaces cut across and connect the (old) Diaspora and Israel, leading to the erasure of previous feelings of belonging and to the evoking of a Tunisian fantasy where the family's *plus beaux jours* are lost. If Israel is certainly one of these new spaces, the other is France—or, better to say, Paris. It is there that the protagonist of *Un été à Jérusalem* wishes to return, and it is also the home of the characters of a second novel by Boukhobza, *Pour l'amour du père*. As we shall see, the family and its complex memory of the Tunisian past are also present in this text—at the center of which, however, is not the absence but instead the omnipresence of the feelings that bind one generation to another, and especially a father to his daughter.

"In that same moment, the *Ville de Tunis* trembled. *On s'en va*, we are leaving .... As the boat departed from the quay, from the land, from Tunis, those words flew from one group of people to the other. It was over. And so it began."[38] *Pour l'amour du père*, published in 1996, narrates the turbulent relationship that, several decades after the migration, still characterizes the life of the members of a Tunisian Jewish family in Paris. The protagonist, Alice, is a successful lawyer who struggles to find love and cope with her father and sisters, one of whom—Sassou—disappeared several years earlier, after the family discovered that she wanted to marry outside of the Jewish community. Even though the entire novel is set in the French capital, the city of Tunis is always in the background. As opposed to Paris, where "it is always gray, it is always bad [weather]," Tunis *el-hedra* (Arabic: "the green") "looked like a garden, with little houses facing the sea."[39] Here, the climate becomes a mirror of the feelings that the protagonists, and especially the father, perceive after the migration: "The father cannot be cured from Tunisia, he always compares everything, he compares the taste of the fruit he ate *là-bas* with those that he buys at the market of Clichy; he says that life was easier under the sun, it had a taste."[40] *Là-bas*, a term that is present in the writings as well as in the memory of many North African Jews and of colonial migrants, stands for a place where everything was better but that is also radically different from what the country of origin has become after the end of colonialism. Similarly to the case of the Algerian *pieds-noirs*, in today's Tunisia "the streets, the shops, the avenues, with their ancient mix of populations are not the same," to the point that the country seems like "an unqualified *là-bas*, whereas France becomes a more or less accepted *ici*."[41]

The echoes of this far away *là-bas* can now be found only in spaces other than Tunis—for example, in the Parisian neighborhood of Belleville. The Tunisian Jewish quarter par excellence, Belleville has been described as "a protective universe where the brutality of assimilation [in French society] was alleviated."[42] It is there that the man goes every Sunday, to meet with three other Tunisians: "*Là-bas* [i.e., in Tunis], he only greeted them nodding his head, he barely said good morning. In Paris, they became like brothers." In their Sunday gatherings, "little by little, [the men] made their neighborhood come back to life in their memory.... For them, it was like going back to their true and most authentic self.... They drink mint tea, eat semolina sweets. They never talk about the present."[43] As Simon and Tapia explain, in the aftermath of the migration, Belleville gave many Tunisian Jews—who, in the 1970s, formed the absolute majority of the Jewish population of the neighborhood—the illusion of being closer to the homeland. People lived as if in a village, surrounded by newly established Tunisian-owned cafés and shops, which often bore names like *La Goulette* or *Dar Djerba*.[44]

Another space that makes Alice's father remember Tunisia is Israel, where he visits his son Gérard: "[In Israel] the father started again with the comparisons with Tunisia.... He said that the fruits were just as big, the watermelon, the peach, the orange.... He began to have an idea of Israel that was related to the white light of Tunis."[45] As already found in novels and memoirs by Israelis of Moroccan origin like Sami Berdugo and Ami Bouganim, the Promised Land paradoxically is the place where the Diaspora comes back to life.[46] This is similar to the Algerian settlers of Maltese origin who nowadays embark on memory voyages to the land of their ancestors, Malta, where most of them have never been and which is therefore experienced as a mediated space to reconnect them to their native Algeria.[47] This kind of transfer—that is, in Freudian terminology, the reproduction of feelings related to repressed experiences and the substitution of the original object of the repressed impulses with someone or something else[48]—occurs throughout *Pour l'amour du père*. For example, in another passage of the book, in a bar Alice meets a young man of Algerian origin who kisses her and who, symbolically, "is like the father when he was young, he is the memory of the father's body." Just like the father, the man longs for a bygone epoch when, on the other shore of the Mediterranean, "we [Arabs and Jews] were like the fingers of a hand."[49] Just as the lives of these two groups were shaped, at a collective level, by violence and the trauma of exile, the same happened at an individual level to Alice, despite the fact that she migrated to France when she was a little child. Both Alice and her father manage to resist exile through specific regimes of memory and the creation of unexpected mnemonic correlations: between Tunisia and Israel, the memory of the father and that of a young Franco-Algerian man.[50]

This said, it is not clear to what extent the protagonist actually believes the idyllic vision of Tunisia transmitted by the father. Alice is very reluctant to remember the past and has forgotten many details of it. For her, it signifies not so much the departure from Tunisia, an event that she almost does not recall, but the death of her mother when she was a child and the disappearance of her sister Sassou. It comes back in the shape of haunted memories and barely comprehensible Arabic words. Arabic is transformed into the repository of her traumas and secrets, into a language "whose words stayed with me like embers," "Arabic, the forbidden language, the language of before the exile, the language of the father. . . . 'What is it you mumbled? I did not understand a word . . .' 'I was inventing words.'"[51]

Additionally, pre-1960s Tunisia, and as it happens also pre-Nasserist Egypt, is portrayed as a cosmopolitan society where Arabs, Jews, Italians, Maltese, and others lived together. In the Tunisian case, Jews and Italians are the ones who feature more prominently—the Italians being the biggest and most ancient community of Europeans present in the country since the mid-nineteenth century, one that, as opposed to the French, remained in a more in-between position that made them neither colonized or colonizers.[52] For them all, the migration ended this world in a definitive manner, unveiling ethno-religious and national cleavages that hitherto had been less visible and crucial. But in France, much of Tunisia is forgotten, as if it never existed: "'You sang us this song [of Farid El Atrach], when we were children,' she says. . . . 'It is true! *Ya Hassra* ["alas"]!' says the father smiling. 'Sing!' 'My voice is lost.'"[53]

As said above, the only moments when the past reappears are experienced in Belleville or in a casual encounter with other exiles—for example, a taxi driver who has been accused of killing his wife and whose family Alice is defending: "This taxi driver," says Alice's father, "he is a bit like myself. He wants to find his land . . . his home. And he does not see anymore his wife or his daughter, because he works, he works. That is how it is, *la ville*."[54] Similarly to the Israel of *Un été à Jérusalem*, here the city of Paris—as opposed to Tunis—is an alienating location where migrants only work and forget about the rest, even about their own family. Despite their alleged previous similarities, North African Jews and Muslims are no longer part of the same milieu: the migration and the life in the metropole have in the long run estranged the two communities from each other. This occurred not only because of the societal reactions to the policies that the French state implemented since the 1960s vis-à-vis the two—which were, generally speaking, more inclusive and less othering for the Jewish than the Muslim immigrants—but also as a consequence of the Palestinian-Israeli conflict and its impact on the identity and self-perception of the Jews of France and of French Muslims.[55] If so, what is left to Alice and her father? How can they continue their life, despite the difficulties at individual, familial, and national levels? Perhaps the answer resides in a feeling to which everyone can cling—love: between the father and his dead wife, between Alice and her companion, for one's *pays perdu*, and for the noisy streets of Belleville, the only place in the whole of Paris where "there are colours, coloured men, *et c'est beau*."[56]

Both *Un été à Jérusalem* and *Pour l'amour du père* present the migration as the beginning of an individual and collective exile, whose marks pass from one generation to another and have a deep impact on family and interethnic relations.

The migration sheds light on memories that often make the protagonists feel displaced, as if they could never find a place to settle and find solace. Furthermore, the Diaspora does not end with the resettlement of the Jews in Israel, let alone in another diasporic country like France, but instead is born again in new forms after the migration. Even in Jerusalem or Paris, the traumatic past and the violence of this event cannot be forgotten. The Jewish migration from North Africa and Egypt, in most cases, did not bring the Jews to wholly foreign spatial-national dimensions where they could reinvent themselves from scratch but to strangely familiar locations—like France, Israel, or, as we shall soon see, Italy—to which they were already connected because of colonialism, feelings of Jewishness, or the belief in the Zionist idea. The result was a difficult process of transmission and continuation of an exilic identity that, in the case of Boukhobza's characters, not only is rooted in vanishing feelings of Tunisianness but—at the same time—draws upon a present characterized by failed attempts to integrate into a postcolonial context in which the protagonists do not feel they have a place.

BETWEEN LIBYA AND ITALY: HISTORIES FROM THE OTHER SHORE

In the history of the Jewish migrations from the Middle East and North Africa, that to Italy probably remains one of the least known and studied. There are two main explanations for that: fewer North African Jews moved to Italy than to France, the US, or obviously Israel; and no less importantly, until today the Italian society largely lacked a profound public debate on colonialism and its aftermath, even more so in relation to the Jewish minority.[57] As Patrizia Audenino has argued, Italy preferred to adopt "a politics of oblivion, more than of memory" vis-à-vis its postcolonial returnees and migrants to avoid the disclosure of events and legacies that would disturb the establishment of fruitful relations with the countries of the southern shore of the Mediterranean and of Africa.[58] Furthermore, colonialism was perceived as an appendix of Fascism more than an integral part of early twentieth-century Italian history, despite the fact that the colonial enterprise had actually begun at the turn of the century and continued during the so-called liberal period—for example, the Ottoman provinces of Cyrenaica and Tripolitania officially became Italian in 1912, ten years before the advent of the Fascist regime in 1922.

To begin narrating this void, it may be worth focusing on the case of Libya, Italy's most important colony, and discussing two books published in Italy in 2003 and 2015 by Jewish authors of Libyan ancestry: Victor Magiar's *E venne la notte* (2003) and Raphael Luzon's *Tramonto libico: Storia di un ebreo arabo* (2015).[59] These texts are not the only ones by Libyan Jews published in Italian; there were earlier ones, like Roberto Nunes Vais's *Reminiscenze tripoline* (1982), and a more recent novel by Daniela Dawan, *Qual è la via del vento* (2018), which I will also talk about. Together, these works allow us to understand how Italy, colonialism, and Libya intersect in the memory of the Libyan Jews and appear in their writings. They explore the gradual demise and vanishing of the daily interactions between Jews and Arabs in times of turmoil in Libyan history, first during the colonial and then, especially in the case of Luzon, in the postcolonial period. *E venne la notte* and *Tramonto libico*, in particular, point to the different ways in which the Libyan Jewish past can be evoked nowadays: as a source of historical knowledge and ethnic pride, as a tribute to one's own family in the context of a wider North African and Sephardi past, or more simply as a story that, despite its historical significance, few people seem to remember. Moreover, whereas the texts of Boukhobza almost exclusively describe the period that followed the migration, those that I will now present concentrate more on the preceding epoch, although this does not imply—especially in the case of Luzon—that they fail to inscribe the memory of the Libyan Jews in contemporary regional and global dynamics, from the Arab-Israeli conflict to the 2012 Libyan uprising.

Victor Magiar was born in Tripoli in 1957 to a family of Sephardi origin. In 1967, the family migrated to Rome, where Magiar has been active in local politics and Jewish communal affairs. His novel *E venne la notte* is among the first published in Italian by a Libyan Jew. In it, he describes the history of the Jews of Tripoli from colonial times to the 1960s, narrating it through the voice of the young Hayim Cordoba and his family. The title of the book refers to a verse of the book of Isaiah (21:11,12)—"Watchman, what of the night? . . . Morning is coming, but also the night"—which depicts the fall of the ancient city of Babylon. However, in Magiar's book, the *notte* that the protagonist sees approaching is the end of the Jewish presence in Libya and the beginning of a new and initially darker epoch for both the Jews and the Libyan nation at large.

As said, Italy today hosts a relatively small North African and Middle Eastern Jewish population that is part of a larger but still small Jewish Diaspora of around thirty-five thousand people in a country of sixty million inhabitants.[60] The Libyans are the biggest and most visible North African Jewish community in Italy, particularly in the cities of Rome and Milan. Even though the migration of Jews from Libya had started already around 1948, the first waves were directed toward Israel and not Italy, where the Jews began to arrive mainly after 1967 and Qaddhafi's coup d'état (1969). It is estimated that around 5,000 of them evacuated to Italy from that year up to the early 1970s, but in the end only around 1,800 decided to remain in the country. The rest reemigrated to Israel, where around 90 percent of the Libyan Jews settled definitively. While still in their land of birth, the Libyan Jews, similarly to the Tunisians, were quite integrated in the local society and economy. Italian colonialism had led to Italianization, especially of the upper echelons of Jewish society, but this had not erased the many ties the Jews had with the Arab culture of Tripolitania and Cyrenaica or with the Arabic language.[61]

In fact, even though in *E venne la notte* the relations between Jews and Arabs are sometimes described as tense, the author acknowledges that at an individual level—and even on the occasion of the infamous anti-Jewish riots that occurred in 1945, 1948, and 1967—Jews and Arabs could be friends or at least good neighbors. The protagonist, Hayim, for example, lives next to an Arab family that will rescue him and his sister during the riots that erupt in Tripoli in 1967 as a consequence of the Six Days War: "Sharìf lets the window down to stretch his left arm with two of his fingers in sign of victory: we are on the side of the protest, belligerent and tense.... We are in the middle of the crowd and no one pays attention to us, since we are protected by the Mercedes that only an Arab notable would drive and by our red hair, which even today make us more European, more *inglìz*."[62] In another section of the book, Hayim plays with Sharìf's son, and even though the children end up arguing about armies and politics, theirs seem to be little more than childhood skirmishes:

> On Radio Cairo they said that "the Arab Nation will cancel Israel from the world map and give the honor back to the Arabs in Palestine." "Honor?" "Yes, *sharàf*, honor." "Yes! The honor that they lost twice in 1948 and 1956! Majority does not always win...." "Are you saying that three million Jews can win against a hundred million Arabs? Are you trying to make me laugh? Not even if you go and ask Nembo Kid and Batman...." "But have you never heard of David and Goliath?" "Sorry, I never watched this movie. Have you?" The *signora* Raffaella intervenes immediately, bread and jam impose a truce.[63]

Magiar presents the two as unaware actors of a history that they barely know and that they interpret using points of reference that are both old and new: the biblical story of David and Goliath and the traditional value of honor, popular movies and characters of American comics like Batman and Nembo Kid (the name given to Superman in its first Italian version). As Daniele Comberiati argues, Magiar stigmatizes all kinds of religious fanaticism and, conversely, embraces the multicultural and multireligious atmosphere that up until a certain epoch allegedly characterized Tripoli.⁶⁴ The city is portrayed in detail through the description of some of its most famous monuments and buildings, which date back to both precolonial and colonial times: Piazza Italia, Corso Sicilia, Bab al-Bahr, and last but not least the old city, where every Sabbath "half of the Jews are preparing the candles, another half are bathing and perfuming with many essences."⁶⁵

As we shall see in the third chapter when we analyze the novel *Benghazi Bergen-Belsen* by the Israeli Yossi Sucary, Libya proves to be ancient and modern at the same time, as it has been perceived by Italian colonial officers and architects: "Tripoli was certainly shaped by European dominance, but it was also a site of numerous countervailing ambiguities, in its architecture, its social policies, and its malleable spatial and political relations."⁶⁶ Such ambiguities became clear in moments of tension during colonial times: "Initially, the Italians respected the traditions and laws of the [Jewish] community, but with the advent of Fascism things changed." In the 1930s, the Fascist governor of Libya, Italo Balbo, wanted to impose Italian civil law with regard to issues pertaining to the *halakhah*, such as marriage, and ordered that all shops—including those owned by Jews—be open on Saturdays. The opposition of the Jews in the end led to the flogging of some in a square of Tripoli.⁶⁷ "The Cordoba brothers," narrates Magiar, "... in that December afternoon, went to the square in front of the *Manifattura dei Tabacchi*, mixed in the crowd.... First the *querelle* on marriages, then the conflict over the Sabbath, lastly the 'racial laws': the future did not bode anything good."⁶⁸

Once the Arab-Israeli conflict broke out, the situation became even more difficult for Libyan Jews such as Hayim. The author talks at length about 1948 and its impact in Libya, interspersing the narration of Hayim's life story with historical summaries printed in another type. From this point of view, *E venne la notte* is both a real story and a fictitious reenactment of the past. If the life of Victor Magiar emerges through the help of literature, on the one hand, and the fictional character of Hayim Cordoba, on the other, his work is not an autobiography and the author's goal is not to reconstruct his own life in detail. Rather, he aims to tell the story of a vanished community—as is clear from the accuracy of the narration, the frequent and intentional usage of Ladino expressions, and the presence of a detailed glossary of Arabic, Ladino, Hebrew, and Turkish words at the end of the volume. The short circuit between history and literature is one of the most interesting aspects of Magiar's book, and it echoes the idea that literature can provide a more intimate and instant reading of the past. As opposed to an autobiography *stricto sensu*, where—according to Lejeune—the author signs a pact with his readers, promising to tell his life story in the truest manner that memory allows him,[69] in *E venne la notte* the young Hayim is the alter ego of Magiar yet also symbolizes an entire community and different generations of Libyan Jews.

Aside from the descriptions of Tripoli, Italy, and the echoes of the Arab-Israeli conflict, the book includes interesting reflections on the relations between Jews and Arabs, and between people belonging to different ethno-religious worlds more generally. For example, at the beginning of *E venne la notte* Magiar describes the school Hayim attends as a space of harmonious coexistence: "in this school, in this city, being different is something normal; it is like our sea with many fishes of different race, or like the trees of the school garden."[70] Difference does not characterize only the school but even Hayim's family. For example, the boy walks with his father in the streets of Tripoli with a world atlas in his hands. This makes him think about his family, scattered in places as different as Australia, Brazil, and Israel. In the meantime, a protest is about to start in the city, and therefore the father warns Hayim in Ladino: "'*No pèdres tiempo!* . . .' Casablanca, Palma de Mallorca, a jump and . . . the *Caffè Gambrinus* becomes our shelter in the middle of the stormy Mediterranean. . . . The cafés on the Corso, a free port for castaways left with no transport."[71] As the situation in Libya and Jewish life in Tripoli become more and more troubled, Hayim concludes that "history is chasing us since generations but my parents still resist on this shore; they do not confront the sea and do not drop the anchor since they are afraid of the storm. But Storm has come after us again, passing by the corniche, up inside our home."[72] Then, at the end of the story, while the protagonist is sitting on a plane to Italy, the sea "that in the daylight divides its lands, in the silence of the night becomes a cradle and hosts its languages, in dreaming it confuses time, mixes epochs and binds civilizations."[73]

These passages vividly illustrate the centrality of Libya and of the Mediterranean in the imagination of the child protagonist and of the author. Libya and its inhabitants sit on the shore of a sea to which Hayim feels connected: a *mare nostrum* ("our sea") that is not what Fascist foreign policy implied, not the heir of the glorious Roman Empire, but a space of passage where familial faces and places interweave with the trauma of the exile.[74] With the migration, the Mediterranean brings Hayim to Italy, which in turn is transformed into a foreign *oltremare* that even before the departure from Libya had caused pain to the Libyan Jews—as the episode of Italo Balbo and the implementation of the Fascist racial laws showed. That said, the image of Libya changes as well: it passes from a space of coexistence, in some ways capable of managing the quotidian relations between its inhabitants, to a faraway territory to which one only returns with memory. Perhaps to overcome the many borders that cut across this trans-Mediterranean itinerary, at the end of the book the author inscribes the history of his community within a larger, global one that binds Tripoli to war-torn Yugoslavia, where Magiar goes in the 1990s with the representatives of an Italian nongovernmental organization: "Not being able to bear the narrowness of the new borders, drawn by invisible differences, by faceless soldiers, we unconsciously searched for a spot with no barriers so as to find again the feeling of unity, the peace of a limitless space that only the sea can give."[75] Thus, the memory of his exile from Libya remains inside him, both as a reminder of the pain that borders and war can generate and as a spark that sheds light on the limitless Mediterranean Sea, onto which Italy, Libya, and Yugoslavia all give.

In 2018, fifteen years after the publication of Magiar's book, Daniela Dawan gave to print the novel *Qual è la via del vento*. Dawan, lawyer by training, had already published a work of fiction, set in interwar Tunisia: *Non dite che col tempo si dimentica* (2010). *Qual è la via del vento* is a semiautobiographical story centered on Micol, a Jewish girl who leaves Tripoli for Italy in 1967 and, several decades later, returns to Libya on an official visit with a delegation of Libyan Jews. Like Magiar, Dawan focuses on the Mediterranean Sea but presents it as an immobile entity, which the protagonist sees from the airplane that is taking her back to Tripoli for the first time: "Micol looks down from the window: the Mediterranean, an immobile slab of steel.... Her balloon, she suddenly thinks. She is smiling: if it still exists, where will it be? Perhaps, flying over Libya and the Mediterranean, it passed exactly from there, it got lost between the clouds.... It was directed to the stars."[76] The balloon, which reminds her of a sister who died very young and was buried in Libya, got lost somewhere over the Mediterranean. The sea then becomes an inanimate entity that, nonetheless, she has to cross in order to come to terms with Libya: "This place is like a lover from whom we separated despite ourselves.... It is not dead, it exists. But it is not for you anymore."[77]

In the 1960s, on the airplane from Tripoli to Rome, Micol and her parents had had very different feelings about the country: "During the voyage, they do not exchange a word, and when they arrive they have the same piercing thought: they are nothing but refugees, now, even though for the time being they can afford living in a hotel.... 'And what are we going to do tomorrow?'... 'We will search for a house. We will buy some clothes.'... 'To start all anew, at my age.'"[78] Here, Libya is a hovering home, whereas Italy looks like a foreign land, where it is difficult to imagine the future. In a way that partly remembers the case of the Jews who resettled in France after the Algerian War, the Jews who left Tripoli and Benghazi arrived in Italy, a country that did not want to remember its colonial past and the troubling postcolonial legacies that still bound it to the other shore of the Mediterranean.[79]

Raphael Luzon's *Tramonto libico: Storia di un ebreo arabo* gives yet another insight into the Libyan Jewish history and the postmigration context, first by opting for self-writing instead of fiction. Born in Benghazi in 1954, Luzon moved to Israel in the 1990s and worked as a journalist and producer for the Italian national broadcasting company. Then he resettled in London. For many years he has been very active in organizing events on Libya and Libyan Jews, and he is recognized as one of the leading public figures of the Libyan Jewish Diaspora at the European level. *Tramonto libico* goes back to Luzon's family's final moments in and departure from Benghazi before moving to a description of the author's life after 1967, first in Italy, then in Israel and Britain, and finally of his voyages to Libya in the 2000s—which culminated in his arrest in Benghazi in 2012. Even though nostalgia for the lost world of his youth is present, from the beginning it is clear that it is not the story's leitmotif and that readers will not be spared the author's numerous difficulties and traumas before and after the migration.

One of the first episodes Luzon remembers from his childhood in 1960s Benghazi is going to the barber, where an Italian called Salvatore—who works for the Arab owner of the shop, Shafik—warns him: "'Be careful young man, soon all you Jews will be slaughtered.' I froze, even though I did not get the inner meaning of the sentence. But I saw the bad gaze of Salvatore in the mirror ... Shafik came to check that the cut was perfect. While he brushed the last hair with precise and sharp gestures, he said quietly with kindness, almost inadvertently: 'It really seems that these days are not going to be happy ones for you Jews.' This time I was not afraid ... after all I knew that being unpopular every now and then was part of being Jewish."[80] It is interesting to note that here the Italian settler Salvatore makes the protagonist much more afraid than the Muslim Arab Shafik. More generally, Arabs are not portrayed as evil characters but often as friendly and generous people. That is the case with Zaineb, the servant of the Luzons. The day before the 1967 anti-Jewish riots, Luzon writes as if he was talking to her directly: "You went to my mother and hugged her and it seemed that you did not want to let her go. I was standing in front of you and ... I saw clearly that tears dropped from your eyes and cut through your cheeks, getting my mother's shoulder wet.... On that day, none of the servants of the Jewish families went to work. None. Only you, Zaineb, came and cleaned our home in your unique way, then you cried and went back to your shacks, to your life, without saying anything."[81]

The affective bonds among Jews and Arabs living in the same household is a recurring theme in many books by North African and Middle Eastern Jews—such as the short story *Iya* (1994) by the Iraqi-born Shimon Ballas, in which the author movingly narrates the migration of the Jews of Baghdad through the perspective of an Arab housekeeper.[82] This kind of episode portrays the family as a large entity, going beyond the nuclear model and including people who are not kin related but who nonetheless are part of the same domestic world. At the same time, it reveals the hegemonic and class dynamics that, especially since the early twentieth century, sometimes existed between Jews and Arabs—and which, together with many other factors, deteriorated the relations between the two groups.[83]

Both Luzon's and Magiar's families belonged to the middle and upper strata of Libyan Jewish society, "more Westernized, more connected to the Arab elite and at the same time to the Italian minority, which had significant economic interests in the country."[84] This is one of the factors that might explain why they stayed in Libya until 1967. In that year, one of the worst moments in the history of the relations between Libyan Jews and Arabs occurred. Anti-Jewish riots started around Tripoli, causing the death of some of Luzon's relatives. The riots were a reaction to the Six Days War and took place in the context of a Palestine Week proclaimed between June 5 and June 12 by the Libyan government. Additionally, at that time the Libyan monarchy was going through a deep crisis. During the riots, about 60 percent of Jewish properties in Benghazi, and other properties owned by Italians and even Muslims, were destroyed. Because of the chaotic situation and the danger the Jews were facing, rescue operations by plane were soon organized, and by early July most of those living in Benghazi and Tripoli had already been brought to Italy.[85]

"And so we left," writes Luzon, "with nothing, leaving our dead behind us, without knowing the fate of our relatives, abandoning our houses to the Arabs, with our heart broken and our traditions, our dearest ones, our recollections [*ricordi*] in the fragile luggage of our memory [*memoria*]."[86] The author explains the trauma of his departure and tells how his family had been obliged to leave everything—in both a material and immaterial sense—behind, to the Arabs. But if *Tramonto libico* is the story of *un ebreo arabo*, of an Arab Jew, as the subtitle of the book claims, who are the Arabs and why do they become other from the Jews? Actually, it seems that the category of Arab Jew is used in a literal and nonpolitical manner, following the definition the Italian best-selling author Roberto Saviano gives in the preface: "These are Jews who felt like and defined themselves 'Arab Jews' because their language was Arabic, because for centuries if not millennia, their roots were planted in those lands of sun, desert, and sea which go from the Middle East to the Maghreb."[87] However, several studies showed that in the nineteenth and early twentieth centuries or even before, few of these Jews defined themselves as Arabs, even less as Arab Jews. One only finds occasional usage of the term in sources and contexts as different as the Arabic press of late Ottoman Palestine, in writings by Jews who lived in modern Iraq, or, later in the 1960s, in the writings of Albert Memmi. As said already, the category of Arab Jew as it is understood today only started to be deployed more or less in the last three decades and mainly in academic circles, becoming commonly used to refer to the whole of the Jews of the Arab lands.

In *Tramonto libico*, the protagonist and his family are defined as Arab Jews insofar as they speak Arabic, eat Arab food, and "have an Arab mentality."[88] Yet, in narratives covering moments of despair and sadness like the migration or the 1967 riots, the category of Arabness refers exclusively to the Muslims and stands in opposition to that of Jewishness. For example, when the author recalls the time his family's Libyan Muslim acquaintances arrived in Italy, after the migration, he writes: "It happened that an *Arab* acquaintance from Libya visited us in Italy, because he felt nostalgia for his *Jewish* friends or out of guilt or only in order to finalize some business that had been left halfway."[89] Throughout the book, Arabs and Jews are portrayed as both neighbors and enemies, or as rivals and relatives, to quote the felicitous title of Harvey Goldberg's study on Libyan Jews:[90] they are part of a shared history of daily interactions, exchanges, and clashes that—as seen in Boukhobza's *Pour l'amour du père*—came to an end with the outbreak of the Arab-Israeli conflict, decolonization, and the road the Arab nation-states took.

In this description, the Italians and the Italian Jews that Libyan Jews encountered after emigration feature as little more than background actors. Italy is portrayed as a shelter where Raphael and his family can start to rebuild their life but also as a space where they faced difficulty and incomprehension, from the precarious situation in the refugee camp of Capua, near Naples, where they settled in the immediate aftermath of their departure from Benghazi, to the insults of Raphael's classmates at the Roman Jewish school, who told him to "go back to Africa." As a result, the protagonist stuck to his family and a Libyan Jewish circle of friends: "We, the boys that had come from Libya, always spent time between us and it would be so up until the day when the first wedding between a Jewess from Tripoli and a Roman Jew was celebrated."[91] Although Libya had been an Italian colony and many Libyan Jews had attended Italian schools and spoke Italian, upon arrival in Rome they were stigmatized as coming from an underdeveloped, *African* country—relegated to a status like that of the Italians of Libya expelled when Qaddhafi rose to power in 1969, of many other colonial migrants, and of the *Mizrahim* in Israel.⁹²

The Jews who arrived in Italy from Libya and other countries of the southern Mediterranean shore felt that their history and identity were not being correctly understood—when not ignored altogether—by a society that until then had been characterized, and for many more years would be, almost exclusively by emigration of Italians abroad more than by immigration of foreigners to Italy.⁹³ Furthermore, the Libyan Jewish migrants possibly reminded many Italian Jews, as well as non-Jews, of Fascism and its disastrous colonial and nationalistic enterprises. Gone were the days when rabbis like Elia Samuele Artom or Gustavo Castelbolognesi were being sent to Tripoli to guide the local Jewish communities and Italian Jewish leaders thought about the possibility of establishing a Sephardi federation that—under their guidance—would unite Jews from all over the Mediterranean.⁹⁴ After all, when the Libyan Jews migrated, only twenty years had passed since the end of the Second World War and the Holocaust, and Italian Jewry had just started to reconstruct itself and find a space of its own in Republican Italy.⁹⁵

As in Magiar's *E venne la notte*, the idea of mobility and of exile as foundational characteristics of the Sephardi Jews appears in *Tramonto libico*. In the 2000s, after Luzon's *'aliyah* to Israel and then his migration to London for professional reasons, he started to organize activities on behalf of the Libyan Jewish diaspora. Luzon's memoir illustrates that the migration from one's country of birth to Europe often is only the first step in the making of a multidimensional diaspora and a transnational itinerary, which in his case intersects Israel, Italy, Britain, and Libya. As a result of his activities on behalf of the Libyan Jews, the Libyan government officially invited Luzon to visit the country. Arriving there with his old mother and his sister, all "hesitant, happy, scared," Luzon suddenly sees "the blue of the sea being torn by the yellow of the earth, like a gash of memory that leaves us dismayed, silent. . . . The sea was marvelous, the only one that had not changed, transparent like the clear sky upon us."⁹⁶ While escorted by Libyan guards, Raphael and his family tour Benghazi and visit, if only from the outside, "our family home" and then also "the synagogue, the school, the three places that made me what I am, that taught me and gave me the strength to be a man and to face all that was soon to come." They even meet an old friend of his mother's, Rasmia, now old and in bad health, who "started to shake and with great efforts but clearly, a word erupted from her mouth . . . : 'Rachele, Rachele, Rachele. . . .' The two women hugged each other and in that hug, which made us all cry, I saw—as if in a revelation—the meaning of our entire voyage."⁹⁷ A meeting with an old neighbor can be found in many memoirs and novels by Jews from the Arab world, for instance in the semiautobiographical novel *Qol tze'adenu* (The sound of our steps; 2008) by the Israeli of Egyptian origin Ronit Matalon—in that case the protagonist's mother, after many decades, visited her old apartment in Cairo and met one of her neighbors. Thanks to that, one learns that time surely fades the memory of the past but never entirely cancels it. On the contrary, memory can come back in tiny details like the color of the Mediterranean Sea—the only thing that appears to have not changed after the migration—or the barely audible words of an elder.

Nonetheless, both Magiar and Luzon feel that not just the neighborhoods and cities but the entire world in which they were born has disappeared and that therefore "there is no place to go back to."[98] They can only go forward, by blending history with fiction and by constructing new identities at the crossroads of Libya, Italy, and the Mediterranean. For them, the memory of the Libyan past is always conceived from an exilic present: even decades after the departure from Tripoli and Benghazi, the world in which they were born has an impact on their life and on how they perceive their surroundings. This very clearly emerges from the description of Luzon's arrest during his last trip to Libya in the summer of 2012, at the time of the uprising that would lead to the ousting and killing of Qaddhafi, when the author was accused of being an Israeli spy and then released several days after the intervention of the Italian authorities and a number of Libyan personalities: "I walked along the perimeter of the cell . . . in an endless half-sleep populated by ghosts, memories, faraway places, forgotten faces and beloved eyes," asking how that could have happened "precisely [to] me, that I had seen everything and forgotten nothing."[99] Ultimately, Magiar's and Luzon's works seem to suggest that the North African Jewish past is perennially oscillating between multiple geographies and chronologies, as if to demonstrate once more the extent to which the experience of exile and trauma "fundamentally shape[s] the temporality of modern memory," and in this case creates original—yet quite ambivalent—correlations between the Italian and Libyan shores, and the two epochs in the authors' lives that these countries represent.[100]

"HA-ROMAN HA-MITZRI" BY ORLY CASTEL-BLOOM: A FAMILY FANTASY

In the early 1950s, a group of young Egyptian Jews affiliated with the Zionist movement Ha-shomer ha-tzair migrated to Israel and settled in kibbutz 'Ein Shemer—in the northeast of the country, near the city of Hadera. Life in the new environment was not easy, and clashes soon broke out between the new *kibbutznikim* and the *vatiqim* ("elders"), the founding members who were mostly of Ashkenazi origin and who started to accuse the Egyptian *gar'in* (lit.: "nucleus") of nothing less than anti-Zionism and Stalinism. But for Henriette, a member of the *gar'in*, things were quite different: "We were cosmopolitans.... We were in favor of equality, brotherhood, solidarity and against all kinds of racism. That is why they threw us out of the *kibbutz*."[101] The history of this bizarre *gerush* ("expulsion")—which challenges, not only from a literary point of view, the idea of the *kibbutz* as an egalitarian space, based on collectivism and Socialist ideals—and of the new life that an Egyptian Jewish family builds for itself in Israel, is at the core of Sapir Prize winner *Ha-roman ha-mitzri* (The Egyptian novel), published in 2015 by Orly Castel-Bloom. It is also, unlike what we have seen so far, an attempt at reconstructing one's own family history, not so much by using memory or the historical records, but by pushing the boundaries of the imagination to the extremes—as if this is the only way to write about a world that is lost forever.

Castel-Bloom was born in Tel Aviv in 1960 and, especially since her acclaimed novel *Dolly City* (1992), has become one of the most important Israeli authors of her generation and an internationally renowned writer.[102] Because of her original style and language, which deconstruct the traditional relations between syntax and lexicon to produce grotesque or even nightmarish descriptions of an Israeli microcosm living in a state of permanent crisis, Castel-Bloom has been defined as the quintessential post-Zionist writer and an emblem of Hebrew postmodernism.[103] *Ha-roman ha-mitzri* is not the first text that the author dedicates to her Egyptian background, which is already present in the short stories *Joe 'Ish Qahir* (Cairo Joe), part of the collection *Svivah 'Oyenet* (Hostile surroundings; 1989), and *Ummi fi-shughul* (Arabic: My mother is at work), which was published in *Sippurim bilti-ratzoniyim* (Involuntary stories; 1993).[104] However, it is the first major work in which the author tackles her family story, albeit in a surreal manner that combines reality and fiction, as is always the case in Castel-Bloom's writings. *Ha-roman ha-mitzri* tells of a family of Egyptians newly immigrating to Israel and their unnamed daughter, *ha-bat ha-gdolah* ("the eldest daughter"), to whose story the author adds episodes in the life of the family's ancestors in Egypt and the Iberian Peninsula.

To understand the milieu from which Castel-Bloom—and the characters of *Ha-roman ha-mitzri*—comes, one has to remember that the majority of the modern Egyptian Jews descended from migrants arrived in Egypt in the second half of the nineteenth century and at the beginning of the twentieth, following the great economic expansion Cairo and Alexandria underwent after the opening of the Suez Canal in 1869, and the boom of the cotton industry in those same years.[105] As thousands of Jews from the eastern Mediterranean, North Africa, and southern Europe settled in Egypt, a new Egyptian Jewish Diaspora came about. It was by and large a middle-class community made of small entrepreneurs, professionals, and business owners that stood at the crossroads of different national and cultural identities: protégés of European powers, Egyptian or stateless, largely but not solely Francophone, deeply modern and at the same time attached to their Mediterranean and Ottoman background and to Jewish traditions.[106]

Of the almost eighty thousand Jews who lived in Egypt in the late 1940s, about 30 percent eventually migrated to Israel. Their 'aliyah was due occasionally to Zionist convictions—even though Zionism had directly involved a minority of the Egyptian Jews—and more often to the fact that for many, especially for those who were stateless, the migration to Israel was the easiest option for leaving Egypt in times of increased nationalistic and anti-Jewish sentiments. In fact, most of the Jews left in the 1950s, after Nasser's Revolution (1952) or during the Suez War (1956).[107] Considering this, it is not surprising that for some of the protagonists of Castel-Bloom's *Ha-roman ha-mitzri*, Zionism is not the driving force behind the migration, let alone their life. For example, for Adèle—another member of the *gar'in*—political ideologies such as "Zionism, Communism, Socialism—beetles, that is what they were like, beetles to be sprayed and get rid of, in order to have everything clean and ready for the things that really counted in life: love, quiet, beauty, an adequate amount of good food."[108] Adèle's husband, Vita, was a member of the Zionist group Ha-'ivri ha-tza'ir ("The young Hebrew") in 1940s Egypt but was also someone who fought to improve the conditions of the Egyptian peasants: "As an Egyptian he felt he had to take part in the harsh demonstrations against the royal police of Faruq, as a Zionist he smuggled Jews out of Egypt. He did these two things putting his own life at risk."[109] In fact, until the mid-1940s, being a young Egyptian Zionist did not mean rejecting feelings of belonging to the Egyptian nation. In an only apparently contradictory manner, Zionist aspirations coexisted with profound cultural and emotional ties to Egypt, as one realizes when reading articles published in Egyptian Jewish pro-Zionist newspapers of the interwar years—for example, *La Tribune Juive*—or when looking at the interactions that at the time still existed between Egyptian and Zionist youth associations and scouting movements.[110]

As said, *Ha-roman ha-mitzri* begins with the *gerush* of the protagonists from a kibbutz. Rejected by and unwilling to adapt to that environment, the parents of *ha-bat ha-gdolah*, Charlie and Viviane Castil, together with the former's brother Vita; his wife, Adèle; and their daughter, *ha-bat ha-yehidah* ("the only daughter"), all move to Tel Aviv. In fact, it is there that most of the Egyptian *'olim* (pl. of *'oleh*, "[Jewish] migrant to the State of Israel) settled and tried to create a home in which to cultivate a more private and barely visible Egyptian Jewish heritage made of memories, family sayings, and old photographs. Like other *Mizrahim*, these migrants found it difficult to adapt to 1950s Israel, which was so different from the urban and middle-class lifestyle to which they were accustomed. As people "who came to young Israel from such modern cities as Baghdad... Algiers, Casablanca, Tangiers, Tehran," some of the *'olim* were "shocked to discover the technological and economic backwardness of the Jewish nation" and deeply resented the fact that they had to leave a generally comfortable life and first settle in a transit camp.[111] The Castils, just like many other new immigrants, "were not the lords of the land and it was better to keep their mouth shut and only express their opinion while sitting among themselves on the balcony at dusk—and even then, not in Hebrew."[112]

The balcony is a recurrent feature in Castel-Bloom's literary architecture and, according to Grumberg, could symbolize the disruption of "the boundaries between the individual and the collective, the person and the place she inhabits, but ends up making them only more apparent."[113] In fact, the characters of *Ha-roman ha-mitzri* seem to look at Israeli society from the outside, from the borders of their balconies that overlook the Tel Aviv boulevards: they are internal outsiders to the nation, as exemplified by the fact that they chat in French but understand and speak Hebrew too. In all the novels by Israelis of Egyptian origin—and in *Mizrahi* literature more generally—from Jacqueline Kahanoff and Yitzhaq Gormezano Goren to Ronit Matalon and Moshe Sakal, Hebrew is presented as a language that the migrants have difficulty in learning and speaking and whose national centrality does not erase the presence of the many different idioms that the migrants brought from the Diaspora—in the case of Egypt, languages such as French, Ladino, Italian, and Arabic—and the cultural complexity that lies beneath this multilingualism.[114] The same happens in the writings of Egyptian Jews now living in France, Italy, or the US, like André Aciman, who—in *Out of Egypt*—describes the lingua franca used by an upper-class Alexandrian Jewish family and their Arab servant: "When Mohammed, our servant, telephoned early one morning from the hospital... he told me, 'Al bambino bita Mohammed getu morto,' meaning, 'The son belonging to Mohammed has become dead.'... This was not even spoken Egyptian, but in its garbled mixture of French, Italian, and Arabic, it allowed Europeans who never cared to learn Arabic to communicate with the local population."[115]

The idea that the Egyptians were among the least Arab among the Jews of the Middle East also emerges from a passage of Castel-Bloom's novel. In it, we read how the protagonist, *ha-bat ha-gdolah*, befriends a classmate from a well-off Ashkenazi family, whose house she frequently visits. There, "between the first and second course, the mother used to light a cigarette and they started talking about Kafka, and everybody took part to the conversation.... The Hebrew they spoke there was different, even from the one taught in school.... The house was full of books, but Hebrew books."[116] Despite the difference in social status between the Ashkenazi girl and *ha-bat ha-gdolah*, the former's mother believes that "her parents [of *ha-bat ha-gdolah*] know better. They are from Egypt, but they speak French at home. The Egyptians are different from all other *Mizrahim*."[117] Even though it would be incorrect to claim that the Egyptian Jews were estranged from the Arab world and from the Arabic language, one cannot deny that in comparison to the Moroccan or Iraqi Jews, they participated less to the local Arabic cultural and literary scene.[118] The emphasis on the Levantine and cosmopolitan atmosphere in which the Egyptian Jewish identity developed also relates to the fact that, up to the 1930s, Egyptian national identity was often conceived not in terms of Arabness but in relation to the Mediterranean and the Pharaonic era.[119]

As regards the Egyptian *'olim*, the underlining of an alleged Europeanness and cosmopolitanism was for many a reaction to the derogatory attitudes that the Israeli establishment initially had toward the *Mizrahim*—who were perceived as uneducated individuals coming from backward countries who needed to be reeducated in the new (Zionist/Israeli) environment.[120] Finally, I would argue that this is related to a sociocultural imaginary that, both before and after the *'aliyah*, was influenced by notions of middle-class distinction and respectability. For many Egyptian Jews, Europe was not the location of a centuries-old Diaspora that Zionism intended to negate but the metaphor of modernity and of a modern world they wished to be part of.[121] Even after the migration, the characters of *Ha-roman ha-mitzri* still perceive themselves as belonging to a middle stratum of society that strives to live "not far from the center of town" and of Israel, to quote the title of Castel-Bloom's first collection of short stories, *Lo' rahoq mi-merkaz ha-'ir* (1987); yet the small distance between the center and their homes suffices to render them outsiders to the political and national landscape with which they are struggling.

As already seen in Boukhobza's *Un été à Jérusalem*, for the protagonists of *Ha-roman ha-mitzri*, the *'aliyah* is only the last step in a long family history of exile, of which the first step had been the expulsion from *Sefarad*. This historical event frequently finds place in the memorial literature by Egyptian Jews, resulting in anecdotes that reinforce one's personal pride and (lost) social status vis-à-vis the difficulties of the postmigration context. For example, the Italian Laura Barile, who descends from an Alexandrian Jewish family, remembers how her grandfather's ancestors had lived in Zaragoza and Salonika: "In Egypt, Albert Gattegno founded a construction and electrical enterprise.... Nobody remembers where exactly he was born."[122] Along similar lines, Jean Naggar says that her grandmother came from a family of "survivors of the inquisition in Spain, [that] had fled to Amsterdam, where they flourished and multiplied greatly before seeking and finding a home in Egypt."[123] As opposed to this, Castel-Bloom narrates *Sefarad* in a defiant way, explaining that most of the Castil family escaped Spain and after a long journey across the Mediterranean arrived nowhere else but Gaza, whereas the other members of the family became *conversos* and therefore were able to continue living in Spain and to work as pig farmers.[124]

This familial fantasy is due not only to Castel-Bloom's writing style, always characterized by irony, but also to the fact that for her generation—that of the children of the first migrants, who, just like the protagonist of *Ha-roman ha-mitzri*, bear no name—the Egyptian Jewish past seems to come back only in the shape of extraordinary memories in a quasi-magical place they do not know personally.[125] Even Israel appears like a land of missed opportunities, where *ha-bat ha-gdolah*, her cousin *ha-bat ha-yehidah*, and their parents constantly search for a better life or fight against illnesses and, while doing so, try to get along while arguing with one another. However, Castel-Bloom's characters always end up overcoming their personal dramas—which, in turn, relate to those of an entire community—with a smile and a bit of irony.[126]

As regards the ethno-national backgrounds of *Ha-roman ha-mitzri*, one cannot avoid noting that the narration rarely includes Arabs, especially Palestinians, who are more or less absent from the story. This occurs not just in this novel but also in previous works by Castel-Bloom, which, even though innovative and subversive in terms of style or in representations of the Levant, never conjoin the history and memory of the *Mizrahim* with those of the Arabs.[127] For example, a day trip to the sea in Tantura, a small village in Galilee a few kilometers north of Zikhron Ya'akov, is portrayed as a moment that brings back unhappy memories of the childhood of *ha-bat ha-gdolah*: "All her life she had dreamt of Tantura, where she had never managed to go. Her parents' friends, from the *kibbutz* 'Ein Shemer, used to go to Tantura during the holidays and rent a bungalow next to the sea, as they had done in their childhood in Port Said or Lebanon. But Charlie and Viviane did not have enough money for Tantura." There, in a grotesque move typical of Castel-Bloom, we discover that the daughter of *ha-bat ha-yehidah*, who could not help crying while swimming in the sea, "was developing a chronic autoimmune illness."[128] Even though no mention of it is made in the book, it is worth remembering that in 1948 the Haganah voided the fishing village of Tantura of its Palestinian inhabitants—some claim that villagers were killed—and next to it the kibbutz Nahsholim and the moshav Dor were founded. In the mid-1950s, the possible commercial and touristic usage of the coast started to be discussed, and shortly afterward what remained of the Palestinian houses were demolished to make space for that vacation village that *Ha-roman ha-mitzri*'s characters happen to visit.[129]

That said, an Arab character does feature in *Ha-roman ha-mitzri*. At the center of one of the final chapters of the novel is an Egyptian man who, having studied Hebrew in Tel Aviv, works as a guide for Israeli tourists in Cairo: "He had a predefined itinerary that started with the Pyramids in Giza, those of Saqqarah, and then back to Cairo—the suq Khan el-Khalil (where Israelis generally bought scarves); after that he brought the visitors to the Egyptian Museum, and finally—and this was for many Israelis the highlight of the visit—the Coptic churches, the old synagogue of Ben Ezra in the *harat al-yahud* [Arabic: "Jewish neighborhood"].... In the end, he liked the Israelis and shared with them a mutual language, even though he never saw such arrogance as theirs."[130] The man disappears in mysterious circumstances during one of the popular protests that took place in Cairo in the years following the 2011 revolution, after having met at the zoo Céleste Sanua, the daughter of the president of the Jewish Community of Cairo, whom he starts to help and date.

The novel then is a continuous overlap of fictional and surreal stories, on the one hand, and episodes that instead refer to the history of the Egyptian Jews in more or less accurate terms, on the other. In contrast with more conventional testimonies and life stories written by Egyptian Jews, which often present a sentimental picture of pre-Nasserist Egypt and the cosmopolitan golden era that they allegedly experienced,[131] *Ha-roman ha-mitzri* does not wish to commemorate the past but to reimagine it as a collection of fragments that, altogether, form the contours of a family to which everyone can feel attached. "Telling a story, be it by a writer or a historian," Alon Confino contends, "is a way of looking outward and offering a way of seeing the world, of being in it. This way of seeing is possible when we open our imagination . . . or when we sense a pain of recognition."[132] If this is true, by bringing together distant times and places, and by trying to reconcile Egypt with Israel through the recourse to fantastic stories, Castel-Bloom constructs an alternative memorial itinerary that offers a perhaps more humane vision of the past and of the other. Her extravagant narration reinterprets the Egyptian

Jewish memory of the Castil family as a series of unresolved exiles whose stories are waiting to be told, of seemingly unsurmountable boundaries that only literature can cross.

To anyone familiar with the writings of Egyptian Jews, Castel-Bloom's mixture of fiction and truth will immediately bring to mind the Israeli novelist Yitzhaq Gormezano Goren, who was born in Alexandria in 1942 and migrated to Israel with his family as a child, and the Italian saying he repeatedly cites in the *Trilogiah 'Aleksandronit* (Alexandrian trilogy): *Se non è vero, è ben trovato* ("If it is untrue, it is well conceived"). For Gormezano Goren, the story he wishes to tell is not true or false but forcedly both, and thus he cannot call himself a witness.[133] Even though *Ha-roman ha-mitzri*'s grotesque elements render the distinction between the real and surreal dimension more easily discernible than in Gormezano Goren's works, we can still trace a similar reasoning that views literature as a refuge from reality, a space in which to resist the frontiers that traverse Israeli society and the Mediterranean region more broadly.

The Castil family narrative can be compared to those of other Middle Eastern and North African Jews, as they all reflect an exilic history that traverses the centuries and is destined to continue after the establishment of Israel. This country, while being the national and geographic home of a new generation of Castils, does not end their feeling of uprootedness and of always being en route. As I already argued, this appears to be the most significant characteristic of the identity of the Middle Eastern and North African Jews—and, even more so, of the ways in which it is imagined and narrated—as well as of other exiled communities, such as the Italians of Tunisia, the Greeks of Egypt, or the Algerian *pieds-noirs*. "It goes back, I believe," notes Teresa Cremisi, born in Alexandria and partly of Jewish background, "to that period, the feeling that everything was temporary, for us, for the others, for the entire mankind. It was pointless to make fuss, some were more exiled than others, but they easily got used to that idea."[134]

Whereas before the migration the absence of a clear national identity and the idea of belonging to a broad Levantine world did not constitute a problem, from the 1950s and 1960s, and in the aftermath of the resettlement of the Jews to another country, it became a troubling yet defining trait of diasporic communities that did not seem to have a place inside the new—postcolonial or Zionist—nation-state. Thus, to understand the place of the Castil family, one can only go back in time to *Sefarad* or to pre-Nasserist Egypt, travel to a surreal contemporary Cairo, and end in an apocalyptic Tel Aviv, which, in contrast to the polar winter Castel-Bloom described in the 2002 novel *Halaqim 'enoshiyim* (Human parts), is now hit by "a hot and disheartening winter, that followed a series of arid winters, as a result of global warming.... Nobody had ever witnessed such weather. Air conditioners. August in the middle of November."[135]

The lives of the Castils cannot be included in a linear historiographic narrative but must be told as a sequence of events that intersects with them and whose recollection brings the past back into the present, erasing the boundaries between the two and giving life to a third dimension dominated by fantasy. Ultimately, the Castil family itself is the fantasy that the protagonists—from *ha-bat ha-gdolah* to her parents and their friends—like to tell, so as to put aside an Israeli reality that is often too harsh. As opposed to Raphael Luzon's claim to have forgotten nothing of his premigratory past, *Ha-roman ha-mitzri* originates in the quasi-complete oblivion of a past, and to an extent a present, that the Castil family does not want to remember and therefore reinvents with the imagination.[136]

REDRAWING THE BOUNDARIES

Based on a Jewish literary and historical perspective, this chapter has looked at the Sephardi and *Mizrahi* past as it comes out of memorial writings rooted in the migration, exile, and resettlement experienced by the Jews of North Africa and Egypt in the second half of the twentieth century. The writers I analyzed use different approaches: Boukhobza describes families torn between France and Israel who still maintain Tunisia as a crucial, albeit vanishing, *lieu de mémoire*. The autobiographical writings by Luzon and Magiar, on the other hand, examine the Libyan past and portray it through the perspective of their migratory itinerary to Italy and the troubled relations that Libya and that country have entertained from Fascism to postcolonial times and until today, and in doing so, these writings build complicated chronologies and geographies that traverse the Mediterranean. Thirdly, Castel-Bloom uses the historical memory of her Egyptian family as a palimpsest against which to construct a deeply creative literary fantasy: in it, the present is much more at stake than the past, which always is narrated in a surreal manner.

Sometimes, these authors reflect on the past in positive and nostalgic terms, for example indulging in the cosmopolitan atmosphere of a Libyan school once attended by both Jews and Arabs. In other instances, they focus on the more negative aspects and their troubling legacies—like the dull life that Tunisian elders endure in the southern Israeli periphery, or the antisemitic riots that occurred in 1960s Tripoli. Despite these differences, the four of them conceive of the country of origin as a foundational imaginative landscape in which to situate their identity. The southern shore of the Mediterranean is presented as an entity characterized by a plurality of nations and languages, by movements of people that connect and divide the two shores. In addition to people, ideas and imaginaries circulated, in this case not only from north to south but—especially after the migration of the Jews—vice versa. So, if it is true that at least since the first half of the twentieth century Europe and colonialism have had an impact on the identity of the Jewish migrants, after the 1950s and 1960s, when they resettled in places like the Parisian neighborhood of Belleville or in the desert city of Beer Sheva, so have these same migrants tenaciously brought their recent Arab past with them to the other side of the Mediterranean.

Literary writing then helps to disrupt the colonial and postcolonial power relations in which these migrants are imbricated, shedding light on unexpected moments of interaction between Jews and Arabs, old and new habits and lifestyles: think of the depiction of the Egyptian tourist guide who falls in love with one of the last Jews of Cairo in Castel-Bloom's *Ha-roman ha-mitzri*.[137] From this perspective, the distinction between Diaspora and Land of Israel appears less central, as it is substituted with a more ambiguous postmigratory Mediterranean world, of which Israel itself is part. This is not something completely new, as studies on early modern Sephardi culture have already underlined the processes of rediasporization that Jewish migrants experienced in the aftermath of the expulsion from Spain, reconceived as a second exile after that from the Land of Israel.[138] Thus, these North African and Middle Eastern Jewish writers help us to clarify that the postmigratory diasporic identity certainly reflects the contingencies of a new and different historical period but at the same time results from an almost permanent history of migration that goes back to the antiquity and that the birth of the State of Israel did not end.

This history is mirrored in the many memorial ties that bind the Arab Muslim world—from which the Jews come—to Europe and Israel and that bring about the formation of *noeuds de mémoire* that go beyond the present boundaries of nations and continents.[139] Certainly, the country of immigration plays a great role and deeply marks their memorial itinerary. But nonetheless, it is not the sole or even most important point of reference, as it is always evoked together with other spaces—from the city of birth to a school, a neighborhood, and of course the country of origin—and is part of a composite picture populated by Jews and Arabs, French and Tunisians, Ashkenazi and *Mizrahi* Israelis, and so on. Within this panorama, one finds stories that, despite having different settings and chronologies, coalesce into a homogeneous narrative of exile in which shared tropes and modes of remembrance can be found: suffice it to mention the central place ascribed to one's Sephardi ancestry in Castel-Bloom's

Ha-roman ha-mitzri and Magiar's *E venne la notte*, or the ambivalent representation of the Arabs—comrades, lovers, and enemies—in Boukhobza's *Pour l'amour du père* and Luzon's *Tramonto libico*.

At the same time, these tropes do not tell us in a straightforward manner how, for example, the Arabs *were* conceived by Tunisian Jews living in 1980s Paris but how they *could* be conceived. By saying so, I follow a reading of memory "as an outcome of the relationship between a distinct representation of the past and the full spectrum of symbolic representations available in a given culture."[140] In other words, the literary elaboration of the past is constructed against the background of different versions of it, which interact with one another and pave the way to ever-changing itineraries of remembrance. While this may seem a naivete, it is important in order to correctly redraw the boundaries between the literary past and the historical reality, even more so in the case of communities who lived through traumatic experiences of displacement, like the Jews of the Middle East and North Africa, and whose history can be—and, in fact, often has been—subject to contrasting yet equally rigid nationalistic interpretations: either as one of cohabitation ended first because of colonialism and then Zionism and the birth of Israel, or of innate Muslim antisemitism and *dhimmitude*.[141] Thus, the literary itineraries that these four writers elaborate can be read as an attempt to conceive of the past as a collection of geographies of migration embedded in a multidimensional "history that we did not know"[142]—or, perhaps, we had all forgotten about—made of lost proximity to and increased distance from the other, of nostalgia for the country of origin, and of feelings of estrangement and unhomeliness for the country of immigration.

NOTES

1. Gini Alhadeff, *The Sun at Midday: Tales of a Mediterranean Family* (New York: Anchor Books, 1997), 3.

2. Here I can only refer to a few seminal studies: Peregrine Horden and Nicholas Purcell, *The Corrupting Sea: A Study of Mediterranean History* (London: Blackwell, 2000); David Abulafia, *The Great Sea: A Human History of the Mediterranean* (Oxford: Oxford University Press, 2011); and of course the classic by Fernand Braudel, *La Méditerranée et le monde méditerranéen à l'époque de Philippe II* (Paris: Armand Colin, 1949). See also Iain Chambers, *Mediterranean Crossings: The Politics of an Interrupted Modernity* (Durham, NC: Duke University Press, 2008); Julia Clancy-Smith, *Mediterraneans: North Africa and Europe in an Age of Migration, c. 1800–1900* (Berkeley: University of California Press, 2011).

3. For a sociopolitical usage of the notion of *Mediterranean neighborhood*, see Tobias Schumacher, "Introduction: The Study of Euro-Mediterranean Cultural and Social Co-operation in Perspective," in *Conceptualizing Cultural and Social Dialogue in the Euro-Mediterranean Area*, ed. Michelle Pace and Tobias Schumacher (London: Routledge, 2007), 3–12; Stefania Panebianco, "The Euro-Mediterranean Partnership in Perspective: The Political and Institutional Context," in *A New Euro-Mediterranean Cultural Identity*, ed. Stefania Panebianco (London: Frank Cass, 2003), 23–46; Federica Bicchi and Richard Gillespie, eds., *The Union for the Mediterranean* (London: Routledge, 2012).

4. Maryline Crivello, "Les arts de la mémoire en Méditerranée," in *Les échelles de la mémoire en Méditerranée (XIXe–XXIe siècle)*, ed. Maryline Crivello (Arles: Actes Sud, 2010), 28–29.

5. Michael Rothberg, "Introduction: Between Memory and Memory: From Lieux de Mémoire to Noeuds de Mémoire," *Yale French Studies*, no. 118–19 (2010): 7. See also Astrid Erll, "Travelling Memory," *Parallax* 17, no. 4 (2011): 4–18.

6. For another perspective on the subject, consider the monographic issue of the journal *Expression Maghrébines* 11, no. 2 (2014) on "Nouvelles expressions judéo-maghrébines" and Ewa Tartakowsky, *Les Juifs et le Maghreb: Fonctions sociales d'une littérature d'exil* (Tours: Presses Universitaires François-Rabelais, 2016); Thomas Nolden, *In Lieu of Memory: Contemporary Jewish Writing in France* (Syracuse, NY: Syracuse University Press, 2006), esp. 164–212.

7. Albert Memmi, *Juifs et Arabes* (Paris: Gallimard, 1974), 57. See also Emanuela Trevisan Semi, "Entre le contexte oublié et l'hégémonisation du 'fait juif': quelques réflexions à partir du narratif sioniste," in *Socio-anthropologie des judaïsmes contemporains*, ed. Chantal Bordes-Benayoun (Paris: Honoré Champion, 2015), 101–9.

8. On the *longue durée* effects of the decree on the Jews of Algeria, see Joshua Schreier, *Arabs of the Jewish Faith: The Civilizing Mission in Colonial Algeria* (New Brunswick, NJ: Rutgers University Press, 2010), esp. 168–75; Maud Mandel, *Muslims and Jews in France: History of A Conflict* (Princeton, NJ: Princeton University Press, 2014).

9. Tabea Alexa Linhard, *Jewish Spain: A Mediterranean Memory* (Stanford, CA: Stanford University Press, 2015), 7.

10. Roger Chartier, *Au bord de la falaise: L'histoire entre certitudes et inquiétude* (Paris: Albin Michel, 1998); Ivan Jablonka, *L'histoire est une littérature contemporaine* (Paris: Seuil, 2014).

11. Carlo Ginzburg, "Just One Witness," in *Probing the Limits of Representation: Nazism and the "Final Solution,"* ed. Saul Friedländer (Cambridge, MA: Harvard University Press, 1992), 95.

12. Miccoli, *Histories*, 8; Julia Clancy-Smith, "Twentieth-Century Historians and Historiography of the Middle East: Women, Gender, and Empire," in *Middle*

East Historiographies: Narrating the Twentieth Century, ed. Israel Gershoni, Amy Singer, and Yakan Hakan Erdem (Seattle: University of Washington Press, 2006).

13. Monique R. Balbuena, *Homeless Tongues: Poetry and Languages of the Sephardic Diaspora* (Stanford, CA: Stanford University Press, 2016), 12–18; Lital Levy and Allison Schachter, "A Non-universal Global: On Jewish Writing and World Literature," *Prooftexts* 36, no. 1–2 (2017): 1–26. See also Dario Miccoli, "Introduction: Memories, Books, Diasporas," in *Contemporary Sephardic and Mizrahi Literature: A Diaspora*, ed. Dario Miccoli (London: Routledge, 2017), 1–9.

14. Paul Sebag, *Histoire des Juifs de Tunisie: Des origines à nos jours* (Paris: L'Harmattan, 1991); Lucette Valensi and Abraham Udovitch, *The Last Arab Jews: The Communities of Djerba, Tunisia* (New York: Harwood Academic, 1984). On the *grana*, see Leila El Houssi, "The Qrana Italian Jewish Community of Tunisia between XVIII–XIX Century: An Example of Transnational Dimension," *Studi Emigrazione*, no. 186 (April–June 2012): 361–69.

15. Laurence Podselver, "L'alya des Juifs de France: de la communauté à la nation, premiers éléments d'une recherche," in *Socio-anthropologie*, ed. Chantal Bordes-Benayoun, 335–46.

16. Tartakowsky, *Juifs*.

17. Madeleine Dobie, "For and Against the Mediterranean: Francophone Perspectives," *Comparative Studies of South Asia, Africa and the Middle East* 34, no. 2 (2014): 398.

18. Chochana Boukhobza, *Un été à Jérusalem* (Paris: Balland, 1986), 35–36.

19. Boukhobza, *Un été*, 135, 137.

20. Boukhobza, *Un été*, 21.

21. Nathan P. Devir, "Midrashic Bodies: Prostitution as Revolt in Chochana Boukhobza's *Un été à Jérusalem*," *Nashim*, no. 23 (2012): 129–44.

22. Nina B. Lichtenstein, "North Africa, France, and Israel: Sephardic Identities in the Works of Chochana Boukhobza," *Sephardic Horizons* 3, no. 2 (2013), http://www.sephardichorizons.org/Volume3/Issue2/Identities.html.

23. Shmuel Yosef Agnon, *Tehillah* (Tel Aviv: Shocken, 1977). See also Dekoven Ezrahi, *Booking Passage*, 34.

24. See Oren Yiftahel and Eretz Tzfadia, "Between Periphery and 'Third Space': Identity of Mizrahim in Israel's Development Towns," in *Israelis in Conflict*, ed. Adriana Kemp, David Newman, Uri Ram, and Oren Yiftahel (Eastbourne: Sussex Academic, 2004), 203–35; Aziza Khazzoom, "Did the Israeli State Engineer Segregation? On the Placement of Jewish Immigrants in Development Towns in the 1950s," *Social Forces* 84, no. 1 (2005): 115–34; Seymour Spilerman and Jack Habib, "Development Towns in Israel: The Role of Community in Creating Ethnic Disparities in Labor Force Characteristics," *American Journal of Sociology* 81, no. 4 (1976): 781–812.

25. Boukhobza, *Un été*, 47.

26. André Nahum, "L'exil des Juifs de Tunisie: l'échec d'une continuité," *Pardès* 34, no. 1 (2003): 244. Consider also Esther Schely-Newman, *Our Lives Are but Stories: Narratives of Tunisian-Israeli Women* (Detroit: Wayne State University Press, 2002); Navah Sarah Yardeni, *Yehudei-Tunisiah be-Israel: 'Edot ve-te'ud* [Tunisian Jews in Israel: Testimony and documentation] (Lod: Orot Yahadut Maghreb, 2009).

27. Boukhobza, *Un été*, 32.

28. Boukhobza, *Un été*, 192.

29. Eliezer Ben-Rafael and Yochanan Peres, *Is Israel One? Religion, Nationalism, and Multiculturalism Confounded* (Leiden: Brill, 2005); Eliezer Ben-Rafael, *The Emergence of Ethnicity: Cultural Groups and Social Conflict in Israel* (London: Greenwood, 1982); Judith Shuval, *Immigrants on the Threshold* (New Brunswick, NJ: Aldine Transaction, 1963).

30. For a similar interpretation, see Laurel Plapp, *Zionism and Revolution in European-Jewish Literature* (London: Routledge, 2008), esp. 167–69.

31. Boukhobza, *Un été*, 55.

32. Boukhobza, *Un été*, 117–18.

33. Marianne Hirsch and Leo Spitzer, *Ghosts of Home: The Afterlife of Czernowitz in Jewish Memory* (Berkeley: University of California Press, 2010), 293–300.

34. Boukhobza, *Un été*, 208.

35. Boukhobza, *Un été*, 253–55.

36. As an overview, I refer to Laurence J. Silberstein, *The Postzionism Debates: Knowledge and Power in Israeli Culture* (London: Routledge, 1999).

37. Michel S. Laguerre, *Global Neighborhoods: Jewish Quarters in Paris, London, and Berlin* (Albany: State University of New York Press, 2008), 32–34. Laguerre talks about the anti-Jewish incidents that took place in Paris in 1982, especially the bombing of a Jewish-owned restaurant in the Marais. For a more general overview, see Marianna Scherini, "The Image of Israel and Israelis in the French, British and Italian Press during the 1982 Lebanon War," in *Global Antisemitism: A Crisis of Modernity*, ed. Charles Asher Small (Leiden: Brill, 2013), 187–202.

38. Chochana Boukhobza, *Pour l'amour du père* (Paris: Seuil, 1996), 50.

39. Boukhobza, *Pour*, 86.

40. Boukhobza, *Pour*, 10.

41. Michèle Baussant, *Pieds-noirs: mémoires d'exil* (Paris: Stock, 2002).

42. Patrick Simon and Claude Tapia, *Le Belleville des Juifs tunisiens* (Paris: Autrement, 1998), 49.

43. Boukhobza, *Pour*, 50–51.

44. Simon and Tapia, *Le Belleville*, 107–17.

45. Boukhobza, *Pour*, 46.

46. Emanuela Trevisan Semi, "Lifewriting between Israel, the Diaspora and Morocco: Revisiting the Homeland through Locations and Objects of Identity," in *Contemporary Sephardic and Mizrahi Literature: A Diaspora*, ed. Dario Miccoli (London: Routledge, 2017), 84–97.

47. Andrea Smith, *Colonial Memory and Postcolonial Europe: Maltese Settlers in Algeria and France* (Bloomington: Indiana University Press, 2006).

48. Jonathan Lear, *Freud* (London: Routledge, 2005), 122–24.

49. Boukhobza, *Pour*, 104–5.

50. Michael Rothberg, "Remembering Back: Cultural Memory, Colonial Legacies, and Postcolonial Studies," in *The Oxford Handbook of Postcolonial Studies*, ed. Graham Duggan (Oxford: Oxford University Press, 2013), 359–79.

51. Boukhobza, *Pour*, 102, 109.

52. On the Italians of Tunisia, see Daniela Melfa, *Migrando a Sud: Coloni italiani in Tunisia (1881–1939)* (Rome: Aracne, 2008); Leila El Houssi, "Italians in Tunisia: Between Regional Organisation, Cultural Adaptation and Political Division, 1860s–1940s," *European Review of History/Revue Européenne d'Histoire* 19, no. 1 (2012): 163–81. Consider also the memoir by Marinette Pendola, *La riva lontana* (Palermo: Sellerio, 2000).

53. Boukhobza, *Pour*, 147.

54. Boukhobza, *Pour*, 126.

55. Here, I am elaborating on Kimberley Arkin, *Rhinestones, Religion, and the Republic: Fashioning Jewishness in France* (Stanford, CA: Stanford University Press, 2014), esp. 62–64. On this crucial and hotly debated topic, consider Mandel, *Muslims and Jews*; Katz, *Burdens*; Shepard, *Invention*; Colette Zytnicki, "Du rapatrié au séfarade"; "Circulations et migrations des Juifs du Maghreb en France, de la veille de la Première Guerre Mondiale aux années 1960," ed. Valérie Assan and Yolande Cohen, special issue, *Archives Juives* 53, no. 1 (2020); Doris Bensimon-Donath, *L'intégration des Juifs nord-africains en France* (Paris: Mouton, 1971).

56. Boukhobza, *Pour*, 187.

57. Giampaolo Calchi Novati, "Mediterraneo e questione araba nella politica estera italiana," in *Storia dell'Italia repubblicana*, ed. Francesco Barbagallo (Turin: Einaudi, 2005), 2:197–263; Angelo Del Boca, "The Myths, Suppressions, Denials and Defaults of Italian Colonialism," in *A Place in the Sun: Africa in Italian Colonial Culture from Post-Unification to the Present*, ed. Patrizia Palumbo (Berkeley: University of California Press, 2003), 17–36; Daniela Baratieri, *Memories and Silences Haunted by Fascism: Italian Colonialism MCMXXX–MCMLX* (Bern: Peter Lang, 2010).

58. Patrizia Audenino, *La casa perduta: La memoria dei profughi nell'Europa del Novecento* (Rome: Carocci, 2015), 142.

59. On the memorial literature of the Libyan Jews, see Daniele Comberiati, "'Province minori' di un 'impero minore': Narrazioni italo-ebraiche dalla Libia

e dal Dodecaneso," in *Fuori centro: Percorsi postcoloniali nella letteratura italiana*, ed. Roberto Derobertis (Rome: Aracne, 2010), 95–110; Piera Rossetto, "Writings of Jews from Libya in Italy and Israel: Between Past Legacies and Present Issues," in *Contemporary Sephardic and Mizrahi Literature*, ed. Dario Miccoli (London: Routledge, 2017), 69–83; Raniero Speelman, "Ebrei 'ottomani'—Scrittori italiani. L'apporto di scrittori immigrati in Italia dai paesi dell'ex impero ottomano," *EJOS* 7, no. 2 (2005): 1–32.

60. The number refers to the people officially registered in one of the Italian Jewish communities. See Enzo Campelli, *Comunità va cercando ch'è sì cara... Sociologia dell'Italia ebraica* (Milan: Franco Angeli, 2013), 15.

61. Maurice Roumani, *Gli ebrei di Libia: dalla coesistenza all'esodo* (Rome: Castelvecchi, 2015), 264. On the Jews of Libya, see Renzo De Felice, *Ebrei in un paese arabo: gli ebrei nella Libia contemporanea tra colonialismo, nazionalismo arabo e sionismo (1835–1970)* (Bologna: il Mulino, 1987), esp. 335–39; Piera Rossetto, "Mémoires de diaspora, diaspora de mémoires: Juifs de Libye entre Israël et l'Italie, de 1948 à nos jours" (PhD diss., Ca' Foscari University/EHESS Toulouse, 2015); Stefano Tironi, "La comunità ebraica tripolina tra la Libia e Roma" (MA diss., Ca' Foscari University, 2002). On the Libyan Jewish middle and upper classes during the monarchy period, see Eyal David, "Hayey-ha-yomyom shel ha-yehudim bney-ha-ma'amad ha-beyinoni-gavoah ba'ir Tripoli be-Luv (1951–1967)" [The everyday life of upper-middle-class Jews in the city of Tripoli, Libya (1951–1967)] (MA diss., Hebrew University of Jerusalem, 2015), kindly provided by the author.

62. Victor Magiar, *E venne la notte: ebrei in un paese arabo* (Florence: Giuntina, 2003), 202.

63. Magiar, *E venne*, 174.

64. Comberiati, "'Province minori,'" 102–3.

65. Magiar, *E venne*, 29.

66. Mia Fuller, *Moderns Abroad: Architecture, Cities and Italian Imperialism* (London: Routledge, 2007).

67. De Felice, *Ebrei*, 183–258.

68. Magiar, *E venne*, 40.

69. Philippe Lejeune, *Le pacte autobiographique* (Paris: Seuil, 1975). On the connections between reality and fiction in historical narratives, I shall refer at least to Carlo Ginzburg, *Il filo e le tracce: Vero, falso, finto* (Milan: Feltrinelli, 2006).

70. Magiar, *E venne*, 19.

71. Magiar, *E venne*, 163.

72. Magiar, *E venne*, 235.

73. Magiar, *E venne*, 268.

74. On mare nostrum in Italian foreign policy during the liberal age and under Fascism, see Stefano Trinchese, ed., *Mare nostrum: percezione ottomana*

e mito mediterraneo in Italia all'alba del '900 (Milan: Guerini, 2005); Daniel Grange, *L'Italie et la Méditerranée: les fondements d'une politique étrangère* (Rome: Ecole française de Rome, 1994). For a critical discussion of the term, see Claudio Fogu, "From Mare Nostrum to Mare Aliorum: Mediterranean Theory and Mediterraneism in Contemporary Italian Thought," *California Italian Studies* 1, no. 1 (2010), http://escholarship.org/uc/item/7vp210p4#page-13.

75. Magiar, *E venne*, 270.
76. Daniela Dawan, *Qual è la via del vento* (Rome: e/o, 2018), 159.
77. Dawan, *Qual è la via del vento*, 164.
78. Dawan, *Qual è la via del vento*, 129.
79. Robert Watson, "Memories (Out) of Place: Franco-Judeo-Algerian Autobiographical Writing, 1995–2010," *Journal of North African Studies* 17, no. 1 (2013): 1–22.
80. Raphael Luzon, *Tramonto libico: Storia di un ebreo arabo* (Florence: Giuntina, 2015), 14–15 (my emphasis). The book has also been translated into English as *Libyan Twilight: The Story of an Arab Jew* (London: Darf, 2016).
81. Luzon, *Tramonto*, 17.
82. Shimon Ballas, "Iya," in *Keys to the Garden: New Israeli Writing*, ed. Ammiel Alcalay (San Francisco: City Lights Books, 1996), 69–99.
83. Daniel Schroeter, "A Different Road to Modernity: Jewish Identity in the Arab World," in *Diasporas and Exiles*, ed. Howard Wettstein (Berkeley: University of California Press, 2002), 150–63; Robert Tignor, "The Economic Activities of Foreigners in Egypt, 1920–1950: From Millet to Haute Bourgeoisie," *Comparative Studies in Society and History* 22, no. 3 (1980): 416–49.
84. De Felice, *Ebrei*, 378–79.
85. Roumani, *Gli ebrei*, 250–55.
86. Luzon, *Tramonto*, 33.
87. Luzon, *Tramonto*, 7.
88. Raphael Luzon, interview, Canale 5, October 2015, http://www.video.mediaset.it/video/tg5/tg5_la_lettura/raphael-luzon_567655.html.
89. Luzon, *Tramonto*, 50 (my emphasis).
90. Harvey Goldberg, *Jewish Life in Muslim Libya: Rivals and Relatives* (Chicago: University of Chicago Press, 1990).
91. Luzon, *Tramonto*, 57.
92. Audenino, *La casa*; Barbara Spadaro, *Una colonia italiana: incontri, memorie e rappresentazioni tra Italia e Libia* (Firenze: Le Monnier, 2013). See also Piera Rossetto, "'We Were All Italians!' The Construction of a Sense of Italianness among Jews from Libya (1920s–1960s)," *History & Anthropology*, https://www.tandfonline.com/doi/full/10.1080/02757206.2020.1848821.
93. See Donna Gabaccia, *Italy's Many Diasporas* (Seattle: University of Washington Press, 2000); Mark Choate, *Emigrant Nation: The Making of Italy*

Abroad (Cambridge, MA: Harvard University Press, 2008); Michele Colucci, *Storia dell'immigrazione straniera in Italia: dal 1945 ai giorni nostri* (Rome: Carocci, 2018).

94. Michele Sarfatti, *Gli ebrei nell'Italia fascista* (Turin: Einaudi, 2000), 17–18.

95. Guri Schwarz, *Ritrovare se stessi: Gli ebrei nell'Italia postfascista* (Rome: Laterza, 2004).

96. Luzon, *Tramonto*, 89–90.

97. Luzon, *Tramonto*, 93, 94.

98. Audenino, *La casa*, 202.

99. Luzon, *Tramonto*, 1–2.

100. Rothberg, "Remembering Back," 361.

101. Orly Castel-Bloom, *Ha-roman ha-mitzri* [The Egyptian novel] (Tel Aviv: Ha-kibbutz ha-meuhad, 2015), 43.

102. V. Figuière-Cagnac, "Dolly City ou la jungle de la vie," *Zafon*, no. 33–34 (1998): 55–56; Deborah Starr, "Reterritorializing the Dream: Orly Castel Bloom's Remapping of Israeli Identity," in *Mapping Jewish Identities*, ed. Lawrence Silberstein (New York: New York University Press, 2000), 220–49; Uri Cohen, *Liqro' 'et-Orly Castel-Bloom* [Reading Orly Castel-Bloom] (Tel Aviv: Ahuzat Bayit, 2011); Anna Bernard, *Rhetorics of Belonging: Nation, Narration, and Israel/Palestine* (Liverpool: Liverpool University Press, 2013), 115–28.

103. Yaron Peleg, *Israeli Culture between the Two Intifadas: A Brief Romance* (Austin: University of Texas Press, 2008), 17–20.

104. Deborah Starr, *Remembering Cosmopolitan Egypt: Literature, Culture, and Empire* (London: Routledge, 2009), 107–9.

105. See David S. Landes, *Bankers and Pashas International Finance and Economic Imperialism in Egypt* (Cambridge, MA: Harvard University Press, 1958); Robert L. Tignor, *Modernization and British Colonial Rule in Egypt, 1882–1914* (Princeton, NJ: Princeton University Press, 1966); Panayotis J. Vatikiotis, *The History of Modern Egypt from Muhammad Ali to Mubarak* (London: Weidenfeld and Nicholson, 1991).

106. Miccoli, *Histories*, 3–8. On the Jews of Egypt more generally, see Jacob Landau, *Jews in Nineteenth-Century Egypt* (New York: New York University Press, 1969); Gudrun Krämer, *The Jews of Modern Egypt, 1914–1952* (London: IB Tauris, 1989); Joel Beinin, *The Dispersion of Egyptian Jewry: Culture, Politics and the Formation of a Modern Diaspora* (Berkeley: University of California Press, 1998).

107. Krämer, *Jews*, 217–20; Michael Laskier, *The Jews of Egypt, 1920–1970: In the Midst of Zionism, Anti-Semitism, and the Middle East Conflict* (New York: New York University Press, 1992); Miccoli, *Histories*, esp. 151–57. On the Suez War, see W. Roger Louis and Louis Owen, *Suez 1956: The Crisis and Its Consequences* (Oxford: Clarendon, 1989).

108. Castel-Bloom, *Ha-roman*, 19.

109. Castel-Bloom, *Ha-roman*, 78.

110. Miccoli, *Histories*, 156–57.

111. Sami Shalom-Chetrit, *Intra-Jewish Conflict in Israel: White Jews, Black Jews* (London: Routledge, 2010), 20.

112. Castel-Bloom, *Ha-roman*, 49. On the kibbutzim founded by Egyptian Jewish immigrants, see Beinin, *Dispersion*, 121–41.

113. Karen Grumberg, *Place and Ideology in Contemporary Hebrew Literature* (Syracuse, NY: Syracuse University Press, 2011), 83.

114. Dario Miccoli, "Another History: Family, Nation and the Remembrance of the Egyptian Jewish Past in Contemporary Israeli Literature," *Journal of Modern Jewish Studies* 13, no. 3 (2014): 321–39. On Egyptian Jewish Francophone and Anglophone authors, see Aimée Israel-Pelletier, *On the Mediterranean and the Nile: The Jews of Egypt* (Bloomington: Indiana University Press, 2018).

115. Aciman, *Out of Egypt* (New York: Picador, 1994), 220–21.

116. Castel-Bloom, *Ha-roman*, 68.

117. Castel-Bloom, *Ha-roman*, 75. On Francophone Israelis, consider Eliezer Ben-Rafael and Miriam Ben-Rafael, *Sociologie et sociolinguistique des francophonies israéliennes* (Bern: Peter Lang, 2013).

118. Dario Miccoli, "A Fragile Cradle: Writing Jewishness, Nationhood and Modernity in Cairo, 1920–1940," *Jewish Social Studies* 21, no. 3 (2016): 1–29.

119. Israel Gershoni and James P. Jankowski, *Egypt, Islam, and the Arabs: The Search for an Egyptian Nationhood, 1900–1930* (Oxford: Oxford University Press, 1986); Donald M. Reid, "Nationalizing the Pharaonic Past: Egyptology, Imperialism, and Egyptian Nationalism, 1922–1952," in *Rethinking Nationalism in the Arab Middle East*, ed. James P. Jankowski and Israel Gershoni (New York: Columbia University Press, 1997), 127–49; Reid, *Whose Pharaohs? Archaeology, Museums, and Egyptian National Identity from Napoleon to World War One* (Berkeley: University of California Press, 2002).

120. Ella Shohat, "The Invention of the Mizrahim," *Journal of Palestine Studies* 29, no. 1 (1999): 5–20; Shohat, "Sephardim in Israel: Zionism from the Standpoint of Its Jewish Victims," *Social Text*, no. 19–20 (1988): 1–35.

121. Miccoli, *Histories*.

122. Laura Barile, *Il resto manca: Storie mediterranee* (Turin: Aragno, 2003), 36–37. On this, see Miccoli, *Histories*, 117–120; Jonathan Schorsch, "Disappearing Origins: Sephardi Autobiography Today," *Prooftexts*, no. 27 (2007): 82–150.

123. Jean Naggar, *Sipping from the Nile: My Exodus from Egypt* (Las Vegas: AmazonEncore, 2008), 56.

124. Castel-Bloom, *Ha-roman*, 85–86.

125. Thelma Admon, "'Ha-roman ha-mitzri': 'otobiografiah le-lo' sentimentaliyut u-le-lo' patos" ["The Egyptian novel": An autobiography without sentimentalism and pathos], *Ma'ariv*, January 22, 2015, http://www.maariv

.co.il/culture/literature/Article-460728. On the second generation of *Mizrahi* authors, I refer to Yochai Oppenheimer, "Be-shem ha-'av: 'edipaliyiut ba-sipporet ha-mizrahit shel ha-dor ha-sheni" [In the name of the father: Oedipal themes in second-generation *mizrahi* literature], *Te'oriah u-viqoret*, no. 40 (2012): 161–84.

126. Yotam Shveymer, "'Ha-roman ha-mitzri': biqoret noqevet u-mushlemet" ["The Egyptian novel": a profound and excellent critique], *Yedi'ot 'Aharonot*, January 20, 2015, http://www.ynet.co.il/articles/0,7340,L-4617053,00.html.

127. Starr, "Reterritorializing," 238–39. See also Bernard, *Rhetorics*, 121–28.

128. Castel-Bloom, *Ha-roman*, 56–57.

129. Alon Confino, "The Warm Sand of the Coast of Tantura: History and Memory in Israel after 1948," *History & Memory* 27, no. 1 (2015): 43–82; Confino, "Miracles and Snow in Palestine and Israel: Tantura, a History of 1948," *Israel Studies* 17, no. 2 (2012): 25–60.

130. Castel-Bloom, *Ha-roman*, 148–49.

131. As an example, consider the two collections of life stories: Liliane S. Dammond, *The Lost World of the Egyptian Jews: First-Person Accounts from Egypt's Jewish Community in the Twentieth Century*, with Yvette M. Raby (New York: iUniverse, 2007); Ada Aharoni et Alii, *'Idan ha-zahav shel-Yehudei-Mitzrayim: 'Aqirah ve-tqumah be-'Israel* [The golden age of Jews from Egypt: Uprooting and revival in Israel] (Holon: Orion, 2014).

132. Confino, "Warm Sand," 75.

133. For example, Yitzhaq Gormezano Goren, *Ba-derekh la-'itztadion* [The path to the stadium] (Tel Aviv: Bimat Qedem, 2003), 252. On Gormezano Goren, see Starr, *Remembering*, 122–33; Dvir Abramovich, "Conjuring Egypt in Israeli Literature: Yitzhak Gormezano Goren's *Blanche*," *Australian Journal of Jewish Studies*, no. 22 (2008): 5–25; Miccoli, "Another History," 324–27.

134. Teresa Cremisi, *La Triomphante* (Milan: Adelphi, 2016), 21.

135. Castel-Bloom, *Ha-roman*, 113.

136. Marc Augé, *Les formes de l'oubli* (Paris: Payot, 1998).

137. See Julia Clancy-Smith, "Twentieth-Century Historians," 89.

138. David Wacks, *Double Diaspora in Sephardic Literature: Jewish Cultural Production before and after 1492* (Bloomington: Indiana University Press, 2015), 12.

139. Rothberg, "Introduction."

140. Alon Confino, "Collective Memory and Cultural History: Problems of Method," *American Historical Review* 102, no. 5 (1997): 1391.

141. Mark R. Cohen, "The Neo-Lachrymose Conception of Arab-Jewish History," *Tikkun* 6, no. 3 (1991): 60–64.

142. Jablonka, *L'histoire*, 192.

TWO

(IN)TANGIBLE HERITAGES

Migrant Associations, Museums, and the Internet

THE LITERARY WORKS BY WRITERS of Sephardi and *Mizrahi* origin that I have discussed have already shown how "memory practices can be understood as traversing and at times unsettling national boundaries."[1] At the same time, the nation-state continues to be an unavoidable point of reference in the process of memory and heritage making and still has a central role in the preservation of the past. Having looked at literature as a first crucial space where memory is constructed and reinvented at an individual level, in order to survey the entanglement among the national, transnational, and diasporic dimensions of the identity of the Jews from the Middle East and North Africa, I will now consider some of the public spaces—in the Diaspora and in Israel—where their cultural heritage is visible, as well as the different heritage making practices that make it known to a wider audience.

In the last years, heritage—and its equivalent in other languages: *morashah* in Hebrew, *patrimoine* in French, and *patrimonio* (or *patrimonio culturale*) in Italian—has become a much-debated category through which to make sense of our history. According to the definition by UNESCO, it is "our legacy from the past, what we live with today, and what we pass on to future generations."[2] Its origins, however, are much older than that and can be found at least in the process of nation building that developed in nineteenth-century Europe, when the first national museums were created and heritage—mainly in the form of material traces of the past—became valorized as a foundational aspect of national identity.[3] Actually, according to the architectural historian Françoise Choay, ideas and debates about the *patrimoine*, particularly ancient monuments and their preservation, were present already in early modern France and Italy, signaling the existence of a much longer interest in the conservation and transmission of the vestiges of the past.[4]

Additionally, nowadays one needs to distinguish between tangible and intangible heritage—between real objects and buildings, on the one hand, and, on the other, a vast array of immaterial aspects of the identity and folklore of a community at local, national, and even transnational levels.[5] Even in the case of the Jewish communities of the Arab world, one could argue that in the early modern period individual Jews and Jewish communal institutions were already looking after their tangible and intangible historical legacy for a number of reasons related to, yet not primarily focusing on, preservation. Think of the documents from the Cairo medieval *genizah*, which have survived because they include the name of God and therefore, according to the Jewish law, had to be preserved and could not be destroyed.[6] In other words, the *genizah* documents did not constitute an archive "arranged for storage and retrieval" but resembled "a final resting place" for various types of texts—both useful and useless.[7] Only the advent of systematic practices of communal organization in the late Ottoman period brought a shifting toward more institutionalized approaches to the preservation of the past, which were similar to those developed in European countries. Limiting myself to the modern era, I should cite the publication of books that—through the adoption of modern historiographic methods—investigated a community's history or, especially since the late nineteenth century, the foundation of historical societies.[8] Again with reference to Egypt, one such organization is the Société d'Etudes Historiques Juives d'Egypte, established in Cairo in 1925, whose main goals were the promotion of the knowledge of the Jewish past and the preservation of ancient artifacts and buildings.[9]

That said, another aspect must be taken into account. In the immediate aftermath of the migration to Israel and to countries in the West, the North African and Middle Eastern Jewish migrants were asked to reconsider their past in reference to the new national context in which they were living, such as Israel or France; however, one now sees a more multifaceted approach that—taking the premigratory place of origin as the inevitable point of departure—mirrors both the postmigratory/national dimension and a global/diasporic one. Therefore, reflections on the preservation of the Algerian Jewish heritage nowadays do not exclusively evoke France, but also today's Algeria, global processes of *patrimonialization*, and not least the State of Israel—especially considering this country's role as catalyst for practices of Jewish heritage preservation and musealization. This multivocal perspective is not unique to the Jewish case, and to a certain extent, one could even assume that heritage has always been understood beyond the nation-state and by considering cultural transfers.[10] This is even truer if one thinks about the intangible heritage, which I will discuss more in the next pages. Even though I will sometimes refer to physical objects and to Sephardi and *Mizrahi* material culture, what is at stake in this chapter are the "traditions or living expressions inherited from our ancestors and passed on to our descendants," such as "oral traditions, performing arts, social practices, rituals, festive events, knowledge."[11]

Thus, if heritage is to be understood as "where we have *come from*," can we really think of it "as mobile, in the sense of moving from one place to another, but also as itself capable of transformation and capable of *effecting* transformation"?[12] In the cases under scrutiny, the emphasis on the transnational dimension determined the birth of a shared heritage that in the first place refers to (lost) Sephardi worlds. However, we are talking about Jewish communities that before the mass migration, even though they shared an ethno-religious background and a number of similar traditions, did not necessarily perceive themselves as part of a larger Sephardi—let alone *Mizrahi*—Diaspora. It is interesting to remember that, for example, the idea of *Judaïsme nordafricain*—instead of a myriad of Jewries as different as the Sephardis of Tangier, the Frenchified Algerians, or the *grana* of Tunis—only started to gain momentum in postcolonial times, not in earlier periods.[13] The same can be said for Israel, where only from around the 1950s and 1960s did the Jews coming from the Arab world and from Iran begin to be categorized as *'edot ha-mizrah*, and later as *Mizrahim*.[14]

To investigate these issues, I look at a series of public spaces that together compose the contemporary Sephardi and *Mizrahi* heritage landscape: associations, museums and memorials, and lastly the internet. First, I focus on heritage associations founded by Israeli Egyptians and the activities they have undertaken since the 1960s: here issues of cosmopolitanism and Israeliness are debated in relation to the Egyptian Jewish past and its refashioning in a new national context, dominated by different identity and political reference points. Then, I turn to the Jews of Algeria who migrated to France in the 1960s as a community characterized by a *difficult heritage* comprising the troublesome legacies of colonialism and the obstacles that these migrants—who in most cases were, from the point of view of the state, colonial returnees—encountered when attempting to gain space in the French (Jewish) heritage and memorial arena. To do so, I consider Algerian Jewish heritage associations, historical exhibitions on the Jews of Algeria in French museums, and monuments that aim to commemorate aspects of the Algerian Jewish past in today's France. Finally, I consider the digital diasporas that have come about on the internet—a space where, for instance, Jews of Moroccan and Egyptian origin operate websites dedicated to their heritage and interact on social networks through the exchange of photographs, memories, and various kinds of information. Besides showing the internet's relevance to the construction of Jewish identity in the twenty-first century, these diasporas illustrate more generally the opportunities that digital technologies offer in terms of heritage making, allowing more and more people to take part in it.

By connecting these different spaces and the modalities through they are constructed, I shed light on the formation of a multivocal Sephardi and *Mizrahi* heritage at the crossroads of the communal, national, diasporic, and virtual level. Such heritage is a mobile and plural construct originating in the memory of displacement, exile, and the feeling of unhomeliness that these communities share, and it goes beyond any rigid distinction between tangible and intangible.[15] Actually, these different case studies highlight the fact that it is not possible to talk about the existence of a unified Sephardi and *Mizrahi* cultural heritage. We should rather refer to a set of interrelated *heritages*, whose development is concurring to make the Jews of the southern Mediterranean shore more visible on the public scene and allowing them to tell their own story without the mediation of professional historians and scholars. And it is here that another question, to which I will return in the course of this chapter and in the next one, arises: What does this increased visibility stimulate? In other words, are practices of Sephardi and *Mizrahi* heritagization—which have grown and continue to grow both in the Diaspora and in Israel—and what one may call *public history*, providing a better understanding of these communities' past, or are they triggering the consolidation of memories that, while certainly more visible than before, compete with one another without reconciling such a troubled past with an equally problematic present?

THE ASSOCIATIONAL CULTURE OF EGYPTIAN JEWS IN ISRAEL

Migrant associations, which are associations founded by migrants sharing the same or a similar ethno-national origin, have long been regarded by scholars as either spaces that lead to further social segregation or mediating institutions that can ease the process of integration into a new national context.[16] In the case of migrant heritage associations, Rosen-Lapidot and Goldberg argue that the stakes in the groups' activities include both the past, with its much-cherished and its difficult memories, and the contingency of the present—especially for people or communities that have been uprooted from their milieu and whose migration was not, or at least not primarily, due to economic reasons.[17] Here, I look at the Egyptian Jewish associational culture in Israel and read it as an expression of Israeliness—or perhaps of a wish to be included in the context of immigration—based on the transmission of a both tangible and intangible heritage, in which selected aspects of the Egyptian diasporic past are accommodated and mobilized vis-à-vis the present.

Generally speaking, all public expressions of ethnicity should be viewed as a resource that has different political, cultural, and symbolic usages. In the case of Israel, in consideration of the 1950s 'aliyot from the Middle East and North Africa and their societal impact, some sociologists have believed that "when the gaps in income or education . . . are eliminated, ethnic associations or expressions will also cease."[18] However, more than sixty years after these migrations, it seems evident that forms of ethnic display are not destined to disappear anytime soon—even though they certainly will not retain the same characteristics they had in the past. One may argue that the resilience of ethnicity depends on the fact that the socioeconomic and educational cleavages between *Mizrahim* and *Ashkenazim* never vanished entirely[19]—or perhaps that it is an inevitable consequence of a diasporic past that left an indelible mark on Jewish and Israeli identity. Think, for example, of the ongoing presence of heritage associations and museums established by groups that have been more integrated in the Israeli society and national narrative, and for longer, than the *Mizrahim*, like the museums founded in northern Israel by German- and Hungarian-speaking Jews.[20] Such heritage associations may play a less important role in the future. But, for the time being, it is unlikely that expressions of ethnic identity will disappear altogether. On the contrary, the history of the Egyptian Jewish associational culture in Israel shows that forms of Jewish localism and diasporism can adapt in relation to the contingency of time and according to new ethnonational spaces and sociopolitical atmospheres. As already said, they highlight the persistence of the Diaspora as an essential facet not only of Jewish but also of Israeli culture.[21]

To understand the associational world of the Egyptian Jews in Israel, one needs to go back to 1958, when—only a few years after the migratory waves that followed the Free Officers' Revolution and the Suez War—a group of people, including the former chief rabbi of Alexandria Moshe Ventura, founded the 'Irgun nifga'ey ha-radifot ha-'anti-yehudiyot be-Mitzrayim/Association des ex-victimes des persecutions anti-juives en Egypte. Its main goals were:

> 1) to assist members of the Organisation in order to facilitate their integration in Israel and their settlement in the country. 2) to represent members with the central Government Institutions. . . . 3) to act in order to obtain . . .

organisation for the moral and material damages ... suffered in Egypt on account of the anti-Jewish persecutions they [i.e., the members of the 'Irgun] were submitted to since the establishment of the State of Israel. 4) to act in order to obtain for all those members of the Organisation who were interned in Egypt ... the status of "Atzir Zion."[22]

In 1958, a Jewish community of about nine thousand still existed in Egypt. On the other hand, the Egyptian 'olim numbered twenty-eight thousand.[23] The Egyptians were one of the most recent Middle Eastern additions to what was called, in Zionist vocabulary, the *kibbutz galuyiot* ("ingathering of exiles"). It is therefore unsurprising that, at the time, most of the activities of the 'Irgun were related to the restitution of Jewish properties and assets left behind, as well as the status of Jews who were still living in Egypt. The 'Irgun also organized cultural and social activities: for example, the annual celebration, with the support of a number of donors, of the bar mitzvah of indigent boys; the assignment of student scholarships; and the organization of *tiyulim* (pl. of *tiyul*: "walk") aimed at improving the youths' *yediyat ha-'aretz* ("knowledge of the Land [of Israel]").[24] This kind of activity echoes well-established Zionist practices common already in the pre-1948 period, which viewed the physical and geographical knowledge of the land as something that "brought together self, community, and space in a ritual of Zionist affirmation that enacted the nationalist idea in an embodied practice."[25] Activities like the *tiyulim* were of utmost importance even in a period like the 1950s and 1960s, when thousands of Diaspora-born Jews were migrating to Israel from the Arab world, and from Europe too, and the idea of the state as a *kibbutz galuyiot* was still very relevant.

As I have mentioned, the more recent vicissitudes of the 'olim and their problems featured prominently. The 'Irgun's bulletins often mention the Lavon affair and how it was commemorated in Israel. The Lavon affair, also known in Hebrew as *'eseq ha-bish* ("mishap"), consisted of a series of acts of espionage and sabotage undertaken in Cairo in 1954, on behalf of Israel, by a group of Egyptian Jews affiliated with Zionist youth movements. When the Egyptian police discovered them, the saboteurs were arrested and tortured, and two committed suicide in prison. The trial that followed ended with the execution of two others: Shmuel Azar and the Karaite Moshe Marzuq.[26] Thus, every year in the month of *Shvat* (January–February), the Egyptian 'olim celebrated a *yom zikaron le-qedushey-Qahir* ("day of remembrance for the martyrs of Cairo"), and in 1965 they supported the dedication of a street in Holon to the *qedushey-Qahir*. Attending the dedication were the mayor of the city, Pinhas Eilon; Minister of Postal Services Yisrael Yeshayahu; Rabbi Ventura; and the parents of Moshe

Marzuq and Shmuel Azar, as well as those of Eli Cohen, one of the so-called 'oley gardom Dameseq ("those who rose to the gallows of Damascus").²⁷

The choice of a street in Holon probably depended on the significant number of Egyptian 'olim who lived in the city. In fact, according to the association's yearbook for 1972–73, of the approximately thirty-four thousand Egyptian Jews in Israel at that time—a number that seemingly included only Israeli citizens who were born in Egypt and not the Israeli-born sons of the first immigrants— more than half resided in Holon and Bat Yam. The 'Irgun had branches in other towns too, but even these were almost all located near Tel Aviv: for example, in Hertzliyah, Or Yehudah, and Be'er Ya'aqov.²⁸

The bulletin's emphasis on the political dimension of the migration of Egyptian Jews also concerned one of the most active members of the 'Irgun at the time, Shlomo Kohen-Sidon (Tzidon), who in 1965 authored *Dramah be-'Aleksandriah ve-shney hrugey-malkhut* (Drama in Alexandria and two martyrs)—one of the first fictional works written in Israel focused on the Egyptian Jews and set at the time of the Lavon affair. From 1966 to 1969, Kohen-Sidon was a member of the Knesset for *Gahal*, the rightist coalition between *Herut* and the Liberal Party, and he was very active in demanding compensation for the assets and properties the Jews had left in Egypt, even though his attempts did not result in any solution.²⁹

Certainly, the 'Irgun was not primarily a heritage association but a mutual aid society to support the Egyptian migrants, particularly the poorer among them. For example, it paid the legal expenses for members who needed a lawyer, organized bar mitzvah ceremonies, and helped elders to obtain old-age pensions from the National Insurance Institute. The association fought for the lost properties and assets left by the Egyptian Jews in Alexandria and Cairo and wished to highlight the positive role that this Diaspora had played in the establishment of Israel and in the first years of the state: "This great mass of people," the yearbook of 1972–73 stated, "contributed to the building of the state. . . . Also in the recent Kippur War, our sons had a significant role in containing the attacking enemy. But . . . these people neither have a role in the administration of the public affairs or have an adequate representation in national institutions. Our hope is that this situation will not last for long and that this injustice, which affects our people, will be corrected."³⁰

Underlying this kind of discourse was the idea that even though until the 1940s few Egyptians had been actively involved in the Zionist movement or migrated to British Palestine, many supported the *yishuv* and the Zionist movement through philanthropy or economic investments. Think of the Mosseris, one of the most important Cairo Jewish dynasties, who had significant business interests in Palestine at the time of the British Mandate—for example, they founded the famous King David Hotel in Jerusalem.[31] Seen from this perspective, the fact that in Egypt until the late 1940s only a minority of Jews were Zionist and very few were doing ʿaliyah did not contradict the fact that now they were proud and full-fledged Israelis. Rather, it showed how, at least until a certain moment—as seen in Castel-Bloom's *Ha-roman ha-mitzri*—feelings of belonging with Egypt could go together with an attachment to Jewish identity and a philanthropic understanding of Zionism.

The goals of the 'Irgun and of similar migrant associations started to shift more explicitly toward the cultural realm during the 1970s and in the early 1980s, with the ideological and societal changes that Israel as a whole went through: from the victory of the rightist party Likud in 1977, to the gradual weakening of Socialist Zionism, of the idea of Israel as *kibbutz galuyiot* and, following that, the appraisal of ethnicity as something to be valorized instead of dismissed.[32] "Why only now?" asked one of the very first issues of the *ʿAlon moreshet yahadut-Mitzrayim* (Bulletin of the heritage of the Jews of Egypt), in 1985. The answer was that "the difficulties of the ʿaliyah, the time of the adaptation, the worries about earning an income, the building of a home in Israel, the daily commitments of working and bringing up children, all this did not leave us time for thinking," but "now, thirty-seven years after the independence of Israel in her homeland, we want to pass the heritage of the Jews of Egypt to this generation and to the following ones, so as to show our roots to our children."[33] This is a common refrain and may sound like a cliché; however, it does reflect the reality of more or less any kind of migration: the first generation usually is busy rebuilding life in a completely new environment and therefore does not have time—and, perhaps, does not want—to think too much about what has just been left behind, and these tasks are then left to the next generation. In the case of the Jews of Egypt, only at a distance of thirty years, and also after all the changes of Israeli society mentioned earlier, were the ʿolim ready to put aside the most troubling and unsettling aspects of the migration and to concentrate on the preservation of their cultural heritage.

In the case of more or less all Sephardi and *Mizrahi* diasporas, and in the activities of the 'Irgun, we encounter the belief of the elders of being the guardians and last inheritors of a history that no one remembers. In relation to this, in 1990 the president of the association *Goshen* wrote that "of all the communities [of Israel], the Egyptian is the least known. More than forty years passed since the second exodus from Egypt and our memories begin to fade."[34] Even though one may say that the Egyptian ʿaliyah probably was less problematic—if only because of its more limited size—than those from countries like Morocco or

Iraq, the activities that the 'Irgun promoted in the 1960s testify to the difficulties the Egyptian *'olim* also faced. Thirty years later, however, such bitter moments were put aside to celebrate the Egyptians' contribution to the building of Israel and to remember the good old days spent in Cairo and Alexandria. In that spirit, *Goshen* asked its readers "to contribute with texts, comments, and portrayals of how life was in Egypt, so as to enrich our testimonies and our magazine."[35]

The bulletin—written half in Hebrew and half in French—published short autobiographical essays, poems, and letters by Egyptian Jews living in Israel and sometimes even in the Diaspora. Many of those poems are by one of the most renowned of the Egyptian *'olim*, the Cairo-born poet Ada Aharoni. In one of these, *Me-Haifah le-Qahir ha-qrovah ha-rehoqah* (From Haifa to Cairo, so near and so close), Aharoni fantasizes about talking with her old Muslim schoolmate Qadriya at the time of the Kippur War, which opposed Israel to Egypt. Reversing Haim Nahman Bialik's poem *'El ha-tzipor* (To the bird), which was published in 1892 and which talked about a bird that flew back to the Diaspora after visiting the Land of Israel, Aharoni imagines being a bird that has finally come to rest in Israel:

> They told me I am
> only a guest
> even though I was born in the land of the Nile
> ... I spread out my Jewish wings
> and seek a new nest,
> I found it on Mount Carmel
> and here I wish to remain.
> More than anything else,
> today I ask
> to see our fighting sons
> immersed
> under the rays of that peace
> prepared by their mothers
> when they were younger than them.[36]

Goshen also presented the works of art of Egyptian-born amateur painters and artisans, reviews of books on Egypt in general and on the Egyptian Jews specifically, and even a cookery column, *Mi-pinatah shel Esti* (From the corner of Esti), with recipes in both Hebrew and French featuring typically Egyptian dishes as well as more global or even European ones, like onion-and-wine soup, *champignons à la grecque*, and *gâteau aux pruneaux*.[37]

Despite the insistence on more culture-related aspects, politics is not wholly absent from the pages of *Goshen*. For instance, in 1990 the bulletin printed a statement made in that year by the president of the State of Israel, Haim Herzog—whose wife, Orah, was born in Egypt—to praise the strength of the Egyptian Jews who never lost faith and hope, not even in the direst moments of their lives or during the notorious Lavon affair: "Nobody can give back the beautiful years that you lost, but nonetheless we have to try and ease, as much as we can, the suffering that you went through."[38] On another occasion, a few years earlier in 1988, *Goshen* had proudly published a special issue celebrating the fortieth anniversary of the establishment of Israel. At this point, it should be noted that, since the 1980s and throughout the 1990s, the main animator of *Goshen* was the above-cited poet Ada Aharoni. Aharoni authored several volumes of poetry and novels—such as *Mi-piramidot le-Qarmel* (From the pyramids to Mount Carmel; 1985); *Qeruv ha-levavot* (The closeness of the hearts; 2010); and *Ha-'ishah ha-levanah: Zihronot me-'Aleksandriah* (The woman in white: Memories from Alexandria; 2008)—and contributed to a number of Israeli and Anglophone magazines with essays on the issue of Palestinian-Israeli reconciliation and peace. In fact, according to Aharoni, the Egyptian Jews and more generally the *Mizrahim* should act as a bridge between Israel and the Palestinians, and between Israel and the Arab world, because of their intimate knowledge of the Arab culture and mentality.[39]

Through the activities of the International Forum for Literature and Culture, which Aharoni founded in 1999, and the stressing of categories that in her view better connect Muslims and Jews, such as *sulhah* ("reconciliation") and *kavod* ("honor"),[40] Aharoni advances a culturalist agenda that looks at the future more than at the past and utilizes the Egyptian Jewish heritage as a resource for improving Middle Eastern regional politics and the relations between Israelis and Palestinians. At the same time, hers is an Israel-centered understanding of the past, which views it as part of a larger history of Jewish national rebirth. Aharoni supports the idea that both Palestinians and Middle Eastern Jews are to be viewed as "refugees from the same war"—something that, as I will further explain, can be questioned from a historical and even more juridical perspective and that, in some ways, risks minimizing the complexities of the two respective histories. At the same time, at a more practical level she contends that the issue of Jewish property claims against Arab countries by now has become pointless: "Peace is a much greater treasure than money. And, after all, the Arab states are poor, they have no money to give us."[41]

The shifting from politics to culture visible in *Goshen* and then in Aharoni's own activities continues with the last association I will talk about, the Hitahdut

Figure 2.1. Eighth World Congress of Jews from Egypt, Tiberias, 2017. Source: Author.

'Oley Mitzrayim ("Union of Egyptian migrants"). Its goal too is to preserve the history and cultural heritage of the Egyptian Jews and to promote various kinds of related activities. The Hitahdut, which is the more or less direct continuator of the 'Irgun, is based in Tel Aviv, where its members gather on a regular basis for book presentations, lectures, and meetings. For sure, it is the most important of the extant heritage associations, in part because in the 2000s smaller groups based in Haifa and Bat Yam decided to merge with it: *"car l'union fait la force,"* as the association's bulletin explained.[42] At its seat, today one can admire a small exhibition of objects, historical documents, paintings, photographs about life in Egypt, and models of Egyptian synagogues from the time that is remembered as *tor ha-zahav* ("the golden era") of the Egyptian Jews. The Hitahdut publishes a magazine called *Bnei ha-Ye'or* (Sons of the Nile) and—as of 2022—has organized, sometimes in cooperation with Diaspora-based heritage associations, eleven World Congresses of Jews from Egypt, the first held in Tel Aviv in 1983 and the most recent ones in Ein Bokek, on the Dead Sea, in 2019 and in Tel Aviv in 2021 (see fig. 2.1).

The Hitahdut's bulletin, *Bnei ha-Ye'or*—which subsequently changed its name to *Yetziat-Mitzrayim shelanu* (Our exodus from Egypt)—consists of texts discussing the activities of the association, the publications of its members, and specific episodes and personalities of the Egyptian Jewish past, as well as short stories and poems by the association's members. Like *Goshen, Yetziat-Mitzrayim shelanu* hosts articles in Hebrew, French, and occasionally Arabic. In it, one can read what is going on in countries and cities that host the Egyptian Jewish Diaspora, from London to New York—where the Egyptian synagogue of Brooklyn Ahaba ve-ahva, which bears the name of a renowned *yeshivah* founded in Cairo by Rabbi Aharon Choueka in 1928, has been active since the 1970s.[43]

The longing for Egypt and its bygone cosmopolitan era is a recurrent theme among members of the Hitahdut. In a poem that appeared in the very first issue of *Bney Ha-Ye'or* but that had been written for the official visit of the Egyptian president Anwar al-Sadat to Israel in 1979, Ester Vidal-Mosseri writes in a mixture of Egyptian Arabic and French:

> La-Ini ya-massr él-habiba
> la-Ini ya-massr él-amàn ... Etreins-moi bien-aimée Terre
> Etreins-moi o Terre du Salut
> Etreins-moi ... je ne suis pas étrangère
> Je suis ta fille ... de Helwan l'elue.[44]

> [Hold me oh beloved Land
> Hold me oh Land of Salvation
> Hold me ... I am not foreign
> I am your daughter ... from Helwan the chosen.]

Like literature and writing more generally, cookery also evokes past memories. The president Levana Zamir published a book entitled *Mi-ta'amei Mitzrayim* (The flavors of Egypt), which is a detailed compendium of Egyptian (Jewish) cuisine. The book is dedicated "to my mother ... who taught me not just the taste of good food but also the substance, beauty, and essence of life. And to my two *sabra* daughters ... who love their mum's Egyptian food."[45] Here, it is very clear that gathering with fellow Egyptian Jews at the association's seat, writing something for the bulletin, or cooking a *molokhiyah*—a typical Egyptian soup—for the family make the remembrance of Egypt less painful and the past less distant. Cooking in particular acquires a very intimate meaning, as an act that allows lost perfumes, flavors, and memories to return to the surface.[46] All these activities then transpose a lost Jewish Egypt from the individual to the collective level, making it part of a wider narrative and transmitting it to the next generations.

That said, it is undeniable that the first generation of migrants is the one that participates the most in the association's activities. There are different reasons for this. First, very frequently the younger generations are not exclusively of Egyptian origin, since they have grandparents or parents of other backgrounds. Second, even though Israeli migrant associations—which, as seen, began as mutual aid societies and a catalyst for political/economic demands more than as cultural groups—have actually changed their goals through the years, they often continue to be perceived as politicized lobbies that reflect a Zionist, or at least more normative, interpretation of the past, which does not always appeal to the more socially and politically active among the young *Mizrahim*.[47] The involvement of the younger generations is limited also in the case of associations based in the Diaspora, like the French Association pour la sauvegarde du patrimoine culturel des Juifs d'Egypte or the Association Nebi Daniel, despite the fact that they mainly focus on cultural issues and, especially in the first case, take a more detached stance toward, for example, property claims against Egypt.[48]

That said, it would be unfair to focus exclusively on the political dimension of the Hitahdut and not to say that the conferences and meetings of the association are an extraordinary way to keep in contact with friends living in different parts of the world, as well as an occasion to spend time remembering with a hint of nostalgia the *Egypte d'antan*. For example, at the 2014 Eilat World Congress of Jews from Egypt, Egypt was presented as a magical place where "even if you were not rich, still you could have a maid. Everyone enjoyed a good life." Of course, these meetings also serve as a platform for discussing issues such as the recuperation of lost or sequestered assets, as some of the people gathered in Eilat explicitly underlined: "We left so much in Egypt. We all left something: houses, properties, money." In relation to this, others explained how, upon leaving Egypt, some Jews received a *cértificat de refugié* from the United Nations: "We are refugees. So, what is it they have to decide? What are they talking about?" They argued that beneath the difficulty of getting their properties back, first and foremost lay the Arab-Israeli conflict and the consequences that labeling the Jews from the Middle East as refugees might entail vis-à-vis the rights of Palestinians.[49]

It is interesting to note that the loss and the difficulties faced after the migration, far from being a purely economic and political matter, hide emotional and deeply personal concerns. "[Leaving Egypt] for us children was easier. For my parents it was a huge trauma... every year we used to go to Abu Kir, we always went out and now here we were, surrounded by sand in Qiriyat Malakhi" a woman recalled during the 2017 Tiberias conference. In these quotes, the most tangible components of a lost Egyptian Jewish heritage fuse with the intangible ones. In a way that, after all, is not so dissimilar from literature, the activities of the Israeli Egyptian Jewish associations and the effort to accumulate life stories, poems, and photographs; to print bulletins and books; and to get together on a regular basis are an example of how the history of a community that—because of uprooting and exile—possesses few things from the past can gradually rematerialize in the present to avoid disappearing with the passing of time.[50] Family sayings and stories are transmitted from one generation to another, mingling with real objects and artifacts, when and if these still exist. This way, the distinction between tangible and intangible becomes almost irrelevant and what emerges is an *(in)tangible* heritage of sorts, in which objects and memories, past and present, Egypt and Israel inextricably blend.

THE "DIFFICULT HERITAGE" OF THE JEWS OF ALGERIA IN POSTCOLONIAL FRANCE

"You know, for many years, the Jews of Algeria did not have a memory [*mémoire*]; they only had memories [*souvenirs*]."[51] With these subtle words, an Algerian Jew who has lived in France since the 1960s recalled his community's approach to the past during an interview I did with him in Paris. For this man, the Algerian Jews struggled not only to come to terms with their difficult history but also to construct a coherent historical memory of what happened to them from the time of the mass migration of the 1960s—the *exode*, as he called it—to the present day. If the juxtaposition between *mémoire* and *souvenir*—that is to say, between a socially constructed memory and the individual recollection of the past[52]—may seem almost self-evident when it comes to distinguishing between different forms of remembrance, in the case of the Algerians it illuminates a particularly interesting side of the Sephardi and *Mizrahi* memorial dynamics. Perhaps more than others, this Diaspora experienced a painful uprooting from the country of origin to then migrate to a nation, France, in which they actually had already been living—from a juridical, but surely not geographical, point of view—and of which they had been citizens for three or four generations.

Whereas in the previous pages we have seen that the history of Egyptian Jewish associations in Israel points to the emergence of an (in)tangible heritage that crosses different spaces and countries and yet is capable of firmly rooting itself in the Israeli context, the peculiarities of Algerian Jewish history seem to have led to the birth of a more *difficult heritage* that has struggled to find a place in that French national context of which, as said, the Jews of Algeria theoretically were already part. More than in the Egyptian case, Algeria is perceived as a faraway country that is other from the one the Jews had known.

This depends on the past that the Jews of Algeria share but also, and even more so, on the postcolonial reality that has influenced their lives since the migration in the 1960s. By saying that theirs is a *difficult heritage*, I follow the definition provided by Sharon MacDonald, who contends that a heritage is difficult when "it threatens to break through into the present in disruptive ways, opening up social divisions," because it is meaningful yet troublesome—as it does not evoke national or communal achievements and triumphs but rather dramatic or even shameful events.[53] However, this does not mean that the Algerian Jewish heritage is difficult per se, but that it has come to symbolize a history of disruptive colonial relations and a war that deeply marked the contours of contemporary France and Algeria.

Because of the specificities of Algeria in comparison to all the other territories of the French Empire, the Jews who lived in the country faced a process of juridical and social emancipation that differed from and left a much more profound impact than that of the Jews of Morocco or Tunisia. In fact, even though most of the Jews had lived in Algeria for centuries and were more or less Arabized, forty years after the beginning of the French colonial rule, in 1870 with the Crémieux Decree, they obtained en masse French citizenship—the only exception were the Saharan Jews of the M'zab, a region that at the time was not yet fully annexed to French Algeria.[54] In ways that still differed from one city to another, from the coast to the inland, this provoked the distancing of the Jews from the Algerian Muslim majority—and vice versa—which was further accelerated by a process of cultural and social Frenchification in spaces like school, but also in the organization of communal and synagogue life. Certainly, the colonial dimension of the decree should not be seen in isolation from other aspects that lay beneath its promulgation, such as the idea that, since Algeria was considered part of France and was not a colony like the protectorates of Tunisia or Morocco, there could not be a juridical differentiation between the Jews living in metropolitan France and those living in the Algerian *départements*.

As Joshua Schreier has explained, the logic of the Crémieux Decree "depended on grafting the teleology of French-Jewish emancipation to the colonial narrative of civilising" but at the same time aimed to increase the number of French citizens living in a predominantly Arab Muslim Algeria.[55] Thus, in the course of the nineteenth and early twentieth century, many Algerian Jews adopted "a *French identity* . . . that coexisted up to their departure for France with their *religious identity*."[56] Although they were never completely estranged from the Arab-Berber context and in the 1950s and 1960s some even got involved in the anticolonial struggle,[57] the Algerian War (1954–62) determined their departure—juridically speaking a repatriation—for France together with the

European colonial settlers, the so-called *pieds-noirs*.[58] Only years after the migration did the Algerian Jews slowly start to rediscover a multifaceted heritage that includes different memories and pasts: "French *citizens*, they cultivate their *Jewishness* within a *Sephardi* context, that is permeated of *Berber-Arab* culture, and they share with the other Algerian repatriates their feelings for a past, today largely idealized."[59]

Among the distinctive traits of the Algerian Jewish migration history is the fact that, in contrast to all other Middle Eastern and North African Jewries that dispersed over many different countries across Europe, Israel, and the Americas, almost all of the approximately 150,000 Jews who lived in Algeria settled in France, mainly in Paris and its region or in the south of the country. Only about 12,000 people moved to Israel between 1950 and 1962: this was a small but diverse group, composed of religious and Zionist Jews, as well as Jews coming from the rural south and the region of the M'zab.[60] Whereas in Israel the so-called *Mizrahim* had to reconstruct their heritage vis-à-vis the Zionist ideology and the Palestinian-Israeli conflict, in the case of the Algerian Jews in France, one finds a different scenario dominated by the memory politics of that nation and of Europe. Consequently, the heritage of this Diaspora and its memorial legacies reflect—in a way that parallels those of the *pieds-noirs* and of other postcolonial migrants, more than the *Mizrahim*—a past that brings with it the most dramatic moments of colonialism and the Algerian War, as well as the Vichy period, during which the Jews, both in metropolitan France and Algeria, were deprived of French nationality.

These events, and particularly the Algerian War, have stimulated great controversies in the French public arena, not least with reference to the ways in which they should be remembered and transmitted.[61] In the 1960s and the immediate aftermath of the mass migration, many of the Algerian Jews and the Algerian Jewish associations—like the French-based Association des Juifs Originaires d'Algérie (AJOA), founded in 1962 as a successor to the Comité Juif Algérien d'Etudes Sociales of Jacques Lazarus—viewed the *exode* as inevitable and downplayed the cultural and identity interconnections that the Jews shared with the Algerian Muslims. This brought about a collective memory that, according to Ethan Katz, is based on two overarching historical narratives: that of *progrès et patriotisme* under French patronage and of *violence et vulnerabilité*— both due to Muslim anti-Jewish feelings (think of the infamous Constantine riots of 1934) and *pieds-noir* antisemitism.[62] The persistence of these historical narratives relates to the difference in the process of postcolonial integration into France of Algerian Jewish and Muslim immigrants respectively: whereas the former were considered *rapatriés* and members of "a 'religion', compatible with French citizenship, ... to be Muslim was a 'nationality', thus necessarily foreign."[63] This was a reminiscence of the French colonial law as it was applied in Algeria, where the categories of citizenship and nationality were kept distinct and therefore Algerian Muslims generally were French nationals but not citizens, as opposed to the Algerian Jews and the *pieds-noirs*.

As regards the postmigratory relation with the *pieds-noirs*, studies have shown that initially many French *de métropole* actually viewed the Jews of Algeria as the quintessential *pieds-noirs* since they were said to share—for example, in terms of the stereotypical image of the families disembarking from the quay of Marseille—cultural and even physical characteristics considered to be the French Algerian essence.[64] At the same time, in the first decades after the migration, the Algerian Jews—in ways not so dissimilar from the *Mizrahim* in Israel—generally silenced their identity, which they began to express more freely beginning in the 1980s.[65] Since then, Algerian Jewishness has been depicted as a blending of the Arab-Berber tradition and the French-driven process of emancipation begun in the nineteenth century. This is viewed in positive terms as improving the status of Jews, downplaying the *longue durée* consequences it had at a cultural and political level, first and foremost the progressive estrangement between Jews and Muslims.[66] At the same time, as opposed to what occurred in the first phase, the president of the French heritage association Morial—Mémoire et traditions des Juifs d'Algérie (the name is an acronym for the Hebrew Moreshet yehudei 'Algeriah, "the heritage of the Jews of Algeria") argues that the connection between Jews and *pieds-noirs* nowadays has lessened because of the acknowledgment of "the antisemitism of the *pieds-noirs*, the racism" or is limited to more quotidian aspects of their heritage, such as food.[67] As the Algerian Jewish heritage started to be valorized, dozens of books were published by professional and amateur writers such as Albert Bensoussan and Jean Cohen, and singers like Enrico Macìas set to music the theme of Algeria as a vanished *pays du soleil*:

I left my country
I left my home
[...] Oh Sun! Sun of my lost country
of the white cities I loved
of the girls I once knew.[68]

From this point of view, even today the heritage of the Jews of Algeria shares many similarities with that of the *pieds-noirs* and includes memories and immaterial elements like the sunny and warm climate of a magical land on the other side of the Mediterranean Sea—which is in itself an important component of their heritage, especially given that by the mid-twentieth century more than half of the Algerian Jews lived in coastal cities like Algiers, Oran, and Mostaganem. There is another crucial, yet intangible, aspect: the attachment to the French language and culture. With reference to that, the philosopher Jacques Derrida, born in Algiers in 1930, confessed that for him Paris had been "the city of the mother tongue, a faraway country, close but far, not foreign [*étranger*], that would be too simple, but strange [*étrange*], fantastic, and phantasmic."[69] This feeling of double belonging to France and Algeria was already a foundational characteristic of the Algerian Jews before the migration, when they stood in the midst of contrasting legacies, and therefore—after the *exode*—many started to long for a Franco-Jewish Algeria that can never return. Even though the issue of the motherland and of French as a problematic mother tongue can also be found among other Middle Eastern and North African Jews, in the case of the Algerians it is brought to the extreme: "Algeria was not a province [of France]," Derrida continues, "or Algiers a popular neighborhood. For us, *since childhood*, Algeria was a country [*pays*], in the troubling sense of that word, which does not coincide with the state, or with the nation, the religion, and not even, I dare say, with any true community."[70]

For others, like the feminist philosopher Hélène Cixous, the mother tongue is not exactly French but a blending of languages, smells, and tastes that come to construct Oran, her city of birth: "The names of Oran smelled.... The name of Oran smells of the Bible and incense.... Thus I lived in the bosom of Oran, bathing in a dissemination of signifiers that lulled and moved my heart, I was in this language intangible in its totality, elusive compact, and which I could never hold in my mouth."[71] Still other Jews evoke in less idyllic terms the centuries-old ties that bound their families to Algeria, going back to the early modern era and underlining how this land, where several Sephardi Jews had settled to flee the persecution of the Spanish Inquisition, became another place of exile: "What a bizarre fate, little Gabriel, at a distance of five centuries you are going through what your ancestor had gone through. He left Spain to arrive in Algeria and you just left Algeria for the unknown. He had your same name and his father the same name of your father. You read his book and write its last page."[72]

As in the case of the Egyptian Israeli associations or in the novel *Un été à Jérusalem* by the Tunisian Chochana Boukhobza, the idea of belonging to the last generation able to remember the past is a preoccupation common among first-generation migrants. The Algerians fear that their heritage will vanish inside an indistinct French Sephardi Diaspora, a category that seems destined to inglobate the whole of the North African Jews settled in France since the postwar years.⁷³ This parallels what in many ways has happened in Israel, where the specificities of the Middle Eastern and North African *'olim* were put aside to give life to the *Mizrahim*, a new collective opposed to the Israelis of European descent. In the Algerian case as well, this acquires quite painful meanings. The heritage association Morial contends that "our ancestors . . . came from Cyrenaica, Judea or Spain. . . . They lived together with the Berbers, they had moments of happiness and despair. Oftentimes, they bent their back under the yoke of the law of the *dhimmi*. . . . And France arrived . . . the homeland of the *droits de l'homme*. But then, the *déchirement*. . . . We are the last generation of the Jews of Algeria that knew and loved this country."⁷⁴ Interestingly, despite the fact that in Algeria it had been abolished at the onset of the French colonization in 1830, the Islamic juridical category of *dhimma* is said to "continue to haunt the Jewish imaginary" and is evoked as a metaphor for all that precedes the arrival of the French.⁷⁵ However, the explicit reference to and insistence on *dhimma* actually seems a relatively recent phenomenon, relating to today's Jewish-Muslim relations in France and more generally to the fact that—for many Algerian Jews—Algeria and France are reimagined as a double historical wound. But then, which of the two is the country the last generation of Algerian Jews continues to long for? Is it the Algeria they lived in, or the imagined France which many had never seen before the migration?

To answer this question, it may be worth looking more closely at heritage associations. In fact, these also play a relevant role in France. Morial is one of the most active among the French Algerian Jewish heritage groups, and its goal is "to preserve and transmit the cultural and traditional memory of the Jews of Algeria."⁷⁶ Founded in 1995 under the impulse of the twin association Moriel, which already existed in Israel, it has around four hundred members and two thousand sympathizers. Like the Egyptian Hitahdut, the association organizes lectures and conferences on issues of heritage and history: from the Crémieux Decree to the figure of Jacques Lazarus or the Algerian Jews who fought for France during the First World War. On the occasion of the fiftieth anniversary of the *exode* and the Algerian War in 2012, Morial also organized a *Grand concours national* for children and adolescents between eleven and sixteen years old around the theme *Papy, mamy, racontez-moi votre Algérie . . .* asking young students with an Algerian Jewish family background to write essays that take cue from the family history. The winner of the competition was a sixteen-year-old girl who told the story of her grandfather, born in the city of Constantine: "For sixteen years, I have been listening to stories, anecdotes. All brighten his face of a precious flame. . . . Others sadden him, some others make him laugh. . . . And it is for all these happy memories that, for his seventieth birthday, my grandfather went back to Algeria. But he could not find this kind of moment and it is perhaps upon reading about them, that he will be able to live them again."[77]

As in some of the poems published in the Egyptian Jewish bulletins, here one finds the nostalgia for a joyful past tinged with the sadness of exile, the longing for an immaterial heritage and for an Algeria lost forever, which bears little resemblance to this country as it is today. In fact, when it comes to the possibility of visiting Algeria and taking care of its Jewish monuments and sites, the president of Morial talks about "a catastrophe . . . lost properties, synagogues transformed into mosques or shut down," and underlines the difficulty for the association to return on an official mission—as opposed to what happens in the case of Morocco and Tunisia, or even, to some extent, Egypt.[78] For Morial, the Jews of Algeria then are the protagonists of "a carnal and visceral relation to the *Terre*, its environment . . . but also [of] subsequent shocks, coexistence, and, oftentimes, fierce withdrawals and ancestral concerns."[79] Heritage acquires very physical characteristics, signaling the presence of a tangible Jewish Algeria *in Algeria*, made of old buildings and synagogues in need of restoration, of dilapidated tombs that are part of the country's past, and yet also of a largely intangible Jewish Algeria *in France*, embodied by migrants living on the northern shore of the Mediterranean Sea. The past, and Algeria as the location of its vestiges, is reconstructed in a new geographic and symbolic context that reflects one's individual life story as well as the collective memory of the *exode*. In other words, it is as if the heritage of Jewish Algeria can only be transmitted in exile, at a temporal and spatial distance from the country where it was born.[80]

If the relation of the Jews with today's Algeria is critical, certainly that with France, in consideration of the country's turbulent history in the second half of the twentieth century, has been handled in more effective but still complicated ways. As mentioned, 2012 marked the fiftieth anniversary of the Jewish mass migration and of the end of the Algerian War. Therefore, that year saw the organization of several activities related to the commemoration, first and foremost the exhibition Juifs d'Algérie at the Musée d'art et d'histoire du Judaïsme of Paris. Organized under the auspices of a scientific committee headed by one of the most prestigious representatives of French Jewry, the Algerian-born former chief rabbi of France René Sirat, the exhibition included historical documents, objects, ketubot (Jewish marriage contracts), family portraits, and religious items from Algerian synagogues, and multimedia installations allowed visitors to listen to pieces of traditional Algerian Jewish music. The exhibition had the double goal of "understanding . . . what Algeria represented" for the Jews and showing "how they resent, in France, both the disappearance of the Jewish community *là-bas* and the ruptures and echoes of the difficult history between France and Algeria."[81] It constituted a grand-scale opportunity to rethink the role of a Jewish museum in contemporary France and, at the same time, reposition the history of postcolonial French Jewish heritage inside this kind of institution.[82]

This was done through the reconstruction of the Algerian Jewish heritage in a participatory manner, which allowed virtually any Jew of Algerian origin to contribute to Juifs d'Algérie and have a family object or document included in the exhibition, as if it were—and indeed these items are—a piece of history worth displaying. In a case of difficult heritage like that of the Jews of Algeria, this helps one to reconcile with the past and reexperience the motherland, Algeria, in relation to *another* motherland that is also the host country, France. The exile of the Jews, and of their material culture, from Algeria is reconceived here as a homecoming—a repatriation—to France, of which, after all, they had been citizens since birth. Walking through the rooms of the exhibition, visitors could encounter more than two hundred artifacts coming from both institutional and family archives. Many collateral activities, from book presentations to concerts and movie screenings, took place during the months when the exhibition was on display.[83] On the whole, Juifs d'Algérie aimed at showing the public what Algerian Judaism has been and still is, so as not to lose the memory of a community whose migration "changed the traits of French Judaism."[84] The exhibition resulted almost in a direct experience of Jewish Algeria, at least of how this space can be reenacted today, instilling in visitors the idea that this past—*their* past, in the case of those who contributed directly to Juifs d'Algérie—is valuable. Although the remnants of the Algerian Jewish heritage in France are not imposing synagogues or community buildings but more often intangible memories, family photographs, or small objects that survived the migration and passed from one generation to another, the exhibition wished to demonstrate that even these apparently insignificant things are a foundational component of the identity of this Diaspora and of contemporary French Jewry at large.[85]

In November 2021, a major exhibition opened instead at the Institut du monde arabe, always in Paris. It was entitled Juifs d'Orient: Une histoire plurimillénaire and dedicated to the Jews of the Arab world more generally from ancient times to today. The exhibition was co-curated by the Algerian-born historian Benjamin Stora and inaugurated in the presence of the president of the French Republic, Emmanuel Macron. It included artifacts from private and public collections, photographs, videos, and music installations. Noteworthy is the fact that it was the first time that the Institut hosted an exhibition focused on Jewish-related issues and that collaborated with Israeli cultural institutions, allegedly also as a consequence of the 2020 Abraham Accords. For this reason, a petition by intellectuals and academics from the Arab world and elsewhere accused the Institut of "normalizing oppression" and argued that Israel "appropriated the Jewish component in Arab culture and attempted to Zionize it and Israelize it."[86] But, one could ask, is it possible to organize such an exhibition without collaborating in some ways with institutions located in the country, Israel, where today the majority of the Jews of the Arab world and their descendants live?

In different ways, these two exhibitions were of particular relevance because so far no museum dedicated to the Jews of North Africa—or the Arab world more generally—has been created in France or even in Israel, although in this second case museums dedicated to specific Middle Eastern and North African Jewries exist. In France, at the moment a number of initiatives are in place, also in consideration that 2022 will mark the sixtieth anniversary of the *exode*. Morial therefore launched an online *appel à témoignages*, because "memories are disappearing... we have to guard that the light of the flame is passed and is not extinguished."[87] Another initiative is, for example, that of MUSSEF—Musée du monde sépharade, which initially aimed at creating a museum dedicated to Sephardi Jewish heritage from the time of al-Andalus to the present day, by "bring[ing] into existence what is no longer, by tracing the history and culture of these Jewish communities that disappeared within a few years in the middle of the last century without making much noise."[88] An association in support of the creation of the museum—which is headed by Hubert Lévy-Lambert and supported by a scientific committee in which sit the writer Eliette Abécassis and the historian Michel Abitbol, among others—had been created, together with a website where detailed brochures and information on the project can be read. However, at the end of 2021 the museum project was abandoned because of lack of funds in favor of that of establishing a cultural and research institute, to be named IEMS—Institut européen du monde sépharade.

For the time being, if one wants to know more about the history of the Jews of the Sephardi world, one has to turn to the already existing French Jewish museums, like the above-mentioned Musée d'art et d'histoire du Judaïsme or the Mémorial de la Shoah. In fact, the permanent exhibition of the Parisian Mémorial inscribes the history of the Jews of Algeria and of French North Africa in that of the former colonial motherland. Hosted in a building opened in 2005, the Mémorial was first established in the 1950s as a monument to the *martyr juif inconnu*. It now hosts temporary exhibitions on topics related to the Holocaust, a library and documentary center, and pedagogical activities for teachers, children, and adolescents on antisemitism, antiracism, and other subjects. The permanent exhibition presents "a chronological and thematic itinerary... that tells the history of the Jews of France during the Holocaust."[89] Photographs, artifacts, historical documents, videos, and video interviews guide visitors in a voyage that focuses on the Holocaust but does not forget the larger history of the French Jewish community.

As said, the exhibition includes Jewish communities that are located outside today's France but that were part of its colonial empire until the mid-twentieth century, like Algeria or the protectorates of Morocco and Tunisia. Thus, in a panel entitled *La mise à l'écart: Les ghettos*, next to a historic image of the ghetto of Venice and one that portrays the Jews of the town of Metz, in the Alsace-Lorraine region, one finds a photograph of the *mellah*—the Jewish quarter—of Fès, which was established in 1438 "to protect [Jews] from hostile reactions on the part of the Arab population" and which made Morocco the only country of the Arab world with Jewish walled quarters and not simply an open *harat al-yahud* ("quarter/neighborhood of the Jews"), as in Tunis or Cairo.[90] Another panel, on the diversity of nineteenth-century French Judaism, includes among other things a portrait of Adolphe Crémieux, a photograph of a country house owned by the de Rothschilds, and an image of a group of Tunisian rabbis on an official visit to the *bey* in 1910, as well as a postcard portraying the Jewish quarter of Oran in 1917. An entire panel is dedicated to North Africa during the Second World War, highlighting two overarching themes: *Vichy en Afrique du Nord* and the labor camps located in the region. At the core of this section is the explanation of why the Jews of Algeria were subject to the racist laws promulgated under the Vichy government, which stripped them of French citizenship. The captions further mention that the Jews of Tunisia—as I will explain in detail later—were subject to more lenient measures, but because the country was the only one in North Africa to be occupied directly by the German army, about four thousand Jews were interned in labor camps and some were deported to the Nazi concentration camps.[91]

The Mémorial de la Shoah aims to tell the history of the Holocaust to a French Jewish and non-Jewish public. At first glance, the inclusion of Algeria and French North Africa might seem a relic of Orientalist and nationalist readings of the past, as sometimes happens in European museums and heritage centers.[92] However, this probably would be a partial if not biased interpretation of the Mémorial. It has to be remembered that the museum is visited frequently by French Jews, especially children and youth, among whom many are of Algerian or other North African origin. For this reason, the curators likely felt that North Africa needed not just to be mentioned but to be made part of the whole narrative. In turn, the Holocaust becomes part of a shared French Jewish heritage as an event that speaks to this Diaspora in its entirety, regardless of one's family history and place of birth. This is of great significance particularly in the case of the Jews of Algeria, who, since the 1960s, had to prove both their Frenchness and Jewishness to fellow nationals who saw them as distant people coming from a territory that many wished to forget about.[93]

Certainly, more than a few historians question the idea that the vast majority of North African Jews, while suffering from the Second World War and its impact in the region, experienced anything similar to the Holocaust. As concerns Algeria, it has to be mentioned that the Crémieux Decree was abolished in 1940, Jewish assets were sequestered, and a *numerus clausus* limited the presence of Jews in schools, universities, and several professions. These antisemitic measures were not rescinded as soon as the American forces debarked in Algeria but were renewed in March 1943 and abolished only in October, because French officers—to whom the Americans acquiesced—feared that this move could cause unrest among the Algerian Arabs.[94] During the war, some Algerian Jews also took part in the local Resistance movement and what is known as Operation Torch, a coup staged in November 1942 in Algiers by hundreds of Resistance fighters to help the landing of the Allies. In the course of time, the (indirect) experience of the Holocaust and an event like Operation Torch, which according to many Algerian Jews, among others, "literally forked the natural course of the Second World War,"[95] became iconic moments that relate all Jews living in today's France, be they Ashkenazis or Sephardis. So, although the situation for the Jews in North Africa during the war was certainly less dramatic than in Europe, the Algerian and other North African Jewish associations nowadays tend to represent the Holocaust as a chapter in a shared Jewish destiny that connects the two shores of the Mediterranean. More generally, the memory of the Holocaust has acquired global characteristics, migrating beyond the borders of the territories where it took place to become the reference point for other (Jewish) historical experiences of genocide and violence.[96]

However, to prove that the heritage of the Jews of Algeria reflects not only a centuries-old presence in the Arab world but also—and perhaps even more so—the history of modern France, one cannot refer exclusively to the Holocaust. Let us consider a monument built in 2013 in the cemetery of Pantin, Paris, to commemorate the "exodus of the Jewish French [*français Juifs*] of Algeria" and particularly those buried there, whose tombs cannot be visited by relatives or friends now residing out of that country. Supported by the city council of Paris and the Conseil représentatif des institutions juives de France,

Figure 2.2. Memorial of the exodus of the *français Juifs* of Algeria, cemetery of Pantin, Paris, 2016.
Source: Author.

the creation of the monument was an initiative of the Association Nationale Exode des Français Juifs d'Algérie (EFJA).[97] The association's name reflects the assumption that, since the Crémieux Decree, the Jews of Algeria have been first and foremost a group of French citizens like any other, and only in the second place one that also has a particular ethno-religious origin. By arguing this, the members of the association—who consider themselves to be the "executive representatives of the former French departments of Algeria and the Algerian south"[98]—seem in tune with a quintessentially French notion of universalism that is opposed to any form of *communautarisme*, which is perceived as a threat to the existence of the République and its founding values. One could even contend that the association follows a line of thought that goes back to 1789 and Stanislas de Clermont-Tonnerre, the French deputy and advocate of Jewish rights who famously asserted that "everything must be refused to the Jews as a nation . . . and everything granted to the Jews as individuals."[99]

The monument erected in Pantin (fig. 2.2) consists of a wall of black stone engraved with the phrase "Mémorial 1830–1962 Exode des Français

Juifs d'Algérie" and the stylized drawing of a family—mother, father, and son—sitting next to two suitcases, in front of a vessel departing presumably for France. At the left end, the stone is curved in a cylindric manner so as to create a second, smaller monument to "the memory of the brave French Jewish soldiers who died for France 1830–1962." The names of forty Jews are sculpted on the monument, inside whose pedestal, following a public appeal launched in the months before the construction, EFJA walled small silver cases containing the names of dozens of other people. For EFJA's president Georges Benazera, "it has been comforting to see people from all over the world to call in order to have their names sculpted on the memorial.... We are the last generation."[100]

In the memorial, which aims to commemorate both the Algerian Jews who fought for France since the beginning of colonization and all those buried in Algeria, the French Algerian Jewish identity becomes visible through the evoking of the army service and of the dead ancestors. As regards the first aspect, it is worth noting that since at least the First World War, Jews in countries such as France or Italy have interpreted the possibility—which resulted from the nineteenth-century process of Jewish emancipation—and desire to serve in the army as a supreme sign of patriotism and national loyalty. By referring to the conscription in the French army, the monument also seeks to provide a positive perception of soldiers belonging to a minority group and coming from a territory outside the metropole, and by doing so to counter the rather ambivalent view that the French general public might have of them.[101] Secondly, the dates 1830–1962 imply that this is the only period to be commemorated in Algerian Jewish history and in that of the French Algerian Jews—who, however, actually became French only in 1870—overlooking the many more centuries of Jewish presence in an Arab-Berber Algeria, long before the advent of colonialism. As it happens in other cases, this monument, then, can be read—from the point of view of its designers and users—as a site-related text that proposes specific interpretations of the Algerian Jewish past, inscribing it in the French national narrative and emphasizing the sacrifice, literal and symbolic, of this community before and during the Algerian War.[102]

A year before the construction of the memorial, in 2012, EFJA organized a public ceremony to mark the fiftieth anniversary of the exodus. On that occasion, a *livre d'or* was left at the disposal of the public gathered in the Palais du Luxembourg of Paris, where a conference on *La présence juive en Algérie* took place. Why was the memory of the exodus considered to be so important, and how did the Jews of Algeria evoke their past? For one of the attendees, "instead of renouncing their origins and assimilate, this community decided to reconstruct itself in France. In doing this, it has brilliantly contributed to the enrichment of the *pays d'accueil*." Another confessed that, fifty years after migrating from Algeria, "I think about my family, friends, those who are still there and those that are gone. I think of this 'repatriation.' I think of this country that I left, but that has not left me." A daughter of Jews from Algeria wrote, "Born one year after the exodus, I share . . . the nostalgia for that beautiful Algeria, that joyful Judaism, so rich in colors, emotions, and religious teachings." A man further noted that "we really had to celebrate this fiftieth anniversary" and talked about "a nostalgia full of hope and life, because upon leaving Algeria they brought the soil of their homeland under their soles and the sun on their faces." The guest book closes with a melancholic description of the Algerian sun, "our sun," which since 1962 is said to be "sleeping behind the mountains. . . . Half a century has passed, the wound is still open. We are the last—but not the only ones—to acknowledge this torment."[103]

In one of the themes that comes up in several testimonies, the Jews of Algeria are seen as a laborious and quiet Diaspora, a recurring idea also among those who settled in Israel: "If I were to say what is the characteristic of the Algerians, I would say modesty [*tzniyut*]," an Israeli of Algerian origin who now lives near Tel Aviv has told me.[104] Moreover, as this *livre d'or* shows, even though the memory of the motherland can be painful and some declare that they "have turned the page, they do not want to talk," many Algerian Jews still feel the need to remember and "reconstruct a memory, so that I should be able to say: 'Well, you see, I had something.'"[105] In the majority of these personal recollections, the description of the postmigratory identity is linked to feelings of loss, nostalgia, and sorrow, whereas joy and an omnipresent sun pervade almost all that precedes the war and the exodus. A significant space is given to Judaism, conceived of as a warm, familiar set of religious rites and more generally a central component of the community's dispersed cultural heritage. It is not a coincidence that in the early 1970s a group of Jews from the city of Tlemcen opened an Algerian synagogue in the tenth arrondissement of Paris, resembling that of their city of birth: the Synagogue de l'Union Nationale des Amis de Tlemcen. For Susan Slyomovics, opening this synagogue allowed them to reexperience, in spatial terms, a side of their life in Algeria, as did the evoking in France of centuries-old ritual performances such as the pilgrimage to the tomb of Rabbi Ephraim al-Naqawa (1359–1442).[106] Religion is ethnicized and acquires new meanings: both in France and Israel, a synagogue, a pilgrimage—like the one mentioned above, or that by Tunisian Jews in today's Sarcelles, which reenacts the visit to the tomb of Rabbi El Maarabi, located in the region of Gabès—or a holiday like the Moroccan Jewish *Mimouna* do not have only a religious and ritual function.[107] They act also as original sites of memory for displaced people that momentarily recreate places and epochs of their previous lives in the faraway motherland.[108] Think also of the tombs of Moroccan *tzaddiqim* ("saints") transposed from Morocco to Israel, or those of contemporary *tzaddiqim* who died in Israel, like that of Baba Sali—the Moroccan-born rabbi Yisrael Abuhatzeira—in Netivot: each year, his *hillula* ("death anniversary") gathers more than a hundred thousand worshippers, who recreate in a small town in the south of Israel a centuries-old Moroccan (Jewish and Muslim) tradition of saint devotion.[109]

We have encountered different ways of reclaiming the Algerian Jewish cultural patrimony in contemporary France. Together, they construct a *difficult yet vital* heritage that mirrors the French postcolonial reality, as well as the resilient memories of the Algerian War and the *exode*. In comparison to other North African Jewries, the Algerians share a more complex history of migration and resettlement; it is perhaps for this reason that the memory of the Arab neighbors, schoolmates, or friends appears less often in comparison to the general description of Algeria, of one's place of birth, and of the family. The associational culture and museums that I have described, as well as public commemorative practices like the building of the Pantin memorial, highlight the tensions that lie beneath the triangulation of Jewishness/Algerianness/Frenchness—particularly the difficulty of finding a shared memory, capable of speaking to a community that sees itself as an inseparable part of the *Héxagone* but that, at the same time, originates in a land that is other than France. In this sense, the emphasis placed on antisemitic persecution—through the evoking of the figure of the *dhimmi*—or on the Second World War and Vichy, contributes to make their heritage closer to that of the Jews of Europe. However, the Algerian Jews aim to rescue, and make more visible in the present, other and more specific threads of a multivocal past that—while sorrowful and problematic, as in the seemingly unresolvable contrast that today exists between Arabness and Jewishness—can never be forgotten, as it brings with it "the tenacious certainty that it is possible to be at the same time French and Jewish, *républicain* and sympathetic toward religious rites, Western-oriented but forever marked by the East, by Algeria."[110] This mirrors the problematic place that Algeria still represents in the French national consciousness and history, as highlighted by the discussion of the report on Algerian colonization and the Algerian War, commissioned by the president of the French Republic, Emmanuel Macron, to Benjamin Stora and released in January 2021.[111] It remains to be seen how these lost threads will continue to flow against the background of an increasingly fragmented French Judaism, and in the context of a country that in the last years has seen an upsurge of antisemitism and Islamic radicalism, as well as nationalist and xenophobic calls—including that of the journalist turned politician of Algerian Jewish origin, Eric Zemmour, who in December 2021 announced his candidacy for the 2022 presidential elections and launched the far-right party Reconquête ("Reconquest")—and new forms of social and economic tension.[112]

DIGITAL DIASPORAS: EXPERIMENTS IN MOROCCAN AND EGYPTIAN JEWISH HERITAGIZATION

Cultural associations and museums are often the first spaces one thinks of when it comes to heritage, in both a tangible and an intangible sense, and its preservation. Both presuppose a physical and direct relation among the members of a social group or a community and between them and other people who may or may not belong to it—such as museum curators. However, nowadays, and even more so in the aftermath of the COVID-19 pandemic, the internet and virtual means of communication have acquired a great importance and become almost omnipresent in our daily lives, as well as in the preservation of archival material, museum practices, teaching, and the transmission of the past more generally.[113] Many scholars have started to discuss how the digital technologies are modifying our relation to heritage, history, and memory.[114] Some have underlined how these means of communication potentially pave the way to a more polyphonic and open historical narrative and, in doing so, make more visible the heritage of communities that hitherto have been neglected or marginalized.[115] To continue surveying the Sephardi and *Mizrahi* practices of heritagization and diasporization, I will look at how the internet and online interactions between Jews who have lived in countries of the southern shore of the Mediterranean can lead to the emergence of new, digital diasporas that are different from the Sephardi and *Mizrahi* diasporas *stricto sensu*. I will analyze some of the main websites and Facebook groups connected with the Moroccan and Egyptian Jewish communities. This will allow me to explain who the main users of the websites are and which subjects are the most debated. A qualitative reading of the websites and of the messages exchanged by users permits one to reflect on how the internet is influencing the process of identity and heritage making of two groups of Sephardi diasporic subjects.[116]

Before looking at the Moroccan and Egyptian Jewish websites, I shall define what a digital diaspora is. At first glance, one could argue that digital diaspora is yet another addition to diaspora studies, a field that "emerged in fragmentary fashion ... as earlier disciplines dealing with nation, ethnicity, race, migration, and postcolonialism felt the need to adjust their methods and categories to the pressures of new transnational and global phenomena."[117] The notion of diaspora obviously can be interpreted in many different ways, although some aspects of the so-called Jewish paradigm are always valid. For example, a diaspora usually shares one or more common languages, a specific memory of the past, and often a religious belief.[118] In this case, digital diaspora designates a group of people—made firstly of migrants or descendants of migrants and secondly of others who are or feel related to these migrants and their heritage—that connects through the internet, to take part in networks of communication and discussion in which the real and virtual dimensions overlap.[119] In other words, it is a community that interacts online but is related to an identity and group that already exists outside the internet. It is a mobile and changing category that can be modified or enlarged whenever new members join a website or start to interact on an online forum or social network. A digital diaspora is not entirely a new entity but one that utilizes new forms of communication to sustain and develop a preexisting identity. Nevertheless, the usage of new media is not just a technical aspect but something that has a profound impact on the ways in which this diaspora imagines itself and preserves its cultural heritage.[120]

As regards Morocco, I should recall that a Jewish community, the so-called *toshavim* ("residents, inhabitants"), has lived in this country since ancient times. Over the course of centuries, Jews of Sephardi origin (*megorashim*: "expelled") arrived from the Iberian Peninsula, leading to the birth of a heterogeneous yet well-integrated Diaspora. The history of cohabitation among Jews, Arabs, and Berbers halted mainly from 1948 when, after the foundation of the State of Israel, the first Jewish migratory waves occurred. From that moment and then throughout the 1950s and 1960s, more than 280,000 Jews left Morocco for Israel, France, and countries like Canada because of the worsening of the regional political situation and the living conditions of the community.[121] With the migration, Moroccan Jewry gave birth to a new diasporic identity that nonetheless, both in the case of those who went to Israel and of those who settled in France or Canada, continues to perceive Morocco as a vanished but still present homeland to which to return with memory or, since the 1980s and increasingly in the 1990s, on vacation or pilgrimage. Thus, what emerged is a double diaspora, or, better to say, a form of *rediasporization* of Moroccan Jewish identity.[122] The case of the Moroccan Jews is not unique, since other communities—either Jewish or not—who were forced to migrate have developed similar models and equally complex feelings of belonging. For example, some argue that the Egyptian Jews became a more homogeneous community—or, at least, developed a stronger feeling of being one—only after the migration from Egypt in the 1950s.[123] As said, the existence and sharing of a common memory, conceived as a set of individual and collective notions that, altogether, constitute a fundamental resource of knowledge of the past, is the most relevant characteristic of any diaspora, which constructs itself on the basis of the remembrance of a partly lost and mythologized space and time.[124] But then, keeping in mind the case of migrant associations and their role in the preservation and memorialization of the Sephardi and *Mizrahi* heritage, in which ways does the internet function as a new tool with which a diaspora can commemorate and evoke its past? And are there differences between how this is being done by the Jews of Morocco and by those from Egypt?[125] Another question worth asking is whether the internet can ease some of the tensions present in the process of exilic identity and heritage making that these migrants undergo, or in other words to what extent the digital dimension can be a freer space of interaction and an antidote to divisive, or even nationalist, readings of the past.

The first website I will look at is Dafina. Despite the name, its focus is not gastronomy but the cultural heritage of the Jews of Morocco that, nonetheless, a dish like the *dafina* seems to symbolize:

> Who of you knows the unique taste of the *dafina*, the delicious Shabbat dish? Its taste and smell are inscribed in our genes and in our cells in an indelible way. You know why? Because its perfume carries with it all the wonderful memories associated with Shabbat and so reawakens in us the joy of those times, which are buried in our inner self. And that is what we want to create on the Net. We want this site to be as delicious as the *dafina* of Shabbat.... May we reunite and connect through the invisible web of the internet.... At a time when our future both in Israel and in Europe is going through a serious crisis, and the direct witnesses of our life in Morocco are disappearing, it seemed crucial to take the initiative of collecting and preserving our heritage in order to transmit it to future generations.[126]

The *dafina* (in Moroccan Arabic, lit. "covered") is one of the most famous dishes of the Moroccan Jewish cuisine. It consists of beef, chickpeas, potatoes, eggs, and wheat and traditionally is consumed during the meal of the Shabbat. Referring to the dish's flavor and the memories attached to it, Dafina defines itself as *the* website of the Jews of Morocco and aims to contribute to the preservation of the heritage of this community at a point when—as we have read more than once—the passing of time and the gradual disappearance of direct witnesses has made this a pressing need. The website is run by a charitable foundation founded in 1999, the Harissa Foundation, which also owns websites dedicated to the Tunisian (*Harissa*) and Algerian (*Zlabia*) Jewish cultural heritage and which is responsible for organizing events and exhibitions on North

African Jewish culture. Dafina's forum is its major interactive section and the space where the importance of the website for re-elaborating the Moroccan Jewish Diaspora is most visible. It is almost entirely in French, and its users come from virtually all countries where Moroccan Jews live today. Even if the choice of the French language could, in part, orient the profile of the users in favor of those Francophone elements that traditionally belonged to the middle and upper class of the community,[127] the moderators justify this choice by saying that this language was selected because, even though it "is not the language of our ancestors and this compromise is not perfect, [it] is our common denominator on the website," considering that "the forum members come from all corners of the earth [and] do not all understand Hebrew, Arabic or Judeo-Arabic, English, Spanish, or *haketi*."[128]

Dafina's forum has sections focused on many different themes, from the history and current affairs of Morocco to Jewish genealogy. Leaving aside the two generalist sections *Le Maroc* and *Divers*, those that have the largest number of discussions are *Darkoum* ("at your house, at your place") and *Yahsra* (lit. *Ya hasra*). There, the forum is a space to reunite with friends, relatives, neighbors, and classmates and to share memories of the Moroccan past. Dafina acts as a catalyst for discussing and transmitting the peculiarities of the heritage of a diaspora that is now dispersed in several countries. In this way, a global and allegedly borderless means of communication like the internet quite paradoxically serves to strengthen the very localized Moroccan identity of these Jews, as if to remind us of the resilience of "collective identities, despite the process of globalisation, geographic mobility, dispersion and dislocation."[129]

Dafina can be said to fulfill a double function: first, it is the virtual supplement of a well-consolidated associational culture that the North African Jews developed in the aftermath of their migration, and, second, it is a new space where people who may or may not know one another outside the web meet and talk. For example, in a discussion about the town of Souk el Arba, northeast of Rabat, a user fondly writes, "Time passes and memories come back to the surface, as I turn the pages of Dafina. A wonderful website that I just discovered. . . . When I read some of the articles, suddenly my memory awakens."[130] In a long discussion and exchange of pictures of the school of the Alliance Israélite Universelle in Mazagan (El Jadida), another person says with nostalgia and a hint of bitterness, "I am happy to read all these names of *mazaganais*, that despite the [passing of] time are and remain in my memory, suddenly all these faces come back to remember the happy and unhappy sides of the past, of our childhood."[131] These stories and many others introduce the internet as an additional space in which to recreate and reconnect with one's dispersed heritage. Furthermore, the online dimension—thanks to its alleged absence of borders and its timelessness—allows for a prolonged *aller et retour* between Diaspora and homeland, past and present—something that already characterized the Moroccan Jewish identity in the postmigration context but that here acquires new meanings.[132] For example, visits to the tombs of *tzaddiqim* have always been a central aspect of Moroccan Jewish (and Muslim) folklore, and Dafina allows its visitors to perform virtual pilgrimages: photographs of tombs and maps of cemeteries are posted online, and users can express their wishes by writing messages or simply remember their attachment to a particular *tzaddiq*. Whereas a journey to today's Morocco first and foremost reconnects Jewish migrants to their native land, it also makes them experience the changes that have occurred since they left Morocco, but thanks to Dafina, they can return to a lost Jewish Morocco and live again in the world of before the migration, which nowadays only exists in memory. As demonstrated by Marie-Blanche Fourcade's analysis of websites dedicated to the Armenian genocide, users are the authors of their own history, which in turn "takes ... an emotional dimension.... There is no longer just a history based on a unified narrative, but plural stories built from selected memories."[133]

Interestingly, and much more than what occurs in the Algerian or Egyptian Jewish websites that I have accessed, Moroccan Jews are not the only users of Dafina. Among the authors of messages, one finds several Moroccan Muslims and other people who, in one way or another, have had a personal experience of Jewish Morocco. For example, an English woman who in the 1960s was employed by an insurance company in Casablanca wrote, "I wonder if anyone remembers me. Between 1960 and 1962 I worked at Barber with my friend Barbara—two of the best years of my life."[134] A Muslim user expresses the desire to find her mother's Jewish school friends, who lived in the port city of Mogador (Essaouira) in the mid-1950s: "I am a *souiri*, not a Jewish one, but I like to follow your conversations and I am happy that this little town left good memories. All the best friends of my mum were Jewish.... my mother was married at the age of fourteen ... so she has attended school between [19]52–56."[135] There are also messages written by the sons of Jews of Moroccan origin, which reveals the extent to which this heritage is being transmitted from one generation to another: "Hello everyone, here I am, the daughter of A. S. who attended the school of the *Tour Hassan* [and] was born in Rabat in 1944, he told me of this school since I was little and I just found this forum, I am so happy for him ... I know he would be very happy to be in touch with students from his class or school!!! I would be grateful if you could leave a message."[136]

As said, in many ways Dafina is giving life to a new diaspora, which superimposes over the *real* Moroccan Jewish Diaspora and is, at least in part, other from it. It is a new diasporic network that includes not only members of the first generation of Jewish migrants—who were born in Morocco—but also their sons and daughters, some Moroccan Muslims, and other people who have encountered the Jews of Morocco in the course of their life.[137] Similarly to what we have seen for literature, writing a message on this website brings back to life microscopic aspects of one's memory and heritage—especially childhood and youth, the school attended, the street or the neighborhood in which one lived, the food eaten at home, the music—and in doing so deconstructs the hierarchy of events traditionally transmitted by historiography. A new, and more quotidian, history comes out of Dafina and reveals a memory of Morocco that is both real and virtual: a distinction that in the end is impossible to make and that shows the constant intermingling of the offline and online dimensions in the contemporary world.[138] At the same time, while Dafina undoubtedly represents an original archive of memories and a positive experience for its users, which can help to reconcile many with a troubled past, its web pages and forums also alert us to the dangers of a memory that, as Pierre Nora noted, "mocks history and ignores its intervals and sequences, its prose and impediments. . . . That [memory] which abolished the duration of time, so as to transform it into a present without history."[139] Moreover, in some cases interaction on the internet can stimulate divisive feelings—think, for example, about the conflation of anti-Jewish and anti-Israeli attitudes that Aomar Boum found while analyzing Moroccan youth cyberactivism. In that case, the internet provided a way to escape the rigid boundaries of Moroccan politics and bypass the youth exclusion from it but also a space where uncontrolled rumors and ungrounded news—like the idea of Moroccan Jews as spies of Israel—were disseminated.[140] When it comes to Dafina, other problems can be discerned: for example, the website forum hosted a heated debate on the so-called massacre of Petit-Jean, an anti-Jewish riot that occurred in a town near Meknès in 1954 in the context of anticolonial demonstrations that, in Morocco as elsewhere in the Arab world, often targeted foreign residents and members of minorities, such as the Jews.[141] This obviously does not mean that feelings of antisemitism were wholly absent from that context, but in many cases they should be seen as part of a larger picture of (Arab Muslim) nationalist resurgence, in which the Jews as well as many other groups did not fit. Dafina's users commented at length about this event, but when reading the various messages, one realizes that very few knew its factual evidence and that most users only wrote what they had heard from others, regardless of any historical accuracy. Some confused the Petit-Jean episode with other anti-Jewish riots that had occurred in the area of Meknès in the mid-1950s.[142] From this point of view, Dafina and the Egyptian Jewish websites that I will now introduce ultimately tell us more about the present than the past, signaling the resilience of the premigratory homeland and the contradictory ways in which its former inhabitants can mobilize their cultural heritage at individual and collective levels and therefore transmit their own version of the past.

In comparison with the Moroccan one, the Egyptian Jewish digital diaspora first of all is less characterized—because of the political situation in Egypt—by a real *aller et retour* between the old and new homeland. Secondly, the mythologization of the past, and of a heritage that is perceived as unique, plays an even greater role. The majority of the websites on Egyptian Jewish history and identity belong to Egyptian Jewish associations based in Europe, Israel, or the US. Others are run by single individuals, like the French-based Souvenirs d'Egypte of Albert Pardo, the Australian-based Jews of Egypt Foundation by Joe and Racheline Barda, or the photographic albums that can be found on the online photo-sharing application Flickr.[143] Additionally, in recent years groups like Jews of Egypt, Egyptian Jews, The Heritage of the Jews of Egypt, and Les enfants des Juifs d'Alexandrie et d'Egypte appeared on the social network Facebook.[144] The website of the Association pour la sauvegarde du patrimoine culturel des Juifs d'Egypte (ASPCJE) is one of the oldest. The ASPCJE was founded in 1979—the year in which the peace treaty between Egypt and Israel was signed—by a group of Jews who had settled in the Paris region, among whom was the renowned psychiatrist and writer Jacques Hassoun.[145] Its aim was, and still is, to "reopen the pages of our past and get our history back" and, in so doing, "transmit and share ... the cultural diversity" of the community, "beyond the passing of time and our dispersion."[146] Since then, the ASPCJE has organized a reading club and book presentations, and it publishes a bulletin called *Nahar Misraim* ("the river of Egypt," i.e., the Nile), which is sent to about 250 people, as well as an email newsletter.[147] The association's website primarily aims at "informing and keeping [people] updated about our writings and our activities, inviting you to participate." Designed in a simple manner, the ASPCJE home page welcomes visitors with photographs that portray different aspects of life in Egypt—for example, the Cairo neighborhood of Mouski, a view of the Pyramids, two men wearing a *tarboosh*.

Besides sections that summarize the history of the Egyptian Jews—and which include short essays on the Jewish schools in Egypt and the contribution of the Jews to Egyptian cinema—one can find the digital version of two books published by the ASPCJE: the 1984 *Juifs d'Egypte: Images et textes* and the 1978 *A la rencontre des Juifs d'Egypte*.[148] Furthermore, the ASPCJE digitized the *Haggadat Farhi*, an Arabic and Hebrew version published in Cairo in 1917 by Hillel Farhi of the text traditionally read during the *seder* of *Pesah*; a collection of 1930s maps of the city of Alexandria; and old photographs that illustrate different moments of community life and celebrations in interwar Egypt.[149] The material available on the website gives an overview of how Jews lived in pre-Nasserist times, focusing on topics and documents that, however, are not necessarily the most important in a purely historiographic perspective. This confirms what Cohen and Rosenzweig argued when they talked about "the fever to bring the primary sources of the past online that began in the mid-1990s," which led to the online publication of documents, "even if those artefacts do not necessarily have a shared 'provenance' and common association in the manner of a traditional archive . . . these website producers create their own virtual collections, often mixing published and unpublished materials in ways that 'official' archives avoid."[150]

As seen with Dafina, the internet offers the opportunity to give a more personal understanding of the Egyptian Jewish heritage, renarrated as if in a virtual exhibition with its most charming sides highlighted. On the other hand, some of the more problematic aspects, like the issue of Jewish property claims against Arab countries—which were frequently discussed by members of the Israeli-based Egyptian Jewish heritage associations—here are left more on the side. This partially differentiates the French-based Egyptian Jewish associations from the Israeli ones and, in many ways, relates to different national memory politics and the minor importance that issues like the Palestinian-Israeli conflict or the cleavage between *Ashkenazim* and *Mizrahim* have for the French-based Jews of Egyptian origin. It also has to do with the different types of social and economic integration that the Egyptian Jewish migrants faced in France and Israel respectively: whereas the migrants to Israel went through the experience of transit camps and had to cope with a certain marginalization on the part of the establishment, those who went to France were in some cases better equipped to start their lives anew and, more importantly, did not live in a state—like Israel—that fought a series of wars against the Arab countries and in which the Jews from Egypt were one among a myriad of Middle Eastern and North African (as well as other) Jewish communities struggling to be publicly recognized.[151]

In addition to the ASPCJE website, the Facebook group Les enfants des Juifs d'Alexandrie et d'Egypte constitutes another example of how the internet can stimulate the narration and preservation of one's history. The group's description states:

> You are at least fifty years old and you are one of those Jews whose parents were born in Alexandria. Deep in your heart, you feel nostalgia for the history of your parents and grandparents, for dishes such as the *moloheya* or the *kobeba*, for the promenade along the seaside, the card-playing between

friends, of that wholly European elegance typical of the city, [which was] a crossroad of the world's nations.... You never experienced how Egypt was but deep in your heart you all have a small light that turns on when you recognize another son of the Jews of the Nile.... This group aims to exchange recipes, addresses, meetings... but also to get to know each other, to get back in touch, to post yellowed photographs that evocate that bygone world.[152]

As one can read, Les enfants—which had more than 1,800 members as of 2022—intends to disseminate the knowledge of the Egyptian Jewish past and heritage. Despite the name, its members are not only from Alexandria but also from Cairo, and all wish to get together not in the context of an association but more freely online, on the basis of personal memories they share as children and grandchildren of Egyptian Jews or simply as people interested in the Egyptian Jewish past. Its aim is to recreate, in a virtual fashion that is similar to that seen in the Moroccan website Dafina, a country many of the people who write on the Facebook group have never seen but know very well thanks to the nostalgia of their parents or the dishes their mothers and grandmothers used to cook: an aspect that, as already explained in one of the previous sections, is a leitmotif of the remembrance of the Mediterranean Jewish heritage both in Israel and in the Diaspora. The goal of Les enfants is to "exchange recipes, addresses, meetings" and "get to know each other, get back in touch." As opposed to the inevitably more static approach of a website like that of the ASPCJE, which essentially serves to showcase a set of activities conducted offline, the interaction between users is at the core of Les enfants. Here all are asked to contribute in their own way to the reconstruction of the Egyptian Jewish history and to stimulate discussions on topics that relate to it. Therefore, what emerges is a participatory process of heritagization that, in turn, leads to the birth of a virtual world constantly evolving in relation to the written memories and photographs uploaded on the group's page.[153]

For instance, a French member of the group posted a portrait of her great-great-grandfather Aaron wearing a *tarboosh*. Several people commented on it, admiring the beauty of the photograph and the shared memories that it evoked. An Israeli man wrote that his grandfather also "wore [a *tarboosh*] until his death, even after he had arrived in Eretz [Israel]," adding that "that was the time of kings Fouad and Farouk, blessed epochs for the Jews of Egypt." A third member asked if Aaron was "the son of Yehoshua and Behora A." Finally, a fourth added another picture portraying her own grandfather wearing a *tarboosh*, "to keep company to your grandfather."[154] On February 2016, an Israeli woman asked whether "anyone knows the famous *Café Croopy* [i.e.,

Groppi]?"—one of the most renowned cafés of central Cairo and a symbol of *cosmopolitan Egypt*. Almost twenty people replied, answering that "everyone knew the *Café Groppi*," "the ice-creams of *Groppi* were legendary, as well as their cakes and *bombes glacées*," "I was there in 1985 but it was so different from the stories that my mum had told me about its velvet couches and crystal chandeliers." As in Dafina, quotidian details such as a *tarboosh* or the ice creams of the Café Groppi stimulate reflections on the past of the Egyptian Jews and on its almost mythical characteristics. The online circulation of images, and the meticulous comments that members write about them, are important aspects of Les enfants, whose success in uploading sources such as photographs and genealogical information and in reaching relevant audiences can perhaps offer new paradigms of heritage preservation and dissemination for archives and museums.[155]

Additionally, it is interesting to see that politics plays an active role in Les enfants. Members keep an attentive eye on the Egyptian situation, especially considering the turmoil that Egypt has been living through in the last years, following the 2011 Revolution and its long aftermath. For example, after the electoral victory of Muhammad Morsi in 2012, a member posted an article first published on the online newspaper *The Times of Israel* entitled "Egypt's Christians, Facing the Fate of Egyptian Jews," which described the difficult situation for Copts in today's Egypt, comparing it to that of the Jews in the aftermath of the Free Officers' Revolution of 1952.[156] Several members commented on it; one feared that the Copts "too, like us, will be deprived of their possessions and forced to migrate, to say the least," whereas another added that "Morsi, even though he is a Muslim Brother, is far from being as foolish as Gamal Abdel Nasser." The complex political situation in Egypt made people worry, more than before, about the state of Jewish heritage sites in the country. So in 2016 Yves Fedida—a well-known activist of the French-based Egyptian Jewish Association Nebi Daniel—published an appeal to President 'Abd-al-Fattah Al-Sisi asking for the authorization to "1. digitise the Jewish archives, particularly the civil and religious status registers [that are located] in the synagogues. . . . 3. The restoration of the extant synagogues and cemeteries. . . . 5. the creation of a museum for the Jewish heritage inside one of the extant synagogues."[157]

The appeal of Nebi Daniel, together with the activities of the Drop of Milk Association of Cairo—a charitable group headed by Magda Haroun, president of the Cairo Jewish Community, with the goal of preserving the Jewish heritage in Egypt and fostering knowledge about the country's Jewish past—and the lobbying of groups like the American Jewish Committee, in February

2019 led the Egyptian authorities to publicly express interest in projects of restoration of Jewish buildings and cemeteries. After meeting with a delegation of American Jews, which included a descendant of the Cairene rabbi Douek, Al-Sisi assured them that the government, among other things, would provide copies of the communal registers to the Egyptian Jewish associations abroad—as they had been asking for years.[158] One of the most significant results, however, was the fact that following a major restoration, in January 2020 the Eliahou Hanabi Synagogue of Alexandria—built in 1850—was reopened to the public. The official inauguration was attended by Egyptian politicians and several diplomats but only three Jews, and in mid-February it was followed by a sort of second inauguration, a *hanukkat ha-bayit*, "under the patronage of President Abdel-Fattah El Sissi" organized by Egyptian Jewish associations from abroad and in which almost two hundred Egyptian Jews from Israel and countries of the Diaspora took part.[159] While all this signals a change in the relations between the local authorities and Egyptian Jewish representatives, the underlying reasons are multiple. As in the case of other Arab countries, like Morocco, economic and touristic interests and the lobbying activities of Israeli diplomacy and American Jewish groups are playing a role in the increased public interest in these countries' Jewish heritage. On a different level, one may question the involvement of Jewish groups from the Diaspora and Israel—even when driven by a legitimate desire to protect the perishing heritage of their forebears—in projects seemingly related to political, more than cultural, aims and promoted by undemocratic regimes.[160] Certainly, this is a delicate issue on which it is not easy for the people involved to take a definitive stance, and it highlights the more political dimension of heritage, especially in the case of expelled or displaced communities, and its possible uses and misuses.

Going back to the role of the internet, it is obvious that Les enfants is not just a virtual exhibition of Egyptian Jewish community life but a thriving space in which members may reflect on their past and present heritage and propose solutions to the problems of preservation faced by the Jewish monuments of Cairo and Alexandria. On Les enfants, political events intermingle with more private details such as the language typical of the Egyptian Jews, giving life to a diachronic experience of diaspora, in between the private and public sphere, that can be narrated and commemorated. The online discussions on this Facebook group may be interpreted as a form of public history, by which I mean "a movement, methodology, and approach that promotes the collaborative study and practice of history" and that has proved to be particularly effective for "marginalized and forgotten . . . memories" that, thanks to the internet, can regain life and visibility.[161]

The Moroccan and Egyptian cases that I have analyzed offer different, albeit interrelated, approaches for using the internet to come to terms with a lost Middle Eastern and North African Jewish heritage. Whereas the website of the ASPCJE more or less is the showcase of the activities conducted offline by the association, Dafina is a wholly virtual platform for discussing and *returning* to Jewish Morocco and where the Moroccan Diaspora seems to expand beyond its traditional identity boundaries: consider the presence, since the website's inception, of Muslim users and the many ways this mirrors the (lost) Jewish-Muslim cohabitation that for centuries characterized many Moroccan towns. Lastly, the Facebook group Les enfants constitutes a space of discussion for the children and grandchildren of the Egyptian Jews, in which—thanks to the sharing of photographs and other artifacts—to elaborate new and more participatory models of heritage preservation and dissemination. Thus, it is arguable that the Middle Eastern and North African Jews are another example of *connected migrants*: migrants whose identity is characterized by both online and offline presences and traceabilities.[162]

This said, it is important not to confuse a digital diaspora with a diaspora tout court. Websites such as those that I discussed are not the equivalent of the Moroccan and Egyptian Jewish diasporas but rather one of their possible digital projections. Still, the heritage presented and discussed on the internet is not so dissimilar from the one promoted by the migrant associations, to the point that very often the same themes are evoked: food, or the protection of monuments and places of worship located in the motherland. Even the heritage present on the internet is both tangible and intangible, experienced and brought back to life by forms of digital display and preservation. Surely, the greatest advantage of the usage of the internet as a vector of heritage making is its potential to reach a wider audience both inside and outside the Middle Eastern and North African Jewish diasporas and its ability to stimulate a more polyphonic understanding of one's identity: in other words, it helps the members of the diasporic community to reconnect not just among themselves but also with their Arab Muslim and Christian neighbors. But as we have seen, this is not always the case, and just like traditional and better-established heritage spaces—such as museums—the internet can foster divisive approaches or even the misusage of a community's past. Nonetheless, considering the ever-growing importance of digital media in our daily lives, it constitutes an unavoidable and increasingly powerful arena in which even the younger generations—who only rarely take part in the activities of heritage associations—can reconnect to their families' past and therefore ensure its transmission in the future.[163]

THE PAST IN A FOREIGN COUNTRY

In a much-cited book, the historian David Lowenthal recalls the *incipit* of L. P. Hartley's *The Go-Between*, in which the British novelist expressed the somehow irresistible idea that "the past is a foreign country. They do things differently there."[164] In response, Lowenthal argues that the temporal and cultural distance that separates us from our ancestors and the ways in which they lived makes the past a terra incognita that, nonetheless, we continue to inhabit. Additionally, for Sephardi and *Mizrahi* Jews—as in other cases in world history—the past becomes a foreign country in a literal sense. In fact, these people live in places other than those where they were born, which in any case almost always have changed irremediably and appear very different from how they looked only sixty years ago. For these migrants and many of their descendants, even the present is a foreign country, or at least one they have to familiarize themselves with and slowly come to terms with. Their heritage then is constructed on feelings of uprootedness and exile, but also—in what only apparently is a paradoxical effect—on a strong desire to be inscribed in the history of the country, or countries, to which they have migrated.

Egyptian Jewish heritage associations in Israel are an example of how an (in)tangible heritage, the memory of a past life in Egypt, can materialize in the activities that migrants and their children conduct in the postmigratory context—in this case, dominated by the Israeli national narrative and Zionism. The contrast between ethnicity and national identity also has been noted in the case of the Jews of Algeria who resettled in France in the aftermath of the Algerian War. There, the difficulty of finding a place within French—and French Jewish—society reveals that the colonial past and its impact on Jews and Arabs still constitute an open wound, especially in regard to today's growing tensions around radical Islam, terrorism, and antisemitism. Both in Israel and in France, the Sephardi and *Mizrahi* heritage emerges as a multivocal construct, first composed of memories that subsequently are made visible—and more tangible—through the activities of associations, a museum collection or exhibition, and the photographs and objects preserved by individuals and families. The circulation of this heritage is further made possible thanks to the usage of the internet as a vehicle of dissemination and exchange of information. The cases of the Moroccan Jewish website Dafina and of the Facebook group Les enfants des Juifs d'Alexandrie et d'Egypte then shed light on the possible use of the web as a vector of greater interaction among people and generations—not all necessarily belonging to these Jewish diasporas—living in different parts of the world, who wish to commemorate and transmit a past they cannot forget.

The heritage that comes about does not only reveal quotidian and little-known sides in the history of the Jews of the southern Mediterranean shore and in their premigratory identity. It tells how these migrants perceive their motherland from afar—both temporally and spatially—and how the postmigratory context influences its remembrance. Heritage becomes a bridge between history and memory, between the factual reality of life before the migration and the imaginative recollection of the Jews who lived in places like Morocco, Algeria, and Egypt. On the whole, the revival of the Sephardi and *Mizrahi* past in recent years depends not so much on technological innovations, although these certainly are facilitating its dissemination, as on a persistent feeling of displacement and exile from Middle Eastern and North African worlds that many continue to inhabit with the mind, and that feeling is becoming even stronger in an increasingly diasporic world. The result is a set of interconnected *heritages* constantly in the making, involving both old and new territories, objects, and memories. These heritages point to the existence of new postmigratory Sephardi and *Mizrahi* diasporas, with members who, on one side, are not entirely at home in the country of immigration but who, on the other, cannot—and, in most cases, would not want to—go back to their land of birth. This once again reminds us to what extent the Mediterranean region is and always has been a space of rupture and continuity, borders and entanglements.[165]

NOTES

1. I take my cue from the idea of *memoryscape*, on which see Kendall R. Philips and G. Mitchell Reyes, "Introduction: Surveying Global Memoryscapes; The Shifting Terrain of Public Memory Studies," in *Global Memoryscapes: Contesting Remembrance in a Transnational Age*, ed. Kendall R. Phillips and G. Mitchell Reyes (Tuscaloosa: University of Alabama Press, 2011), 3.

2. "About World Heritage," *UNESCO—World Heritage Convention*, accessed January 3, 2022, https://whc.unesco.org/en/about/.

3. Astrid Swenson, *The Rise of Heritage: Preserving the Past in France, Germany and England, 1789–1914* (Cambridge: Cambridge University Press, 2013); John Carman and Marie Louise Stig Sorensen, "Heritage Studies: An Outline," in *Heritage Studies: Methods and Approaches*, ed. John Carman and Marie Louise

Stig Sorensen (London: Routledge, 2009), 11–28; Angelo Torre, "Public History e Patrimoine: due casi di storia applicata," *Quaderni Storici*, no. 3 (2015): 629–59.

4. Françoise Choay, *L'allégorie du patrimoine* (Paris: Seuil, 1992).

5. See "About World Heritage." On heritage in the Middle East, I refer to Rami Daher and Irene Maffi, *The Politics and Practices of Cultural Heritage in the Middle East: Positioning the Material Past in Contemporary Societies* (London: IB Tauris, 2014).

6. Adina Hoffmann and Peter Cole, *Sacred Trash: The Lost and Found World of the Cairo Genizah* (New York: Shocken Books, 2011).

7. Marina Rustow, *The Lost Archive: Traces of a Caliphate in a Cairo Synagogue* (Princeton, NJ: Princeton University Press, 2020), 2.

8. Colette Zytnicki, *Les Juifs du Maghreb: Naissance d'une historiographie coloniale* (Paris: PUPS, 2011).

9. Dario Miccoli, "Moses and Faruq: The Jews and the Study of History in Interwar Egypt, 1920s–1940s," *Quest—Issues in Contemporary Jewish History*, no. 4 (2012): 165–80.

10. Swenson, *Rise*, 3–4.

11. See the UNESCO definition adopted at the 2003 Convention for the Safeguarding of Intangible Cultural Heritage, "What Is Intangible Heritage?," *UNESCO*, accessed January 3, 2022, http://www.unesco.org/culture/ich/en/what-is-intangible-heritage-00003.

12. Sharon MacDonald, "Migrating Heritage, Networks and Networking: Europe and Islamic Heritage," in *Migrating Heritage: Experiences of Cultural Networks and Cultural Dialogue in Europe*, ed. Perla Innocenzi (London: Ashgate, 2014), 54.

13. As noted by Charlotte Siney-Lange, "Grandes et petites misères du grande exode des Juifs nord-africains vers la France," *Le mouvement social* 197, no. 4 (2001): 31.

14. Shohat, "Invention"; Moshe Behar, "What's in a Name? Socio-terminological Formations and the Case for Arabised Jews," *Social Identities* 15, no. 6 (2009): 747–71.

15. Chiara Bortolotto, "From Objects to Processes: UNESCO's Intangible Cultural Heritage," *Journal of Museum Ethnography* 19, no. 21 (2007): 21–33.

16. For an overview, I refer to Jose C. Moya, "Immigrants and Associations: A Global and Historical Perspective," *Journal of Ethnic and Migration Studies* 31, no. 5 (2005): 833–64.

17. Efrat Rosen-Lapidot and Harvey Goldberg, "The Triple Loci of Jewish-Maghrebi Ethnicity: Voluntary Associations in Israel and in France," *Journal of North African Studies* 18, no. 1 (2013): 112–30.

18. Alex Weingrod, introduction to *Studies in Israeli Ethnicity: After the Ingathering*, ed. Alex Weingrod (New York: Gordon and Breach, 1985), XVI.

19. Yitzhaq Haberfeld and Yinnon Cohen, "Ha-hagirah ha-yehudit le-Isra'el: shinuim be-ramot haskalah, sheker ve-hishtalvut kalkalim, 1948–2000" [Jewish immigration to Israel: Changes in the level of education, income, and economic integration], *Megamot*, no. 48 (2012): 504–34; Momi Dahan, "Ha-'im kor ha-hitukh hitzliah ba-sadeh ha-kalkali?" [Did the melting pot succeed in the economic field?], Israel Democracy Institute Working Paper, Jerusalem, October 2013, 1–50.

20. See Tamar Katriel, "Homeland and Diaspora in Israeli Vernacular Museums," in *Memory and Ethnicity: Ethnic Museums in Israel and the Diaspora*, ed. Emanuela Trevisan Semi, Dario Miccoli, and Tudor Parfitt (Newcastle: Cambridge Scholars, 2013), esp. 11–14.

21. Dekoven Ezrahi, *Booking Passage*.

22. Shlomo Kohen-Sidon, "Memorandum regarding the Israeli Organization of Anti-Jewish Persecution Victims from Egypt," *'Irgun nifgaey-ha-radifot ha-anti-yehudiyot be-Mitzrayim: Duah leshnat 1971/Association des ex-victimes des persecutions anti-juives en Egypte*, 10, YBZ XIV B 1701.9.

23. The numbers are indicative since there are great discrepancies in the figures available to researchers. See Sergio Della Pergola, "Ha-demografiah" [The demography], in *Mitzrayim* [Egypt], ed. Nahem Ilan (Jerusalem: Yad Ben-Tzvi, 2008), 34, table 1, table 37, table 3.

24. "Tqasey bar-mitzvah" [The ceremonies of bar mitzvah], *'Irgun nifgaey-ha-radifot 1971*, 62, YBZ XIV B 1701.9.

25. Shaul Kelner, *Tours That Bind: Diaspora, Pilgrimage, and Israeli Birthright Tourism* (New York: New York University Press, 2010), 30.

26. Beinin, *Dispersion*, 94–117; Laskier, *Jews*, 205–51. On the commemoration of the death of Marzuq, see Emanuela Trevisan Semi, "From Egypt to Israel: The Birth of a Karaite Edah in Israel," in *Karaite Judaism: A Guide to Its History and Literary Sources*, ed. Meira Pollack (Leiden: Brill, 2003), 431–51.

27. "Sikum pe'ulot shalosh shanim 1966–1969" [Summary of the activities of the three years 1966–1969] and "Seder ha-yom: Teqes yom ha-zikaron u-vrakhat rabbanim" [Program of the day: Ceremony of remembrance and blessing of the rabbis], *'Irgun nifgaey 1971*, 66, 51, YBZ XIV B 1701.9. Eli Cohen was an Egyptian-born Israeli spy who conducted espionage work in Syria from 1961 to 1965, when the Syrian authorities finally uncovered Cohen and sentenced him to death.

28. "Seder ha-yom," 9.

29. Michael R. Fischbach, *Jewish Property Claims against Arab Countries* (New York: Columbia University Press, 2008), 176–77.

30. "Mavo'" [Introduction], *'Irgun gag yotzey-Mitzrayim be-Isra'el: 'Irgun nifgaey-ha-radifot ha-anti-yehudiyot be-Mitzrayim: Din ve-heshbon leshnat 1972/1973*, 7 YBZ XIV B 1701.9.

31. See Levana Zamir, *Trumot ve-hishgeyhem shel-yotzei-Mitzrayim be-Isra'el be-50 shnot ha-medinah 1948–1998* [Achievements and contributions of Egyptian

Jews in Israel in its first fifty years] (Tel Aviv: Hitahdut 'olei-Mitzrayim be-Isra'el, 2003).

32. Consider, for example, Eliezer Ben-Rafael and Yochanan Peres, *Is Israel One? Religion, Nationalism, and Multiculturalism Confounded* (Leiden: Brill, 2005); Eliezer Ben-Rafael, *The Emergence of Ethnicity: Cultural Groups and Social Conflict in Israel* (London: Greenwood, 1982); Michel Abitbol, "La mémoire occultée et retrouvée: Juifs d'Orient et de Méditerranée en Israel," in *Milieux et mémoire*, ed. Frank Alvarez-Péreyre (Jerusalem: CRFJ, 1993), 353–54.

33. "Moreshet yahadut-Mitzrayim" [The heritage of the Jews of Egypt], *Goshen—'Alon yahadut-Mitzrayim/Bulletin des Juifs d'Egypte en Israel* (henceforth *Goshen*), September 1985, 1, YBZ VI 68.

34. Avner Assahel, "Qol ha-hitahdut" [The voice of the union], *Goshen*, May 1990, 14, YBZ VI 68.

35. Assahel, "Qol ha-hitahdut."

36. Ada Aharoni, "Me-Haifah le-Qahir ha-qrovah ha-rehoqah" [From Haifah to Cairo close and far], *Goshen*, September 1997, 33, YBZ VI 68.

37. "Mi-pinatah shel Esti" [From the corner of Esti], *Goshen*, March 2005, 14, YBZ VI 68.

38. "Mi-divrey nasi' ha-medinah mar Haim Herzog" [From the speech of the president of the state Mr. Haim Herzog], *Goshen*, May 1990, 1, YBZ VI 68.

39. Ada Aharoni, interview by the author, Haifa, May 26, 2014. For an analyis of some of her early works, see Beinin, *Dispersion*, 220–27.

40. For instance, in her documentary *Rimmon ha-sulhah* [The pomegranate of reconciliation], FaceThemLive, 2015, https://www.youtube.com/watch?v=8ABi2mPQnXI.

41. Aharoni, interview by the author. On the risks of comparing the history of the *Mizrahim* with that of the Palestinians, see Shenhav, *Arab Jews*, 110–35.

42. Levana Zamir, "Dvar ha-yoshevet-rosh" [President's foreword], *Yetziat-Mitzrayim shelanu*, January 2012, 3.

43. Levana Zamir, "Hanukat ha-bayit shel 'Ahabah ve-ahvah': beit-ha-knesset ha-mefu'ar shel yehudey-Mitzrayim be-Brooklyn" [Inauguration of 'Ahabah ve-ahvah'], *Bney Ha-Ye'or*, December 2008, 40–41. See also "About Us," Ahaba ve-Ahva, accessed January 3, 2022, http://ahaba.org/default.asp.

44. Esther Vidal-Mosseri, "Poèmes Bessamat El-Màdi," *Bney Ha-Ye'or*, 2005, 18.

45. Levana Zamir, *Mi-ta'amei Mitzrayim* [The flavors of Egypt] (Tel Aviv: Beit Alim, n.d.), 1.

46. Other Egyptian Jews wrote cookery books or include recipes in their memoirs: for example, since the late 1960s the Cairo-born Claudia Roden has written a dozen books on Mediterranean (Jewish) cuisine, whereas Colette Rossant authored *Apricots on the Nile: A Memoir with Recipes* (New

York: Washington Square Press, 1999) and the Israeli Nissim Zohar the autobiographical novel *Ha-molokhiyah shel 'ima'* [Mother's molokhiyah] (Tel Aviv: Yediot Aharonot, 2006). See Nefissa Naguib, "The Fragile Tale of Egyptian Jewish Cuisine: Food Memoirs of Claudia Rosen and Colette Rossant," *Food and Foodways* 14, no. 1 (2006): 35–53. With regard to food and North African Jewish memory and identity, see Joëlle Bahloul, *Le culte de la table dressée: Rites et traditions de la table juive algérienne* (Paris: Metailié, 1983).

47. Consider, for example, the third-generation activism of groups like the literary collective 'Ars Po'etiqah (see Dario Miccoli, *La letteratura israeliana mizrahi: Narrazioni, identità, memorie degli ebrei del Medio Oriente e Nord Africa* [Florence: Giuntina, 2016], 83–96) or the social movement *Tor ha-zahav* ("The golden era"). In different ways, both are critical of the Israeli establishment and politics.

48. Michèle Baussant, "Heritage and Memory: The Example of an Egyptian Jewish Association," *International Social Science Journal*, no. 203–4 (2011): 45–56; Baussant, "'Who Gave You the Right to Abandon Your Prophets?' Jewish Sites of Ruins and Memory in Egypt," *Quest—Issues in Contemporary Jewish History*, no. 16 (2019): 45–71.

49. The quotes from this paragraph come from transcripts of conversations with Egyptian-born Israelis during the Fifth World Congress of Jews from Egypt, Eilat, May 12–14, 2013, and the Eighth World Congress of Jews from Egypt, Tiberias, May 7–9, 2017. For a more detailed discussion of the first event, see Miccoli, *Histories*, 170–76.

50. See Mary Louise Pratt, "Thoughts on Intangibility and Transmission," in *Anthropological Perspectives on Intangible Cultural Heritage*, ed. Lourdes Arizpe and Cristina Amescua (London: Springer, 2013), esp. 79–83.

51. Didier Nebot (president of *Morial—Mémoires et Traditions des Juifs d'Algérie*), interview by the author, Paris, March 23, 2016.

52. On collective memory, see Marie-Claire Lavabre, "La 'mémoire collective' entre sociologie de la mémoire et sociologie des souvenirs?," *Human and Social Sciences*, 2016, https://halshs.archives-ouvertes.fr/halshs-01337854; Guy G. Stroumsa, "Religious Memory, between Orality and Writing," *Memory Studies* 9, no. 3 (2016): 332–40.

53. Sharon MacDonald, *Difficult Heritage: Negotiating the Nazi Past in Nuremberg and Beyond* (London: Routledge, 2009), 1–2. See also William Logan and Reeves Keir, "Introduction: Remembering Places of Pain and Shame," in *Places of Pain and Shame: Dealing with "Difficult Heritage,"* ed. William Logan and Keir Reeves (London: Routledge, 2009), 1–14.

54. On the Jews of the M'zab, who only obtained French citizenship in 1961, see Sarah A. Stein, *Saharan Jews and the Fate of French Algeria* (Chicago: University of Chicago Press, 2014). See also Joshua Schreier, *Arabs of the*

Jewish Faith: The Civilizing Mission in Colonial Algeria (New Brunswick: Rutgers University Press, 2010); Joëlle Allouche-Benayoun, "Les Juifs d'Algérie: du dhimmi au citoyen français," in *Les Juifs d'Algérie, une histoire de ruptures*, ed. Joëlle Allouche-Benayoun and Geneviève Dermenjian (Aix-en-Provence: Presses Universitaires de Provence, 2015), 27–42; Denis Charbit, "L'historiographie du décret Crémieux: le retour du refoulé," in *Les Juifs d'Algérie*, 43–61.

55. Schreier, *Arabs*, 174; see 143–176 for an in-depth analysis of both the Crémieux Decree and the 1865 Senatus-Consulte that preceded it.

56. Allouche-Benayoun, "Les Juifs," 17.

57. Pierre-Jean Le Foll Luciani, *Les juifs algériens dans la lutte anticoloniale: Trajectoires dissidentes (1934–1965)* (Rennes: Presses universitaires de Rennes, 2016).

58. See, for example, Benjamin Stora, *Histoire de la guerre d'Algérie* (Paris: La Découverte, 1993); Jean-Jacques Jordi and Emile Temime, eds., *Marseille et le choc des décolonisations: Les rapatriements, 1954–1964* (Aix-en-Provence: Edisud, 1996).

59. Allouche-Benayoun, "Les Juifs," 17.

60. Joëlle Allouche-Benayoun and Doris Bensimon, *Juifs d'Algérie, hier et aujourd'hui: Mémoires et identités* (Toulouse: Privat, 1989), 337; Haim Sadun, "Ha-tziyonut" [Zionism], in *Algeriah* [Algeria], ed. Haim Sadun (Jerusalem: Yad Ben-Tzvi, 2011), 210.

61. For an analysis of the public initiatives and parliamentarian debates correlated with France's colonial past, consider Romain Bertrand, *Mémoires d'empire: La controverse autour du 'fait colonial'* (Broissieux: Editions du Croquant, 2006).

62. Ethan Katz, "Entre émancipation et antijudaisme: la mémoire collective des Juifs d'Algérie dans la longue durée (1930–1970)," in *Les Juifs d'Algérie*, ed. Joëlle Allouche-Benayoun and Geneviève Dermenjian (Aix-en-Provence: Presses Universitaires de Provence, 2015), 197–224. The Constantine riots occurred in 1931 in the city of Constantine, in Eastern Algeria, after a Jewish man insulted some Muslims washing themselves next to a mosque. This prompted riots against Jews, which lasted for several days and which in the end caused the death of twenty-five Jewish men, women, and children and the destruction of around two hundred Jewish-owned properties. See Geneviève Dermenjian, "Les Juifs d'Algérie entre deux hostilités," in *Les Juifs d'Algérie*, ed. Joëlle Allouche-Benayoun and Geneviève Dermenjian (Aix-en-Provence: Presses Universitaires de Provence, 2015), 135–52; Juan Cole, "Constantine before the Riots of August 1934: Civil Status, Anti-Semitism, and the Politics of Assimilation in Interwar French Algeria," *Journal of North African Studies* 17, no. 5 (2012): 839–61.

63. Shepard, *Invention*, 243. On the ambiguous distinction between *citoyenneté* and *nationalité* (which accorded certain rights to Algerian Muslims but still made them subject to Islamic law, which pertained, for example, to personal status and family law), see Laure Blévis, "Les avatars de la citoyenneté en Algérie coloniale ou les paradoxes d'une catégorisation," *Droit et Société* 48, no. 2 (2001): 557–81.

64. Chantal Bordes-Benayoun, "Unité et dispersion des choix identitaires des Juifs originaires du Maghreb en France contemporaine," in *La bienvenue et l'adieu: Migrants Juifs et musulmans au Maghreb, XV-XX siècle*, ed. Frédéric Abécassis, Karima Dirèche, and Rita Aouad (Casablanca: Centre Jacques-Berque, 2012), 23–36.

65. Colette Zytnicki, "Du rapatrié au sépharade. L'intégration des Juifs d'Afrique du Nord dans la société française: essai de bilan," *Archives Juives* 38, no. 2 (2015): 97.

66. Mandel, *Muslims and Jews*; Katz, *Burdens*.

67. Nebot, interview by the author.

68. Robert Watson, "Memories (Out) of Place: Franco-Judeo-Algerian Autobiographical Writing, 1995–2010," *Journal of North African Studies* 17, no. 1 (2012): 1–22; Claire Eldridge, "Remembering the Other: Postcolonial Perspectives on Relationships between Jews and Muslims in French Algeria," *Journal of Modern Jewish Studies* 11, no. 3 (2012): 1–19; Ewa Tartakowsky, *Les Juifs et le Maghreb: Fonctiones sociales d'une littérature d'exil* (Tours: Presses Universitaires François Rabelais, 2016).

69. Jacques Derrida, *Le monolinguisme de l'autre* (Paris: Galilée, 1996), 73.

70. Derrida, *Le monolinguisme de l'autre*, 74.

71. Hélène Cixous, "The Names of Oran," in *Algeria in Others' Languages*, ed. Anne-Emmanuelle Berger (Ithaca, NY: Cornell University Press, 2002), 185–86.

72. Didier Nebot, *Mémoire d'un dhimmi: Cinq siècles d'histoire juive en Algérie* (Sèvres: Les Editions des Rosiers, 2012), 68.

73. Charlotte Siney-Lange, "Grandes et petites misères du grand exode des Juifs nord-africains vers la France," *Le Mouvement Social* 1971, no. 4 (2001): 29–55.

74. From an undated informative brochure of *Morial*.

75. Benjamin Stora, "L'impossible neutralité des Juifs d'Algérie," in *La guerre d'Algérie 1954–2004: La fin de l'amnèsie*, ed. Mohammed Harbi and Benjamin Stora (Paris: Laffont, 2004), 309.

76. "Présentation," *Morial*, accessed January 3, 2022, http://www.morial.fr/index.php/l-association/presentation-de-l-assoc.

77. From the 2012 *Morial* brochure *Papy, mamy, racontez-moi votre Algérie . . .*

78. Nebot, interview by the author.

79. From the brochure of Morial's 2014 conference, *L'Algérie: L'amour de la Terre Natale*.

80. Here, I draw on Joëlle Bahloul, *La maison de mémoire* (Paris: Metailié, 1992).

81. "Dossier de presse," of the exhibition Juifs d'Algérie, Musée d'art et d'histoire du Judaïsme, Paris, September 28, 2012, to January 27, 2013, accessed January 3, 2022, https://www.mahj.org/sites/mahj.org/files/dossier-de-presse-juifs-d-algerie.pdf.

82. Dominic Thomas, "Museums in Postcolonial Europe: An Introduction," *African and Black Diaspora: An International Journal* 2, no. 2 (2009): 132.

83. "Autour de l'exposition," Juifs d'Algérie, Musée d'art et d'histoire du Judaïsme, Paris, September 28, 2012, to January 27, 2013, http://www.mahj.org/fr/3_expositions/expo-Juifs-d-Algerie-autour.php?niv=2&ssniv=2.

84. "Bande annonce," Juifs d'Algérie, Musée d'art et d'histoire du Judaïsme, Paris, September 28, 2012, to January 27, 2013, http://www.mahj.org/fr/3_expositions/expo-Juifs-d-Algerie-bande-annonce.php?niv=2&ssniv=2.

85. On participatory heritage, see Elisa Giaccardi, "Introduction: Reframing Heritage in a Participatory Culture," in *Heritage and Social Media: Understanding Heritage in a Participatory Culture*, ed. Elisa Giaccardi (London: Routledge, 2012), 1–10.

86. See the catalog from Benjamin Stora, Nala Aoudat, Elodie Bouffard, and Hana Boghanim, eds., *Juifs d'Orient: Une histoire plurimillénaire* (Paris: Gallimard, 2021). As of March 2022, the text of the petition could be read at "An Open Letter to the Arab World Institute in Paris: Culture Is the Salt of the Earth and We Shall Not Allow It to Be Used for Normalizing Oppression," GoogleDocs, https://docs.google.com/forms/d/e/1FAIpQLSfo5DR7RGXkbLwol82jwaW-N8Qu4olKcx46uR9euvWVnddX-Q/viewform?fbclid=IwAR3ameqoljdM-OS2HvzDlqwqWE5DeGk8elulIhokSUeOegbnqmmaERUFECM.

87. "Algérie, 60 ans aprés: appel à témoignages," *Morial*, https://www.morial.fr/temoignage-60ans-apres.html.

88. "Why a Museum of the Sephardic World?," *AMUSSEF—Les Amis du Musée du monde sépharade*, accessed January 3, 2022, https://amussef.org/en/home-2/#pll_switcher. A similar project, which aims to create a *"Mémorial-Musée, centre de mémoire, d'archives, d'étude et de création consacré à l'histoire et à la culture des juifs et autres peuples minoritaires des pays islamisés,"* is supposedly in place in Jerusalem. Jean-Paul Msika, email message to author, April 4, 2018.

89. "Exposition permanente," *Mémorial de la Shoah*, accessed January 3, 2022, http://www.memorialdelashoah.org/evenements-et-expositions/expositions/exposition-permanente.html.

90. See at least Emily Gottreich, *The Mellah of Marrakesh: Jewish and Muslim Space in Morocco's Red City* (Bloomington: Indiana University Press, 2006), 38.

91. Michel Abitbol, *Les Juifs d'Afrique du Nord sous Vichy* (Paris: Riveneuve, 2008).

92. Consider, for the French case, the discussions surrounding the establishment of the Parisian *Cité Nationale pour l'Histoire de l'Immigration*:

Ramon Grosfoguel, Yvon Le Bot, and Alexandra Poli, "Intégrer les musées dans les approches sur l'immigration: vers de nouvelles perspectives de recherche," *Hommes & Migration*, no. 1293 (2011): 6–11; Thomas, "Museums in Postcolonial Europe."

93. See Benjamin Stora, *La gangrène et l'oubli: La mémoire de la guerre d'Algérie* (Paris: Editions de la Découverte, 2005).

94. Hanna Yablonka, *Les Juifs d'Orient, Israël et la Shoah* (Paris: Calmann-Lévy, 2016), 31–35; Stein and Boum, *Holocaust and North Africa*.

95. Jean-Charles Bénichou (president of Moriel—Moreshet Yehudei 'Algeriah be-Israel), interview by the author, Netanya, May 17, 2017.

96. See at least Daniel Levy and Natan Sznaider, eds., *The Holocaust and Memory in the Global Age* (Philadelphia: Temple University Press, 2006); Debarati Sanyal, *Memory and Complicity: Migrations of Holocaust Remembrance* (New York: Fordham University Press, 2015).

97. See the press communiqué by Georges Benazera, president of the *Association Nationale Exode des Français Juifs d'Algérie*, October 9, 2013, http://www.24presse.com/l_efja_annonce_l_installation_d_un_memorial_en_l_honneur_de_francais_juifs_civils_et_militaires_inhumes_en_algerie_au_cimetiere_de_pantin-9911301.html; "Inauguration du mémorial pour les Juifs inhumés en Algérie," *Le Crif en action*, December 23, 2013, http://www.crif.org/fr/lecrifenaction/inauguration-du-mémorial-pour-les-juifs-inhumés-en-algérie/48252. On colonial memorials, see Robert Aldrich, *Vestiges of Colonial Empire in France* (London: Palgrave, 2005).

98. "Qui sommes-nous?," Association Nationale Exode des Français Juifs d'Algérie, http://www.efja.org/qui-sommes-nous/.

99. Stanislas Clermont-Tonnerre, cited in Joan Scott, *The Politics of the Veil* (Princeton, NJ: Princeton University Press, 2007), 75. Consider also Todd Shepard, "Algerian Nationalism, Zionism, and French Laïcité: A History of Ethnoreligious Nationalisms and Decolonization," *International Journal of Middle East Studies*, no. 45 (2013): 445–67.

100. Georges Benazera, cited in Lisa Séréro, "Inauguration à Pantin du memorial pour les Juifs d'Algérie," *Hamodia*, December 2013.

101. Katz, *Burdens*, 22–59.

102. Federico Bellentani and Mario Panico, "The Meanings of Monuments and Memorials: A Semiotic Approach," *Punctum* 2, no. 1 (2016): 28–46.

103. The quotes are all taken from the 2012 *Livre d'or de la commémoration du cinquantenaire* of the EFJA.

104. Ruth Chekroun Cohen (webmaster of *Yahadut Algeriah* and member of Moriel-Moreshet yehudei 'Algeriah), telephone interview by the author, July 19, 2016.

105. Ariel Carsiente, interview by the author, Jerusalem, June 17, 2016.

106. Susan Slyomovics, "Geographies of Jewish Tlemcen," *Journal of North African Studies* 5, no. 4 (2000): 89.

107. *Mimouna* is a typically Moroccan Jewish holiday that is held the day after *Pesah*, and in the last decades it has become popular among a great many Israelis. The holiday marks the Jewish redemption from Egypt and is characterized by a celebratory family dinner in which *hametz* (leavened food) can be eaten again.

108. Laurence Podselver, "Le pélerinage tunisien de Sarcelles: de la tradition à l'hédonisme contemporain," *Socio-anthropologie*, no. 10 (2001), https://socio-anthropologie.revues.org/157. As regards other contemporary Sephardi and *Mizrahi* Jews, consider, for example, the Moroccan synagogues founded in Israel in the 1960s, as noted by Daniel Ben Simon, *Ha-maroqa'im* [The Moroccans] (Jerusalem: Carmel, 2016), 138–40.

109. See Eyal Ben-Ari and Yoram Bilu, "Modernity and Charisma in Contemporary Israel: The Case of Baba Sali and Baba Baruch," *Israel Affairs* 1, no. 3 (1995): 224–36; Eyal Ben-Ari, "Saint's Sanctuaries in Israeli Development Towns: On a Mechanism of Urban Transformation," *Urban Anthropology* 16, no. 2 (1987): 243–72. A *tzaddiq* ("pious, just") is a person—often a rabbi—considered to have spiritual powers and to be worthy of veneration both in life and after death. Even though it also was spread throughout other parts of North Africa, the veneration of *tzaddiqim* was—and partly still is—spread the most among the Jews of Morocco.

110. Benjamin Stora, *Les trois exils: Juifs d'Algérie* (Paris: Stock, 2006), 182.

111. Benjamin Stora, *Les questions mémorielles portant sur la colonisation et la guerre d'Algérie*, January 20, 2021, https://www.vie-publique.fr/rapport/278186-rapport-stora-memoire-sur-la-colonisation-et-la-guerre-dalgerie.

112. For an overview of the relations between different ethnic and religious groups in today's France, see the survey conducted between February and June 2015 (that is, before the terrorist attacks of Paris in November 2015 and of Nice in June 2016) by Chantal Bordes-Benayoun, Dominique Schnapper, Brice Teinturier, and Etienne Mercier, *Perceptions et attentes de la population juive: Le rapport à l'autre et aux minorités* (Paris: Fondation du Judaïsme Français/IPSOS, 2016). On French Jewish identity today, see Erik H. Cohen, *The Jews of France at the Turn of the Third Millennium: A Sociological and Cultural Analysis* (Ramat Gan: Rappaport Center of Bar Ilan University, 2009); Cohen, *The Jews of France Today: Identity and Values* (Leiden: Brill, 2011). On Zemmour, see Glenn Loalerc, "Eric Zemmour, 'son' Judaïsme, 'son' identité française et toutes ses polémiques," *The Times of Israel*, December 5, 2021, https://fr.timesofisrael.com/eric-zemmour-son-judaisme-son-identite-francaise-et-toutes-ses-polemiques/.

113. Bernard Rieder and Theo Roehle, "Digital Methods: Five Challenges," in *Understanding Digital Humanities*, ed. David M. Berry (New York: Palgrave Macmillan, 2012), 67–84. For a Maghrebine perspective, see Bernadette N. Saou-Dufrêne, "Les musées du Maghreb à l'ère numérique: le futur à la rencontre du passé," in *Patrimoines du Maghreb à l'ère numérique*, ed. Bernadette N. Saou-Dufrêne (Paris: L'Harmattan, 2014), 77–113.

114. Consider Daniel J. Cohen and Roy Rosenzweig, *Digital History: A Guide to Gathering, Preserving, and Presenting the Past on the Web* (Philadelphia: University of Pennsylvania Press, 2003); Stefano Vitali, *Passato digitale: Le fonti dello storico nell'era del computer* (Milan: Bruno Mondadori, 2004); Rolando Minuti, *Internet et le métier d'historien: Réflexions sur les incertitudes d'une mutation* (Paris: PUF, 2001); Minuti, ed., *Il web e gli studi storici: Guida critica all'uso della rete* (Rome: Carocci, 2015).

115. Anna Everett, *Digital Diaspora: A Race for Cyberspace* (Albany: State University of New York Press, 2009).

116. See Robert V. Kozinets, *Netnography: Doing Ethnographic Research Online* (London: Sage, 2010); Christine Hine, *Virtual Ethnography* (London: Sage, 2000). I monitored the websites Dafina and ASPCJE and the Facebook group Les enfants des Juifs d'Alexandrie et d'Egypte regularly over a period of about five years (from March 2013 to the end of 2018) and on a more irregular basis up until October 2020. To check previous versions of the website, I also used the application Wayback Machine of the Internet Archive, available at https://archive.org/web/.

117. Kachig Tölölyan, "The Contemporary Discourse of Diaspora Studies," *Comparative Studies of South Asia, Africa and the Middle East* 27, no. 3 (2007): 647.

118. William Safran, "The Jewish Diaspora in a Comparative and Theoretical Perspective," *Israel Studies* 10, no. 1(2005): 36–60.

119. Michel Laguerre, "Digital Diasporas: Definition and Methods," in *Diasporas in the New Media Age: Identity, Politics and Community*, ed. Alonso Andoni and Pedro J. Oiarzabal (Reno: University of Nevada Press, 2010), 49–64; Leopoldina Fortunati, *Migration, Diaspora and Information Technology in Global Societies*, with Raul Pertierra and Jane Vincent (London: Routledge, 2011); Jennifer M. Brinkerhoff, *Digital Diasporas: Identity and Transnational Engagement* (Cambridge: Cambridge University Press, 2009).

120. I refer to the 2003 UNESCO Charter for the Preservation of Digital Heritage, available at http://portal.unesco.org/en/ev.php-URL_ID=17721&URL_DO=DO_TOPIC&URL_SECTION=201.html. See also Fiona Cameron and Sarak Kenderdine, *Theorizing Digital Cultural Heritage: A Critical Approach* (Boston: MIT Press, 2007).

121. Consider Haim Zafrani, *Deux mille ans de vie juive au Maroc* (Paris: Maisonneuve & Larose, 1998); André Lévy, *Il était une fois les Juifs marocains* (Paris: L'Harmattan, 1995); Yigal Bin-Nun, "La négociation de l'évacuation en masse des Juifs du Maroc," in *La fin du Judaisme en terres d'Islam*, ed. Shmuel Trigano (Paris: Denoel, 2009).

122. Stephanie Tara Schwartz, "The Concept of Double Diaspora in Sami Michael's *Refuge* and Naim Kattan's *Farewell, Babylon*," *Comparative Studies of South Asia, Africa and the Middle East* 30, no. 1 (2010): 92–100; Mikhael Elbaz, "Ethnicité et générations en Amérique du Nord. Le cas de la seconde

génération des Juifs sépharades à Montréal," *Revue internationale d'action communautaire*, no. 31 (1994): 63–77; Jean-Luc Bédard, "Mouvances identitaires et restructuration de soi et des autres parmi des Judéo-marocains à Montréal," in *Identités sépharades et modernité* (Levis: Les Presses de l'Université Laval, 2007), 175–90. On return voyages to Morocco, see André Levy, *Return to Casablanca: Jews, Muslims, and an Israeli Anthropologist* (Chicago: University of Chicago Press, 2015).

123. Beinin, *Dispersion*.

124. Martine Hovanessian, "Diasporas et identités collectives," *Hommes et Migrations*, no. 1265 (2007): 8–21.

125. For other case studies, see Ella Shohat, "By the Bitstream of Babylon: Cyberfrontiers and Diasporic Vistas," in *Drifting: Architecture and Migrancy*, ed. Stephen Cairns (London: Routledge, 2004), 271–87; Rosen-Lapidot and Goldberg, "Triple Loci"; Marie Blanche Fourcade, "La mise en ligne des mémoires du génocide armenien," *Ethnologie française* 37, no. 3 (2007): 525–31.

126. From the introductory statement of the website Dafina, accessed January 3, 2022, http://dafina.net/accueil.htm.

127. Bédard, "Mouvances identitaires."

128. See "Règles du forum Darkoum," *Dafina*, http://dafina.net/forums/read.php?50,70807. *Haketi* or *haketiah* is the variety of Ladino traditionally spoken by Jews of Sephardi origin in cities such as Tetouan and Tangiers.

129. Victoria Bernal, "Diaspora, Cyberspace and Political Imagination: The Eritrean Diaspora Online," *Global Networks* 6, no. 2 (2006): 161–179.

130. Message of Rubio, d.[iscussion] *Les anciens du quartier Tour Hasan—Rue d'Avignon*, s.[ection] *Yahsra*, January 19, 2009, http://dafina.net/forums/read.php?55,240652.

131. Message of Bebert75, d. *Alliance Israelite Universelle, Mazagan, Dafina*, s. *Yahsra*, January 3, 2012, http://dafina.net/forums/read.php?55,95413,page=4.

132. Emanuela Trevisan Semi, "L'année prochaine à . . . Ouazzan: des usages socio-politiques d'un culte d'un saint juif," in *Visions du monde et modernités religieuses: Regards croisés*, ed. Noureddine Harrami and Imed Meliti (Paris: Publisud, 2011), 219–26.

133. Fourcade, "La mise en ligne," 527.

134. Message of Carol Bamber, d. *Une jeune anglaise à Casablanca*, s. *Le Maroc*, May 2, 2013, http://dafina.net/forums/read.php? 52.324371.

135. Message of Naeema, d. *Ecole Alliance de Mogador*, s. *Yahsra*, November 4, 2012, http://dafina.net/forums/read.php?55,90507,page=5.

136. Message of Ocemaelyo, d. *Rabat, anciens de l'école de la Tour Hassan*, s. *Yahsra*, March 20, 2013, http://dafina.net/forums/read.php?55,139222,page=13.

137. See Emanuela Trevisan Semi and Hanane Sekkat Hatimi, *Mémoire et representations des Juifs au Maroc: Les voisins absents de Meknès* (Paris: Publisud, 2011); Watson, "Memories," 1–22.

138. Nathan Jurgenson, "The IRL Fetish," *New Inquiry*, June 28, 2012, http://thenewinquiry.com/essays/the-irl-fetish/. On the importance of childhood memories, see Leila Sebbar, ed., *Une enfance juive en Méditerranée musulmane* (Saint-Pourçain-sur-Sioule: Bleu autour, 2012).

139. Pierre Nora, "La génération," in *Les lieux de mémoire*, ed. Pierre Nora, vol. 3, table 1 (Paris: Gallimard, 1992), 959.

140. Aomar Boum, *Memories of Absence: How Muslims Remember Jews in Morocco* (Stanford, CA: Stanford University Press, 2013), 141–48.

141. For example, as in the case of anti-Jewish riots in Cairo in the late 1940s and early 1950s. See Beinin, *Dispersion*, 64–65; Miccoli, *Histories*, 157–68.

142. From the discussion *PETIT-JEAN Massacre de meknassis en Aout 1954*, https://dafina.net/forums/read.php?52,189238.

143. See *Souvenirs d'Egypte par Albert Pardo*, September 2014, http://albert.pardo.free.fr/souvenirs-egypte.htm; Jews of Egypt Foundation, "Introduction," accessed January 3, 2022, http://www.jewsofegyptfoundation.com/Introduction.html; "Les Juifs d'Egypte," *Flickr*, accessed January 3, 2022, http://www.flickr.com/groups/juifsdegypte/pool/with/2358492774/#photo_2358492774.

144. *Jews of Egypt*, https://www.facebook.com/groups/23156188376/; *Egyptian Jews*, https://www.facebook.com/groups/16410059267/; *Les enfants des Juifs d Alexandrie et d Egypte—Jews from Egypt*, https://www.facebook.com/groups/176948023247/.

145. Hassoun authored several books on Egyptian Jewish history and folklore, such as Jacques Hassoun, *Histoire des Juifs du Nil* (Paris: Minerve, 1990).

146. "Naissance de l'association," *ASPCJE*, http://aspcje.free.fr/index.php/notre-association/naissance-de-l-association; "Bienvenue sur le site de l'ASPCJE," *ASPCJE*, http://aspcje.free.fr/.

147. André Cohen (secretary of the ASPCJE), telephone interview by the author, November 19, 2012.

148. See Gilbert Cabasso, ed., *Juifs d'Egypte: Images et textes* (Paris: Editions su Scribe, 1984); Cabasso, *A la rencontre des Juifs d'Egypte* (Paris: Nahar Misraim, 1978).

149. "Nos publications," *ASPCJE*, accessed January 3, 2022, http://aspcje.free.fr/index.php/publications.

150. Cohen and Rosenzweig, *Digital History*, http://chnm.gmu.edu/digitalhistory/exploring/3.php.

151. Michèle Baussant, "Travail de la mémoire et usage public du passé: l'exemple des Juifs d'Egypte," in *Mémoire des migrations, temps de l'histoire*, ed. Marianne Amar, Hélène Bertheleu, and Laure Teulières (Tours: Presses Universitaires François Rabelais, 2015); Miccoli, *Histories*, esp. 167, 175.

152. *Les enfants des Juifs d'Alexandrie et d'Egypte*.

153. Elisa Giaccardi, "Introduction: Reframing Heritage in a Participatory Culture," in *Heritage and Social Media: Understanding Heritage in a Participatory Culture* (London: Routledge, 2012), 13–29.

154. *Les enfants des juifs d'Alexandrie et d'Egypte*.

155. Melissa Terras, "Digital Curiosities: Resource Creation via Amateur Digitisation," *Literary and Linguistic Computing* 25, no. 4 (2010): 426. See also Johan Oomen and Lora Aroyo, "Crowdsourcing in the Cultural Heritage Domain: Opportunities and Challenges," in *Communities and Technology '11: Proceedings of the Fifth International Conference* (New York: ACM, 2011), 138–49.

156. Maikel Nabil, "Egypt's Christians, Facing the Fate of Egyptian Jews," *Times of Israel*, September 28, 2012, http://blogs.timesofisrael.com/egypts-christians-facing-the-fate-of-egyptian-jews/.

157. "Allow Implementation and Preservation of Jewish Heritage," *Collectif des Associations Nationales des Juifs d'Egypte*, April 2016, https://www.change.org/p/president-sisi-allow-implementation-and-preservation-of-jewish-heritage-autorisez-la-mise-en-oeuvre-de-la-préservation-du-patrimoine-juif?recruiter=485414474&utm_source=share_petition&utm_medium=email&utm_campaign=share_email_responsive.

158. Ariel Ben Salomon, "Why Is Egypt Intent on Restoring Jewish Heritage Sites in a Country Devoid of Jews?," *JNS Jewish News Syndicate*, January 9, 2019, https://www.jns.org/why-is-egypt-intent-on-restoring-jewish-heritage-sites-in-a-country-devoid-of-jews/; Herb Keinon, "Sisi: 'If Jews Return to Egypt, We'll Build Synagogues,'" *Jerusalem Post*, February 25, 2019, https://www.jpost.com/Middle-East/Sisi-If-Jews-return-to-Egypt-well-build-synagogues-581664?fbclid=IwAR1T3yLD_Wgqi5q6jn7nrVJ_cVZ1Tn-gahwmOPoxEzH_3asNGIYiRf5NiBE.

159. "Voyage en Egypte," *Association pour la sauvegarde du patrimoine culturel des Juifs d'Egypte*, email communication, January 2, 2020. On the inauguration, see, for example, Amanda Borschel-Dan, "Worshipers Fete 'Very Emotional' Shabbat in Refurbished Alexandria Synagogue," *Times of Israel*, February 16, 2020, https://www.timesofisrael.com/over-180-jews-gather-in-alexandria-to-celebrate-shabbat-in-refurbished-synagogue/; "Ricordi d'Egitto," *Sorgente di vita*, Rai2, March 2020, https://www.raiplay.it/video/2020/03/Sorgente-di-Vita-ricordi-degitto--b39988f9-9511-436e-8d68-515123323ea8.html.

160. In this perspective, the case of Egypt is particularly emblematic, but clearly it is not the only one in the region. See Susan Gilson Miller, "Sensitive Ruins: On the Preservation of Jewish Religious Sites in the Muslim World," in *Synagogues of the Islamic World: Architecture, Design, and Identity*, ed. Mohammed Gharipour (Edinburgh: Edinburgh University Press, 2017).

161. Serge Noiret, "'Public History' e 'Storia pubblica' nella rete," *Ricerche storiche* 39, no. 2–3 (2009): 280, 313.

162. Dana Diminescu and Benjamin Loveluck, "Traces of Dispersion: Online Media and Diasporic Identities," *Crossings: Journal of Migration and Culture* 5, no. 1 (2014): 23–39. See also Sandra Ponzanesi and Koen Leurs, "On

Digital Crossings in Europe," *Crossings: Journal of Migration and Culture* 5, no. 1 (2014): 3–22.

163. Rosen-Lapidot and Goldberg, "Triple Loci," 126.

164. Leslie Poles Hartley, cited in David Lowenthal, *The Past Is a Foreign Country* (Cambridge: Cambridge University Press, 1985), XVI.

165. Clancy-Smith, *Mediterraneans*. On borders in today's world, I refer in particular to Etienne Balibar, *We, the People of Europe: Reflections on Transnational Citizenship* (Princeton, NJ: Princeton University Press, 2003); Sandro Mezzadra and Brett Neilson, *Border as Method, or, The Multiplication of Labor* (Durham, NC: Duke University Press, 2013).

THREE

AN UNFINISHED PRESENT

Migrations of Sephardi and *Mizrahi* Memory

THE INVESTIGATION OF LITERATURE ON the one hand and forms of heritagization on the other has shown to what extent different generations of Sephardi and *Mizrahi* Jews perceive themselves as exiled communities and diasporas that can be foreign both to the country of emigration and to that of immigration. As I have already explained, this does not mean that Sephardi and *Mizrahi* Jews feel that they belong nowhere but, on the contrary, that they maintain multiple, and sometimes problematic, ethno-national and cultural attachments that cannot be contained easily inside the borders of one country or adhere to the national ideology that lies beneath it—for example, Zionism in the case of Israel.

To conclude my voyage along the Sephardi Mediterranean and its memories, now I want to turn to how the North African and Egyptian Jewish diasporas are included in the historical narratives of the country of immigration and how this inclusion has stimulated the elaboration of original ways to deal with their presence specifically, but also with that of migrants and refugees more broadly. I focus on what can be called edges of Sephardi and *Mizrahi* past, which is to say events and memories that can be understood—even in ways that are not always in agreement with the historical reality—as crossing the border between the history of the Jews of the Arab world and that of other groups, be they the Jews of Europe, Palestinians, or today's Muslim migrants. Shedding light on the Jews of the Middle East and North Africa from this specific angle will make it possible not only to counter the historical marginality this group has had until not so long ago but also to better expose—in a sort of multidirectional manner—the current ethno-religious and societal divides between Israelis and

Palestinians, between Jews and Arabs, and lastly between allegedly conflictual geopolitical and imaginative entities such as Europe and North Africa.

Secondly, the chapter wishes to highlight how the present, more than the past, eventually results in the main temporal horizon of the Jews of the Middle East and North Africa—a present, however, that is already shifting and can be interpreted as a form of migration in itself, since it is situated between a constantly reimagined past and a seemingly unattainable future, perhaps in a third space between the two. This is reminiscent of François Hartog's argument about the contemporary *régimes d'historicité* and the present as the dominant category from which we observe the past and future—with the latter often conceived as a threat instead of an opportunity.[1] But then what are the implications of this particular mnemonic framework for the Jews of the Middle East and North Africa? And what can their historical trajectory tell us about the Mediterranean region as a site of contested identities and memories?

This chapter starts with an analysis of the Holocaust as an absent past, which even without being part of the personal or family history of the majority of the Jews of the Arab world nonetheless has acquired over the last years a central role in their (postmigratory) identity and imaginary, partly through cultural media such as literature and cinema. As we shall see, this phenomenon relates not only to Jewish memorial dynamics but to the importance gained by the Holocaust as a global category of memory and the quintessential paradigm of trauma.[2] The increased relevance of the Holocaust goes hand in hand with a second phenomenon, which is visible especially in the political sphere: the representation of Sephardi and *Mizrahi* Jews as refugees and of their twentieth-century history as the Middle Eastern and North African equivalent of what occurred to the Jews of Europe almost at the same epoch. The Jews from Arab Lands and Iran Day—established by the Israeli Parliament in 2014—provides an example of the probably unavoidable, yet perilous, interplay among memory, politics, and history that the Sephardi and *Mizrahi* past are also experiencing and of the impact the Holocaust and the Palestinian-Israeli conflict have on it. As a possible alternative to that, the last section shifts the gaze to Europe, searching for interstices where possibilities of dialogue between the past and present of these Jewish diasporas, and more generally between them and other experiences of migration and displacement, can be found. Thus, I look at the work of Jewish-Muslim associations in Italy and France—the Florentine Donne per la Pace and the Parisian Amitié Judéo-Musulmane de France—and contextualize them vis-à-vis discussions on Europeanness and the place of migrants in today's Europe.

What comes out is, on the one hand, a greater visibility of the Middle Eastern and North African Jewish heritage, as mentioned at the end of the previous chapter, and, on the other hand, the politicization of memory, both in the Diaspora and in Israel. This makes one wonder if the sole way for this memory to emerge is its usage as a lens through which to understand present phenomena, in renunciation of the attainment of more objective and less evocative results. Moreover, it reveals that the history of these Jewries actually did not finish with the migration to Israel or Europe but is continuing in a new manner, which reconceptualizes the postmigratory diasporas to which they belong as sites of knowledge where a plurality of memories circulate and are mobilized to tell and rewrite such a history.[3]

Paradoxically, the proliferation of Sephardi and *Mizrahi* memories, similar but not identical to one another, goes hand in hand with the emergence—at least in the public sphere and in terms of initiatives promoted by state actors—of an artificially homogeneous memory that equates the Jews of the Arab world and their experience of migration and uprooting to (European) Jewish historical events like the Holocaust. That conflation reduces a centuries-old Jewish presence in the Arab world to a series of episodes of violence and persecution that, eventually, would be seen as prelude to the anti-Jewish and anti-Israeli sentiments that today can be found in that region or in sectors of the European Muslim population. Certainly, there are also attempts to construct a pluralistic, and more historically grounded, vision of the past. But one cannot deny that over the last years, the juxtaposition of unnaturally fixed Arab and Jewish identity has become more and more common, standing in sharp contrast to the rather nuanced descriptions that often come out of memorial literature or individual memories. Stuck between the ghosts of a vanished past and a hopeful future that may seem unlikely to ever materialize, Sephardi and *Mizrahi* Jews are constrained to live in an *unfinished* present: one that is always in progress and never fully accomplished but that perhaps precisely for this reason can also be reenvisioned thanks to a variety of cultural and political perspectives, which reflect an ongoing history of migration and exile.[4]

THE PAST OF AN ABSENCE? THE HOLOCAUST IN THE CONTEMPORARY NORTH AFRICAN JEWISH IMAGINATION

The absence, or limited presence, of the historical experience of the Holocaust is probably one of the most immediate differences seen when comparing the history of the Jews of the Middle East and North Africa to that of the European Jews. In fact, during the Second World War, the former did not go through episodes of persecution and antisemitic violence as tragic as the Holocaust, which directly affected only a minority of the Jewish communities of the Arab world. In Libya, around two thousand Jews holding French citizenship or of Tunisian origin were deported to prison camps in Tunisia and Algeria. About eight hundred Libyan Jews who held a British passport were instead transferred by the Italian authorities to Italian prison camps because they were citizens of a country at war with Italy, and more than half of them—almost five hundred people—were eventually deported to Nazi concentration camps in Europe. Still other Jews were interned in Libyan prison and labor camps, such as the infamous camp of Giaddo, where about six hundred died of hunger or illness.[5] In Tunisia, which remained under German occupation for six months between 1942 and 1943, around five thousand Jews were sent to labor camps in Tunisia itself, such as that of Bizerte, and twenty were deported to German death camps because of their Socialist activities. Notably, during the German occupation of the country, the Jews of the city of Sfax were forced to wear the yellow Star of David.[6] Although this situation is not comparable to that of the Jews deported en masse to the Nazi concentration camps in Europe, the living conditions of those confined in the North African labor camps were extremely hard and left indelible memories on the detainees: "more than the lack of hygiene, the terrible working conditions, what troubled us most was the morale. To feel like a derided being ... like an object."[7]

Also in Algeria and Morocco—where Jews were subject to the Vichy antisemitic laws and, in the first case, were deprived of French citizenship—internment camps were opened, and some Jews, together with other people, were confined there, but none seem to have been deported to the Nazi concentration camps.[8] The situation in Egypt was much less difficult thanks to the fact that the Allied powers defeated the Axis forces in the battle of El Alamein in 1942, and the latter never reached Alexandria or Cairo.[9] Different, and more tragic, was the fate of the historic Sephardi community of Rhodes, in the southeastern Mediterranean, to whom more than a few Egyptian Jews were family related. The island, along with a number of smaller islands of the Dodecanese archipelago, at the time formed the Isole italiane dell'Egeo, which remained an Italian colonial territory from 1912 until 1947. Since the early twentieth century, however, many Jews of Rhodes had started to migrate—first for economic reasons and then because of the 1938 Italian antisemitic laws—to Egypt, the US, and countries as different as Argentina, the Belgian Congo, Rhodesia, and South Africa. Following the signing of the armistice between Italy and the Allies in 1943, Rhodes was occupied by the German army. As the Germans arrived, almost all of the two thousand Jews who still lived in the island were deported to Auschwitz-Birkenau, and less than two hundred survived.[10]

Despite this very diverse historical context, it is arguable that nowadays the Holocaust has become a foundational trope of Jewish identity for most Middle Eastern and North African Jews—regardless of their personal and familial history, be they from Libya, Egypt, or even Iraq. Therefore, the vicissitudes of these communities at the time of the Second World War are being not only increasingly highlighted but also put in contact with other events—like the Iraqi *farhud* or the anti-Jewish riots that occurred in cities like Cairo in 1948 or Tripoli and Benghazi in 1967—and interpreted as part of what some have started to call the *Mizrahi* Holocaust. As already mentioned, the memory of the Holocaust has ceased to belong only to those who experienced it firsthand and is being appropriated by a larger number of people who commemorate it and inscribe their life stories in a global (Jewish) narrative of violence and antisemitism. It is true that in the 1940s and immediately after, some Jews from the Arab world were already writing about the Holocaust. Think of the *Megillat Hitler* (Hitler's scroll) published in 1940s Morocco, or the 1950s poems of the Iraqi rabbi Menashe Shahrabani. However, this first wave of little-known poets and writers mainly signaled the desire of non-European Jews to find an explanation for the Holocaust, which oftentimes was subsumed in a longer history of anti-Jewish violence and historicized through the recourse to religious categories or the evoking of biblical stories of persecution.[11]

This is no longer the case with contemporary Sephardi and *Mizrahi* authors, who instead make the Holocaust part of their own memory and life story, regardless of whether this event relates to them directly. I am thinking of Kobi Oz, a *Mizrahi* writer who was born in Israel to Tunisian parents and who did not experience the Holocaust but for whom, nonetheless, it is a sort of nocturnal memory, a nightmare that comes to disturb his sleep: "I had a strange dream. And in the dream I was a boy with lice . . . and then I woke up with a word that haunts me, Buchenwald."[12] The dissonance that exists between the memory of the Holocaust as an (inescapable) aspect of being Jewish and Israeli today, on the one hand, and the fact that it may not be part of one's family history, on the other, is present also in the 1993 short story *Ummi fi shughl* (My mother is at work) by Orly Castel-Bloom, in which the protagonist explains, "I am not a Holocaust survivor . . . but lately I have been dreaming that I am. As a matter of fact, my parents are from Cairo."[13] That said, there are also authors from the Diaspora who write about the Holocaust and the direct relations it has with the history of the North African Jews. For example, the Second World War and the Holocaust are at the center of the novel *La valise de Mlle Lucie* (2008) by the Tunisian-born Nine Moati, which tells the story of a Tunisian Jewish girl living in 1940s Paris. The war and Holocaust are also mentioned in some of the books of the Moroccan Marcel Bénabou.[14] One could cite other media, like visual art and music, that increasingly deal with these subjects: think of Nava Barazani's paintings that portray her mother's experience in the Libyan internment camp of Giaddo.[15]

In the next pages, I look at the Franco-Tunisian movie *Le chant des mariées* (2008) by Karin Albou and then move to the Israeli novel *Benghazi Bergen-Belsen* (2013) by Yossi Sucary. The first is set in Nazi-occupied Tunisia and recalls the hard moments endured by the Jews of Tunis in the winter of 1942–43; the second is a fictional account of the Holocaust experience of the Libyan Jews, based on the story of Sucary's maternal family. These works decenter the European gaze on the Holocaust and, at the same time, reassess the historical weight of this event for two artists who evoke it on the basis of cultural imaginaries and memories different from—but nonetheless interconnected with—those of the Jews of Europe. By choosing the two North African diasporas that have the most to do with the experience of the Holocaust and of Nazism, I underline the fact that a difference should be made between them and other Jewries of the Arab world, for whom the Holocaust is mainly a memorial trope that can be mobilized for different reasons and not a personal or family memory.

Karin Albou, born near Paris in 1968 to an Algerian Jewish father and a French mother not of Jewish origin, made herself known with the acclaimed 2005 movie *La petite Jérusalem* (Little Jerusalem), which portrays a family of North African Jewish origin living in Sarcelles, near Paris, and focuses on the love affair between the young Jewish philosophy student Laura and the Algerian Muslim worker Djamel. Before *La petite Jérusalem*, Albou had realized short movies and a documentary on the Jews of Tunisia, *Mon pays m'a quitté* (My country left me; 1995), about a group of Jews who, decades after leaving Tunisia, return there on pilgrimage. *Le chant des mariées* tells the story of the Jews of Tunis at the time of the Nazi occupation from the point of view of two young girls, the Jewish Myriam and her Muslim friend Nour. The first is engaged to Raoul, a much older doctor who comes from a well-off Jewish family of Leghornese origin and whose marriage with Myriam, in the eyes of the girl's mother, will inaugurate a better life for the entire family. On the other hand, Nour is in love with her cousin Khaled, but the marriage is being postponed until he finds a job. In the meantime, the Germans land in Tunis and impose a series of antisemitic measures; the daily life of Myriam, as well as her relationship with Nour, deteriorates. Nour's prospective husband, Khaled, tells her that the Jews always supported the French colonial occupants and that therefore she should not be friends with Myriam. When Raoul—who in the meantime marries Myriam—is sent to a labor camp outside Tunis, Nour decides to come to help and saves her friend's life by declaring to German officers who are chasing Jews inside a *hammam* that Myriam is her sister. The movie ends with the two protagonists praying aloud in Hebrew and Arabic inside an underground shelter during an air raid on the city.

Le chant des mariées is not the first literary work that describes the German occupation of Tunis: think at least of Albert Memmi's famous novel *La statue de sel* (The pillar of salt; 1953). Although in very different ways, in that case the war generated an identity crisis in the Jewish protagonist, the young Benillouche, who started interrogating himself about his place in Tunisia and his relationship with his religious community.[16] The characters of *Le chant des mariées*—from the well-off Tunisian Jewish doctor belonging to the Leghornese elite to the poor orphaned girl and the vaguely antisemitic young Muslim—certainly are more schematic than Memmi's Benillouche, but they construct an original fresco of a world in crisis, of its feelings, and, even more, of the powerful memories that it still provokes today. Reviewers highlighted the important role assigned to the bodies of the two young protagonists, as objects of sexual desire and as sensual yet tender shelters that Myriam and Nour utilize to go through the difficulties of the war.[17] As concerns the representation of the Second World War, Albou's movie shows how this event disrupted a Jewish-Muslim cohabitation that was already challenged by colonialism and the emergence of Arab nationalism. In *Le chant des mariées*, the families of Nour and Myriam live in the same *riad*, testifying to a history of shared domesticity and proximity. This Jewish-Muslim cohabitation allowed the two groups to know each other directly and experience each other's rituals and holidays. Nevertheless, as shown in Joëlle Bahloul's *La maison de mémoire*—in which the author recalls growing up in a building in the Algerian town of Sétif, where both Jews and Muslims lived—it did not mean automatically that they were friends.[18]

In the Tunisian case, the cultural proximity between Jews and Muslims diminished not only because of increased anti-Jewish feelings on the part of the Arab population but, especially in the initial years of colonialism, also because of the gradual Frenchification of Jewish society—which depended on the diffusion of educational institutions like the Alliance Israélite Universelle and more generally on the social and cultural appeal that France and Europe had for members of ethno-religious minorities. In fact, these minorities often acted as middlemen between the local population and the colonizers.[19] In *Le chant des mariées*, Myriam—as opposed to Nour, who does not go to school—attends a French institute and speaks to her mother half in French and half in Arabic. Myriam represents a generation of Tunisian Jews educated in French schools who dreamed of a mythical Europe while still living in the middle of an Arabized milieu from which they were removing themselves almost inadvertently. "I was, myself," the Tunisian-born writer Albert Memmi confesses, "a guest of the French language. Even worse, I was an eternal guest, never entirely at ease with the others, I could not think of going back to where I belonged. Sooner or later ... the Tunisians and Algerians would go back to their language, their home. But in which house, which home ... was I finally to rest one day?"[20]

Aside from recognizing colonialism's role in separating Jews from Muslims, Albou's movie also hints at the ideological intersections between streams of Arab nationalism and Nazism. In fact, *Le chant des mariées* opens with the impressive frames of a meeting between the great mufti of Jerusalem and Hitler, whose voice can be heard in the background. In other segments we find elements and scenes that further connect the history of Tunisian Jews to that of Nazism and to the Holocaust. For example, we see Jews getting on train cars at the central station of Tunis and others who are wearing a *tallit* boarding a German jeep. These frames reflect the historical episode known as the *rafle* ("roundup") of Tunis, which in December 1942 led to the arrest of about two thousand Tunisian Jews by the German authorities. By evoking the figure of the great mufti, Albou sheds light on figures and tropes that refer to the Holocaust imaginary and shows their unexpected presence in a North African setting, highlighting that 1940s Tunis was another location within a global geography of war and antisemitism. At the same time, the film director—who decided to shoot the movie after reading some of the letters her non-Jewish Algerian grandfather had sent his Jewish wife during the war, while interned in a German prison camp—portrays the war as an event that did not always remove Jews from Muslims, as it made some of them closer than they had been.[21]

In fact, if the German occupation brought about a new set of racial categorizations and impositions, it also triggered feelings of friendship between neighbors. The friendship between Myriam and Nour continues despite the war and, in some ways, is strengthened by it. As mentioned, when the Germans enter a *hammam* seeking Jewish women, Nour declares that Myriam is her sister so the girl will not be arrested. As I will explain further in one of the next sections of this chapter, during the war some Muslims helped or hid Jews in Tunisia and Europe. Think of a curious episode that occurred in Vichy times, when after the promulgation of antisemitic legislation in 1940 some Maghrebine Jews, especially in the Marseille region, decided to disguise themselves as Muslims—and for this reason "administratively ... became akin to Aryans," or of the controversial history surrounding the imam of the Great Mosque of Paris Si Khaddour Benghabrit.[22] This is not surprising considering that the history of the Holocaust, and even more the popular culture surrounding its memory, is populated by figures of saviors, from Oskar Schindler to many others. However, the motivations that drove someone to help and in some cases rescue Jews are difficult to decipher, as they ranged from feelings of humanity toward strangers to affection and love for a friend or much more mundane issues.[23]

In *Le chant des mariées*, we notice a profound feeling of companionship and mutual support binding Nour and Myriam, which drives the former to help her Jewish friend. Although in a different manner, they both go through the war as if through a rite of passage from adolescence to adulthood, changing them from naive girls to grown-up women. In the end, the movie proposes an interesting, gendered reading of the conflict and of the relations between Jews and Muslims: women act as caretakers of their communities' past and of a still uncertain future. For this reason, in the final scene it is Myriam and Nour who pray together, each according to her own religious belief, reciting the Jewish *Shema' Israel* and the Islamic *Fatiha*. Before that, Nour's grandfather had made the girl read some verses from the Koran that say that people of all faiths—that is, Jews too—will reach heaven. In previous segments, *Le chant des mariées* showed viewers very private sides of the girls' life: the ceremony of the *henna*, the shaving of Myriam's body in preparation for her marriage with Raoul, and finally a fake sexual intercourse between Nour and Khaled. The juxtaposition of all these different episodes recomposes the magic of a lost Tunisian folklore and signals how Jews and Arabs, especially those belonging to similar social strata, as in the case of Myriam and Nour, shared a cultural heritage made of rituals and celebrations, as well as norms of moral and gendered behavior.[24]

Going back to Karin Albou, one could assume that, as in the case of second- or third-generation Holocaust survivors, her decision to talk about her family story takes its cue from a forgotten or hidden memory, which has come to the surface accidentally and at a distance of several decades. But *Le chant des mariées* does not talk about the family of Albou's father, who actually came from Algeria, and their vicissitudes under Vichy rule. The movie focuses instead on Tunisia, reinscribing bits of Albou's family story in another context: in fact, the figure of Myriam's mother seems to be constructed along the traits of Albou's paternal grandmother.[25] The director's goal was not to tell a personal story but to shed light on a little-known episode in the history of the Holocaust, and Tunisia seemed to her a more effective cinematic location because, as opposed to Algeria, the Nazi army did arrive there to "spread the Shoah."[26] From a historical point of view, the situation is probably more nuanced, to the point that some scholars contend that the Germans, if they did impose communal taxes on Tunisian Jews and force some to wear the yellow badge, never thought about their mass deportation. According to Michael Laskier, by the time they reached Tunisia in late 1942, the Nazis already "were in panic and frustrated by the bombings and other military operations and thus did not deal with this issue" and, moreover, "did not succeed in organising an effective propaganda apparatus."[27] However, other historians, like Maurice Roumani, explicitly claim that if the deportation of North African Jews did not occur, that was "only by chance" and because of the specific circumstances of the war.[28] In any case, it is true that the 1940s history of Tunisian Jews concerns (Nazi) antisemitism and the Second World War, more than the Holocaust specifically. Moreover, the story of Myriam and Nour and the Nazi occupation of Tunisia should not obliterate the fact that the cohabitation between Jews and Muslims in Tunisia did not end with the war but continued, although with increased difficulty, up to the mass departure of the Jews in the 1950s and 1960s—as other movies, like *Un été à la Goulette* (1996) and *Villa Jasmin* (2007), have shown.[29]

Whereas *Le chant des mariées* deals with life under German occupation and describes the coming of age of two girls in the turmoil of 1940s Tunis, *Benghazi Bergen-Belsen* by Yossi Sucary talks about the Holocaust more directly. The book tells the story of a Jewish girl from Benghazi deported to the infamous Nazi concentration camp. As opposed to the more impersonal and detached approach of Albou, Sucary wrote this novel to shed light on a history in which his Libyan family took part. Sucary explains that most people, both in Israel and the Diaspora, rarely realize that there were Jews from Libya who died in the Holocaust.[30] At the same time, the author noted that in today's Israel "everyone is tied to the Holocaust," an event that in the course of time acquired a foundational role in the national consciousness.[31] Before publishing this novel, Yossi Sucary—born in Ramat Gan in 1959—had obtained success with *Emiliah u-melah ha-'aretz* (Emilia and the salt of the earth; 2012), which was based on the life of his Holocaust survivor Libyan grandmother and which talked about the difficulties she encountered upon arriving in Israel in the 1950s. Libyan and North African Jews' experience of the war and of the Holocaust had already been the subject, in 2005, of the two-part documentary *She'elah shel zman* (A question of time), by the Israeli film director Marco Qarmel. The documentary—which was screened in several festivals in Israel, Europe, and the US—was based on the personal testimonies of people interned in Giaddo and in other prison camps, as well as those of Libyan Holocaust survivors deported to Bergen-Belsen, and it included interviews with historians from Yad Vashem. Its aim was not to equate the war experience of the Jews of North

Africa to the Holocaust, but to shed light on a then virtually unknown historical episode before all the witnesses disappeared. In fact, in its final scenes the film director explains that the Holocaust is not just part of the history "of the European Jews, but of the Jewish People" and therefore of the Jews of North Africa as well.[32]

In a departure from that point of view, at the center of *Benghazi Bergen-Belsen*—which has been translated into English and from which a theatrical play has been made[33]—is Silvana Haggiag, a Jewish girl from Benghazi living in the middle of the Second World War, when Libyan Jews were subject to the Italian antisemitic laws and then, from 1941, to the direct presence of the German army. As the title makes evident, the novel recounts the tragic voyage of Silvana and her family, together with other Libyan Jews, from the warm and familiar world of Benghazi to the concentration camp of Bergen-Belsen, in northern Germany. As opposed to what happens to the Tunisian Jews of *Le chant des mariées*, for them the Holocaust is not a possibility but a reality.[34] The novel can be read as a thick description of Silvana's world and inner self, with particular attention given on the one hand to the gendered dimension and on the other to feelings such as friendship—as in *Les chant des mariées*—but also love for one's family and nostalgia for a faraway homeland that the protagonist may never see again.

As in Magiar's *E venne la notte*, the reader encounters a now largely forgotten Libya, in which the desert mingles with colonial and Islamic heritage. From the beginning of the narration, Benghazi is a city that, although familiar, is populated by frightful German soldiers, from whom Silvana runs away: "One after the other the streets of Benghazi appeared before her, obeying the authority of darkness without the slightest protest. She saw the moonlight bathing only momentarily in the sea and the faint light of the lanterns of the *Lungomare*, the promenade. She quickly crossed the street and began to run along *Via Corso Italia*. Seeking a lit passage, she deviated from her usual path and turned to *Piazza Pene*. It prolonged her way, but the area surrounding the old mosque was always lit, excluding the recent months in which British planes bombed the city."[35] Similar descriptions of the architectural heritage of Libya emerge frequently in the pages of magazines published nowadays by Libyan Jewish heritage associations, like Levluv/Germogli of the Israeli 'Irgun 'olami shel yehudei yotzei-Luv ("World organization of Jews from Libya")—in which Benghazi and Tripoli have the contours of multilayered spaces made of contrasting identities and legacies.[36] The same motif also comes out in the rooms of the Libyan Jewish Heritage Centre of Or Yehudah (fig. 3.1), near Tel Aviv, where visitors—while listening to Arab traditional music or to an *aria* from Giuseppe

Figure 3.1. Museum of Libyan Jews, Or Yehudah, 2018.
Source: Author.

Verdi's opera *Nabucco*—can get an idea of the multidimensional identity of "a living community" that, according to the museum curators, will change again "in the next hundred years."[37]

Silvana is the heroine of *Benghazi Bergen-Belsen* and, with her parents and sister, embodies the strength of an entire community that does not want to vanish and that hopes to survive the difficulties of the war. But as violence against the Jews increases and the Haggiags' house is ravaged, the family becomes the only shelter left to her: "'*Ya ma, nehabbek bezzayid* [Mum, I love you so much],' she whispered to her, and in her heart she wished her words would be like another home. '*Anche io ti voglio bene* [I love you too],' her mother answered."[38] Here, one finds another feature that appears several times in the novel: the melding of words in Libyan Arabic, Italian, and—as the story unfolds and moves from Libya to Europe—broken English and German. This gives readers a direct sense of how the Jews of Benghazi spoke and contrasts with the more literary Hebrew that Sucary uses in the descriptive parts of the book. This writing style shows in a vivid manner the attachment of the Jews to their Arab heritage and the Arabic language, as well as the fact that this community was an inner component of Benghazi's everyday life.

While the first chapters of the book are set in Libya and portray Silvana and her family's last months in Benghazi and then in a Libyan prison camp, the following ones narrate the sea voyage from Libya to Italy—where the Haggiags will spend a few months in the camp of Civitella del Tronto, in the central southern region of the peninsula—and then to Bergen-Belsen. Even in Libya, Silvana begins to feel that her world and family are disintegrating: her father, till then the undisputed patriarch, weakens and no longer knows what to do. Her own identity as a modest and educated Benghazi Jew is put into question by the violent behavior of the German soldiers, who treat her as a Black African: "That was the first time she thought of herself as an African. Few times, Black Africans had come to Benghazi but her father never spoke about them as inferiors.... With difficulty she tried to control herself and not shout at the German soldier. She really wanted to shout at her father, but she did not. The soldier urged her and the others: 'Juden. Afrikaner. Schneller.'"[39]

The idea of the Jews of Libya as Black and African recurs throughout the book, particularly in the part set in Bergen-Belsen—where Silvana and the other Libyans are treated badly not only by the Nazi soldiers but also by some European Jews, who see them as bizarre coreligionists who speak unknown languages and seem to arrive from another planet. Moreover, whereas the violence Silvana suffers while in Bergen-Belsen obviously originates in the Nazi ideology and in the deportation from Libya organized by the Germans, at an everyday level it depends also on the Ashkenazi Jewish inmates who assault her verbally and physically, ending with her rape by three Dutch *kapos*: "Who would save her? Her own white Jewish brethren, who treated her as if she were a human animal that weaseled her way into their group?"[40] By insisting on this aspect, Sucary reflects on the inner ethnic hierarchies within Judaism that, years after the events, will find an echo in the troublesome integration the *Mizrahim* faced upon arrival in Israel. At the same time, it was not only Libyans who faced intra-Jewish discrimination and differentiation in the concentration camps: think of the many Greek Jews, particularly the Ladino-speaking Salonikans, whose Ashkenazi inmates viewed as strange, albeit physically strong and courageous, fellow Jews.[41] The Libyans' Holocaust experience was an extraordinarily marginal one, and therefore when Sucary, as a child in 1960s Israel, would tell the teachers that his family had suffered from the Holocaust, they would reply: "You're mistaken. Only the European Jews were in the Holocaust."[42] The idea of the Jews of the Arab world as quasi-Black people can be found also in Israeli writings and public discussions of the 1960s and is even evoked in the name of the most renowned *Mizrahi* emancipatory movement of the 1970s: *Ha-panterim ha-shehorim* ("The black panthers"), which according to its founders took its cue from the African American Black Panthers. On a different level of analysis, it is worth mentioning that since the late 1980s a number of scholars using the tools of postcolonial studies have interpreted the *Mizrahi* question as a case of subalternity between people belonging to different—if interrelated—sociocultural backgrounds.[43]

Because of the influence of the context of immigration, as well as the personal story of the author, *Benghazi Bergen-Belsen* clearly stems from a different position than *Le chant des mariées*, whose goal was only to portray a lost Jewish-Arab coexistence. Sucary's novel talks little about life in Libya, or about the relationship between different ethnic and religious communities there, choosing to focus on the Holocaust as a revelatory moment of tensions internal to Jewish—and, in an indirect manner, Israeli—society. The only exception seems to be Rivka, an Ashkenazi girl whom Silvana meets in the camp and who soon becomes her best friend. Rivka is the only one who understands how, despite their physical appearance, all Jews are the same, as—in a paradoxical manner—a German soldier tells her in the camp, "If you think that you are different because she [i.e., Silvana] is Black, then you are making a big mistake. Jews are always Black in the inside. Sometimes you can see that also from the outside and sometimes you cannot."[44] But the friendships between Rivka and Silvana and between Nour and Myriam from *Le chant des mariées* have more differences than similarities. Aside from the context in which the friendship develops, the main difference is the fact that Nour and Myriam belong to two religious communities but to the same world, whereas Rivka and Silvana are both Jews but come from very different universes and probably would not have met otherwise.

Silvana Haggiag's story should be viewed as part of a larger context involving feelings that go beyond her Jewish identity; think for instance about her enduring nostalgia for the Arabic language and for Benghazi: "[Silvana] longed especially for the days when her father all of a sudden decided that he had had enough of working, and in the late afternoon took her to *Via Roma* and *Via del Municipio*, bought her . . . white almond candies, or some *croccanti*."[45] While staying at Rivka's barrack, alone after the death of her father and the transfer of her mother and sister Toni, Silvana is left only with the Arabic songs learned during childhood: "The Arabic that for her was like a well-protected home, also provoked the loathing of the others [i.e., the Ashkenazi inmates]."[46] Her isolation from the other survivors also is visible at the end of the novel, when, following the liberation of Bergen-Belsen by the Allies, despite her frailty Silvana wants to be part of a group of former deportees who will be filmed singing *Ha-tiqvah*, the Zionist and then Israeli anthem. Initially the girl keeps silent, but as the anthem reaches the end, Silvana starts to sing, "stressing as much as possible her Arabic accent, so that everyone would know: 'She had been there too, with them.'"[47] This scene inscribes the story of Silvana in that of the Holocaust and of Israel but does so by underlining the extreme difficulty of telling, and hearing, what happened to the Libyans in Bergen-Belsen. Theirs is a past that features little in the Holocaust narrative or in the *Mizrahi* story of displacement and resettlement. As a result, the Jews of Libya consider themselves to still share—in their opinion, more than other Jewish diasporas—"a dominant and innate identity . . . and remain attached to traditions, both from a religious point of view and for what concerns habits and customs."[48] At the same time, this marginality may depend also on the fact that—in comparison to other North African Jewries—the integration of Jews from Libya in Israeli society "was relatively successful, or more precisely, relatively quiet," thanks to the limited size of the community and the fact that most people had already immigrated between 1949 and 1951, before the great *'aliyot* of the mid-1950s.[49]

Nonetheless, it must be mentioned that during the Eichmann trial in 1961 Jerusalem, the vicissitudes of the Jews of Libya, as well as of Tunisia, already were silenced—to the dismay of the Organisation des Originaires de Tunisie en Israël, whose president wrote a letter of complaint to Attorney General Gideon Hausner: "It is true that one cannot compare the persecution of the Jews of Tunisia to that of the Jews of Europe, but this does not diminish the culpability and criminal responsibilities of the Germans against the Jews of Tunisia."[50] Thus, *Benghazi Bergen-Belsen* and the fictional story of Silvana Haggiag—given the fact that Sucary based his work on historical material and interviews with real Libyan Holocaust survivors—becomes a vehicle through which the forgotten Libyan Jewish Holocaust returns to the surface. If this novel legitimately wishes to inscribe the modern history of the Jews of Libya in that of the Holocaust, there is a risk that at the level of the general public a new Libyan memorial landscape associated with the Holocaust will overshadow the rest of their historical experience. It is clear that the case of *Benghazi Bergen-Belsen* and of the Libyans is different from that of, for example, the novel *Pere' 'Atzil* (Noble savage; 2003) by the Israeli Dudu Busi—in which the protagonist is an Iraqi Jewish artist who reflects on his imaginary relation to the Holocaust.[51] But although Libyan Jews were deported to Bergen-Belsen, their history, tragic as it may be, cannot stand for the twentieth-century history of the North African and Middle Eastern Jewish communities as a whole.

The belief in the existence of a loosely defined *Mizrahi* Holocaust in many ways reflects "a strong desire to engrave the missing gene into the DNA of Mizrahi identity in order to be affiliated with the superior group that possesses the legitimacy in Israeli society," more than anything else.[52] This is not to deny or minimize the tragic fate of the Libyans or to propose an idyllic reading of the relations between Jews and Arabs. In fact, one could even contend that the emphasis placed on the Holocaust in some cases has obfuscated other traumatic memories of events that, when they occurred and during the first decades after the establishment of Israel, seemed to have a greater impact on the Jews of Libya: think about the 1945 anti-Jewish riots in Tripolitania, which took place in a moment of deep political and economic uncertainty and led to the death of 130 Jews, instigating the first great wave of Jewish emigration from the country.[53] If it is true that for some North African Jews the Holocaust indeed was until recently an absent past that had been erased from their memory, we should not take this event as the sole or main narrative to which all Jewish history should now conform.[54] In other words, it is one thing to say that the Holocaust is part of the history and memory of the Jewish people in its entirety and quite another to include in it events that are not directly related or to infer that, since some Libyan Jews are Holocaust survivors, all Jews from the Arab world who suffered from war violence and antisemitism should be considered as such.

The movie and novel that I have analyzed are two among the many that in recent years were dedicated to the Sephardi and *Mizrahi* experience of the Holocaust. These works of art aim to extend, each in its own way, the traditional geographic and imaginative boundaries of the Holocaust by focusing on *peripheral* spaces that were imbricated in it and in the Second World War. Even though, as explained, the cases of the Jews of Tunisia and Libya are different from those of other Middle Eastern and North African Jewries, the increased visibility of the North African Holocaust certainly relates to a general Sephardi and *Mizrahi* decentering of this historical tragedy: a shifting thanks to which "the Holocaust loses its quality as index of the specific historical event and begins to function as metaphor for other traumatic histories and memories."[55] *Le chant des mariées* and *Benghazi Bergen-Belsen* therefore act as memory bridges connecting the normative history of the Holocaust with, on the one hand, that of North African Jews who suffered from Nazi persecution or deportation and, on the other hand, that of the many more Jews of the Arab world who, in the mid-to-late 1900s, experienced antisemitism, uprooting, and mass migration but not the Holocaust itself. Nonetheless, particularly in the Israeli context, the Holocaust has become a foundational element of the *Mizrahi* cultural memory, as if "this page of Jewish history were a page of their own history."[56] The act of remembering the Holocaust, in fact, has helped members of these communities to feel more at home in the (Israeli) Jewish context of immigration. But at the same time—as I shall now explain—this often comes with a downplaying of the Arab side of the identity of most of the so-called *Mizrahim* and an embrace of an ambivalent narrative of quasi-permanent persecution and Arab anti-Jewish sentiments that corresponds to contemporary political and ideological reasoning more than to the historical reality.

MEMORY, ETHNICITY, AND POLITICS: THE ISRAELI EXIT AND EXPULSION OF JEWS FROM ARAB LANDS AND IRAN DAY

A family walks through a desolated landscape: father, mother, children, grandmother. The man wears headgear and a tunic; the women's hair is covered by a scarf. They are, says the caption, "a Yemenite Jewish family in the desert on the way to a refugee camp" run by the American Jewish Joint Distribution Committee near the city of Aden. This photograph—displayed at the entrance of the exhibition *I rifugiati ebrei dai paesi arabi* (Jewish refugees from the Arab lands), held between December 2015 and February 2016 at the Jewish Museum of Rome in cooperation with the Embassy of Israel in Italy (see fig. 3.2)—introduces Middle Eastern and North African Jews as refugees whose history, identity, and culture need to be protected and preserved. The exhibition was promoted in the context of the Exit and Expulsion of Jews from Arab Lands and Iran Day (henceforth: Jews from Arab Lands and Iran Day), an observance that the State of Israel officially established in 2014.[57]

The idea underlying *I rifugiati ebrei dai paesi arabi*, and its implementation by the Israeli Ministry of Foreign Affairs, was to have a moveable exhibition that could be relocated easily to different cities and venues on the occasion of the Jews from Arab Lands and Iran Day and at other times.[58] The thirteen panels included photographs with captions describing different aspects of the history and culture of the Jews from the Arab world: from The Islamic Conquest to Education, Sport, Discrimination and Pogrom up to Integration in Israel and Justice and Quest for Peace. The first panel explained that "according to the Islamic law, the Jews were considered *dhimmi*.... In 1860 the *Alliance Israélite Universelle* was created in order to fight against *pogroms* and discrimination.... Throughout the centuries, the conditions of the Jews were precarious. There had been numerous attempts to massacre them and of ethnic cleansing ... in the 1930s and 1940s there were anti-Jewish massacres inspired by Nazism in Libya, Egypt, Algeria, and the cruelest one in Baghdad." Other panels focused on issues such as the contribution of Jews to Middle Eastern

Figure 3.2. The exhibition *I rifugiati ebrei dai paesi arabi* (Jewish refugees from the Arab lands), Jewish Museum of Rome, 2016.
Source: Author.

sports and music. Finally, the migration and arrival in Israel were presented with a description of "the human capital, courage, talent, and experience of the Jews from the Arab lands [that] contributed significantly to the successes of Israel." Even though *I rifugiati ebrei dai paesi arabi* was displayed inside the so-called Libyan room of the Jewish Museum of Rome, which is normally dedicated to the history and culture of the Libyan Jews who arrived in the city in the 1960s and which was renovated at the end of 2017 in conjunction with the fiftieth anniversary of their migration, there was not an explicit connection between the exhibition and this story, to the point that—probably because of the limited space available—most of the Libyan artifacts were hidden behind the panels of the temporary exhibition and were barely noticeable to the visitors. The exhibition fulfilled an official duty of remembrance, signaling Israel's willingness to transform the newly established Jews from Arab Lands and Iran Day into a permanent anniversary on the Israeli civil calendar. So far, this calendar has been centered on commemorative days like *Yom ha-Shoah* (Holocaust

Remembrance Day) and *Yom ha-'Atzmaut* (Independence Day).⁵⁹ That Israeli civil holidays and rituals are inscribed in the calendar of Jewish communities in the Diaspora is not surprising; in fact, the Israeli days of remembrance—like the above-mentioned *Yom ha-'Atzmaut*—are now celebrated throughout the world as part of a post-1948 landscape of remembrance that binds Israel and the Diaspora together in new ways.⁶⁰

Considering all that, the Jews from Arab Lands and Iran Day can be interpreted as an initiative that rightly aims at expanding the public awareness of the history of the Jews of the Middle East and North Africa but does so by focusing almost exclusively on very selective issues—such as property claims against Arab countries and Arab antisemitism—and on the image of these Jews as refugees. In the rationale of the memorial day, these topics are much more at stake than the Sephardi past or the cultural heritage of these communities per se. In that case, what kind of memorial event is the Jews of Arab Lands and Iran Day, and which past does it evoke? And why now?

The Jews of Arab Lands and Iran Day was created with an ad hoc law of the Israeli Parliament in 2014, during Biniyamin Netanyahu's third premiership. Among the promoters of the *hoq yom le-tziyun ha-yetziah ve-ha-gerush shel ha-yehudim me-'artzot 'arav u-me-'Iran* were the Moroccan-born Shimon Ohayon, at the time a member of the Knesset for the center-rightist party Yisrael Beiteinu; Minister of Regional Cooperation Silvan Shalom, who was born in Tunisia; and the representatives of a number of migrant associations like the already cited Hitahdut 'oley-Mitzrayim be-Israel.⁶¹ The law, Ohayon explained, deals with "a story [that] touches about half the residents of Israel, but is almost unknown" and constitutes "an important element for any future peace and reconciliation between Jews and Arabs in the Middle East."⁶² The law designates November 30 as the day for remembering the mass migration and expulsion of the Jews of the Arab world and Iran and envisages three main lines of action: an official commemoration by the Minister for Senior Citizens; educational activities in all state schools, supervised by the Ministry of Education; the commemoration of the day; and—as the Roman case shows—the dissemination outside Israel, via the Ministry of Foreign Affairs and the Israeli embassies, of information about these Jewish refugees and their history.⁶³

Before we look at some of these activities, it may be interesting to reflect on the name of the law and the date chosen. As said, the official name is *yom le-tziyun* (lit. "day for marking") the *yetziah* and *gerush* of the Jews from the Arab Lands and Iran. The Hebrew words *yetziah* and *gerush* (respectively "exit, departure" and "expulsion, exile") reflect the difficulty of finding a univocal definition for the migration of these Jewries. They also point to the fact that some Jews were expelled, including some of the Jews from Egypt accused of being Zionists or Communists, whereas others left voluntarily or for a variety of reasons ranging from Zionism to feelings of being in danger. The law focuses on the expulsion, on the very end, of the history of these communities and inscribes them inside the Israeli memorial landscape by way of their being—just like the Jews of Europe—victims of a history of antisemitism and persecution, terminated with the final homecoming to Israel.[64] Furthermore, most Jews and Hebrew speakers are likely to relate the two terms evoked in the name of the law to two central episodes in Jewish history: the biblical *yetziat-Mitzrayim* ("exodus from Egypt") and the fifteenth-century *gerush Sefarad* ("expulsion from Spain"). The choice of these two terms confirms that, as Lucette Valensi explained, Jewish (and Israeli) memory often can be read as a blending of secular and sacred times and spaces that relate both to the recent past and to older events. In our case, the law establishes a double connection with a contemporary and secular history of antisemitism and anti-Jewish persecution and with religion-based or mythologized episodes like the exodus from Egypt and the expulsion from the Iberian Peninsula.[65] At first glance, it seems that emphasis is placed on the presentation of the Jews of the Arab world as victims and passive actors of an expulsion, rather than active protagonists of their *'aliyah*. But as we shall see, things are more ambivalent because these communities are paradoxically presented both as Zionist pioneers and as powerless exiles.

The date selected by the Knesset can be considered as another indicator of the interpretative framework given to the history that is being commemorated. November 30, 1947, is the day after the United Nations passed the Partition Plan for Palestine, when, as an American commentator wrote in 2015 on the first anniversary of the Knesset's establishment of Jews of Arab Lands and Iran Day, "Violence, following bloodcurdling threats by Arab leaders, erupted against Jewish communities. The riots resulted in the mass exodus of Jews from the Arab world, the seizure of their property and assets and the destruction of their millenarian, pre-Islamic communities."[66] From a historiographic point of view, it is questionable whether the Partition Plan was the principal and most direct cause of the anti-Jewish violence that erupted in 1947 and in the following years in cities as different as Cairo, Baghdad, and Tripoli. Even though these episodes were obviously connected to the outbreak of the Arab-Israeli conflict, they depended also on local factors and were inscribed in larger Middle Eastern and North African anticolonial struggles. This was the case, for example, of the 1952 Cairo fire, whose targets were the Western powers, foreign residents, and religious minorities in general, more than the Jews specifically.[67] That the 1947 Partition Plan was not the main event behind the expulsions and migrations is further demonstrated by the fact that most Jews did not leave the Middle East and North Africa at that time, or even in 1948, but—according to different chronologies, which also concern the political and economic situation of the country of origin—in the course of the 1950s and 1960s.⁶⁸ By saying this, obviously I do not intend to minimize the profound impact that the birth of the State of Israel had on the Jews of the Arab world but rather to underline once more that many other factors contributed to the demise of these communities: particularly the process of decolonization and the spreading of new and less inclusive forms of Arab nationalism that, in some cases, even predated the 1948 war and did not concern Palestine.

The text of the law clarifies why this particular date was chosen. The law introduces the *palit* ("refugee"), a category that, even though absent from the name of the day, plays a crucial role in it: "The Minister of Foreign Affairs will coordinate activities . . . to improve the international knowledge about the Jewish refugees . . . and their rights of compensation."⁶⁹ The discussion of whether the Jews of the Middle East and North Africa, especially those who settled in Israel, are refugees is not new. In 1953, the Israeli anthropologist Raphael Patai argued that in his view a Jew from the Muslim world was not a refugee but an immigrant because "after leaving his habitual residence he is permitted to enter a new country . . . he is . . . aided by the government and by public agencies . . . he is legally entitled to acquire citizenship."⁷⁰ Even though many—if not the majority—of the Jews who left the Arab Muslim world did so "owing to well-founded fear of being persecuted for reasons of race, [and] religion," to quote the 1951 Geneva Convention, it is equally true that because of the Law of Return, those who went to Israel formally entered the country as citizens and not as refugees.⁷¹ The same can be said for Jews who emigrated to a European country of which they were nationals, like the Jews of Algeria who went to France.⁷²

Since its inception in the 1950s and 1960s, the debate over the refugee status of the Middle Eastern and North African Jews never stopped, but it undeniably became much more visible in the last twenty years. First, during the Camp David Summit (2000), President Bill Clinton stated that any agreement between Israelis and Palestinians should include a fund for compensating both Palestinian *and* Jewish refugees. Clinton's statement was preceded by the activities of several US-based Jewish groups and nongovernmental organizations, first and foremost the World Organization of Jews from Arab Countries (WOJAC), which functioned from 1975 to 1999.⁷³ A second group that came about soon after Clinton's declaration is Jews Indigenous to the Middle East and North Africa (JIMENA), founded in 2001 when "a group of former Jewish refugees from the Middle East and North Africa decided it was time to share their personal stories of religious oppression, displacement, material loss and fractured identities."[74] Finally, a third is Justice for Jews from Arab Countries (JJAC), whose aims are "a) to represent the interests of Jews from Arab countries; b) to recognise the legacy of Jewish refugees from Arab countries."[75] As regards the State of Israel, in 2008 the Knesset approved a Law for the Preservation of the Rights to Compensation of Jewish Refugees from Arab Countries and Iran, which explicitly underlined the need to include this issue in any peace agreement between Israel and its Arab neighbors.[76]

If we take into account the legal definition of *refugee*, some might suggest that labeling the totality of the Jews from the Middle East and North Africa as such deprives them of much of their individual agency and does not take into consideration that at least some decided to migrate to Israel of their own will. This is why the Knesset speaker Yisrael Yeshayahu, originally from Yemen, in 1975 contended that "we did not want to call ourselves refugees. We came to this country before the establishment of the state.... We had messianic inspirations."[77] At the same time, it would be simplistic to claim that since Israel granted citizenship upon arrival to all of the *'olim*, none of these can be considered a refugee. The Jews who fled the Libyan cities of Tripoli and Benghazi in 1967 were really seeking refuge from persecution and—as had happened to many Jews of Europe in the 1930s and 1940s—were forced to leave their country of residence, in most cases after having their assets and properties seized by the local government. The comparison with the European Jews becomes further evident in light of the fact that, in Israel, Jewish refugees from Libya and Tunisia nowadays are eligible for monetary compensation as Holocaust survivors and that Jews from Algeria and Morocco who suffered from antisemitic measures during the Second World War—as well as Jews who suffered from the 1941 Baghdad *farhud*—since 2015 have the right to a small annual allowance.[78]

Perhaps these Jewish migrations can be historicized using categories that evoke neither the figure of the refugee nor the Zionist *'oleh* but a more ordinary transnational migrant. It is worth quoting the poetic words with which the writer Ronit Matalon—born in Israel in 1959 to Egyptian Jewish parents— refers to one of the Egyptian-born characters of her novel *Qol tze'adenu* (The sound of our steps; 2008), arguing that hers was not an *'aliyah* but a *hagirah* ("migration"), after which "[all] the good things disappeared. Something terrible . . . had happened in her eyes in the itinerary of the migration, in the geography itself of our migration."[79] Oral evidence, in addition to recently declassified sources, reveals that a number of Moroccan migrants living in 1950s and 1960s Israel wrote letters to relatives still in Morocco, advising them not to come to Israel and, in some cases, even complaining about feeling exiled in the Promised Land and wishing to return to their true North African homeland: "Please send me a ticket so that I can return. [Israel] is a waste of time."[80] These are only two examples that illustrate the impossibility of imposing an overarching meaning on these migrations. The Middle Eastern Jewish migrant—just like any other migrant—was and still is an ambivalent and sometimes *absent* figure, to quote the Algerian sociologist Abdelmalek Sayad, whose history can be reconstructed reading along the grain official names and categories, the legal documents produced in this case by the Israeli bureaucracy, and the labels that the Jewish migrants have chosen for themselves.[81]

The Jews from Arab Lands and Iran Day is inscribed in a civil calendar that so far has been dominated by the remembrance of the Holocaust, on the one hand, and the celebration of the Israeli independence after the 1948 war, on the other. At the same time, we began to notice how labeling the Jews of the Arab world as refugees relates their vicissitudes not only to the Holocaust but also to the history of the Palestinians. An article by an Israeli of Lebanese Jewish origin that appeared in the daily *Yediot 'Aharonot* on November 30, 2015, explicitly claimed that "we Jews have a Nakba too. . . . Unfortunately, our Nakba is private, as it has no international or even national support, it has no Israeli and foreign organisations which recognise it and work to raise Israeli and international awareness of its existence." Here, the Palestinian *Nakba* is reframed and mobilized vis-à-vis the *Mizrahim* and with an eye to compensation rights, since, according to the author, "in any future negotiations to solve the Palestinian refugee problem . . . both Palestinian and Jewish refugees will receive the same theoretical and practical treatment."[82] In 2015, one of the first *'olim* from Iraq declared in an article in *Ha-'Aretz* that "the state [of Israel] almost forgot the atrocities that forced the immigrants to flee for their lives. . . . Unfortunately, it seems their rich culture and folklore did not receive the exposure it deserved. But the authorities have come to their senses and begun to repair the injustice that was done."[83] Finally, as evidence of the impact of this memorial day's first celebration on the general public, *Israel Ha-yom* mentioned that "the heritage of the Jews who fled Arab and Muslim lands will be celebrated with much fanfare on Nov. 30 at the Malha Arena in Jerusalem. This is the first time such a large, state-sponsored event is held in memory of those Jews."[84] In 2019, the *Jerusalem Post* mentioned that "a global *kaddish*," the Jewish prayer for the dead, had been organized by dozens of synagogues throughout the world to "commemorate this painful day."[85] In November 2020 during the COVID-19 pandemic, the Ministry of Jerusalem and Heritage and the Ministry of Social Equality sponsored an online show called *Eretz Tzion ve-Yerushalayim* (Land of Zion and Jerusalem; a quote from the Israeli national anthem) that gathered "Israel's finest performers... continuing the tradition of earlier generations and bringing the creativity and cultural richness of Eastern Jewry to the twenty-first century."[86] The event included Zoom rooms dedicated to all the various Middle Eastern and North African Jewish communities, from Morocco to Iran; ad hoc talks; and videos. Finally, in 2021, a delegation of Israeli associations of Middle Eastern and North African Jews took part in a commemorative ceremony at the official residence of the president of the State of Israel, Yitzhaq Herzog, in Jerusalem.[87]

Albeit in different ways, both the issue of property rights and the idea of the North African and Middle Eastern Jewish past as a hitherto unheard of and unknown story lie at the center of these activities and of the articles that since 2014 have appeared in Israeli and international newspapers every year around November 30. However, what emerges is a memory in the making based on selected historical episodes to the detriment of others: Zionist activities in the Arab lands, Arab antisemitism, and an event like the Iraqi *farhud* are at the forefront of the narration, whereas the more positive sides of the historical encounter between Jews and Arabs—as well as the problems the migrants faced after arriving in Israel and while in the *ma'abarot*—receive much less attention. As for the comparison with the Palestinians, for Yehudah Shenhav it "embroils members of the two groups in a dispute" that might eventually harm future peace agreements between Israel and the Arab states.[88] Regardless of whether one agrees with Shenhav or with the article that appeared on *Yediot 'Aharonot*, it seems unquestionable that evoking the *Nakba*—or the Holocaust and Nazism—in relation to the *Mizrahim* at least produces a competitive memory and zero-sum thinking that do not capture in any way the complexity of the Sephardi and *Mizrahi* identity.[89]

Certainly, transmitting the knowledge of a history characterized by mass displacement and uprooting is not an easy task, particularly when it comes to the educational system. In the case of the Holocaust, already in the 1960s—following the establishment of *Yom ha-Shoah* and the Eichmann trial—Yad Vashem had decided to survey how the history of the event was being taught in Israeli schools, with the idea of systematizing and improving the pedagogical framework that teachers should follow.[90] As regards the *Mizrahim*, given the absence of a centralized institution as authoritative as Yad Vashem, the issue of how to teach the history of these communities and how to deal with the November 30 memorial day seems—for the time being, and despite the existence of national guidelines by the Ministry of Education, which I will talk about later—to remain more open to teachers' choices. At the same time, official state curriculum, Israeli and foreign think-tanks, and academics specialized in didactics are also playing a role. Among the think-tanks is the Kedem Forum for Israeli Public Diplomacy—a nongovernmental organization devoted to "1) protect[ing] the heritage and interests of modern-era Jewish refugees from Arab countries, and 2) deploy[ing] the unique assets of this multilingual and multicultural Jewish community in the cause of truth, peace, and reconciliation in the Middle East."[91] The founders of the Kedem Forum highlight the pedagogical aims of their organization, especially in relation to the memory of the Jewish refugees from the Arab world: "We all know about Kishinev," the infamous pogrom that occurred in 1903 in what nowadays is the capital of the Republic of Moldova, "but we do not know what happened in Baghdad or Cairo."[92] Similar concerns emerge from a law proposal formulated at the end of 2020 by a member of the Knesset and grandson of Iraqi Jews, Ofir Katz, to establish a national memorial day for the victims of the Iraqi *farhud*.[93]

On the occasion of a 2015 one-day workshop on *Mizrahi* and Sephardi history designed for Israeli high school teachers, the Kedem Forum presented ad hoc brochures describing activities students can do on November 30, including "an interview with family members [born in the Middle East and North Africa]" or "visiting museums or the Babylonian or Libyan Jewish Heritage Centres."[94] Such activities do not represent a novelty in the Israeli educational curriculum, which always has asked students to research their family roots through specific assignments (*'avodat shorashim*, lit. "assignment on roots") and which—as we have seen when talking about the first Israeli Egyptian Jewish association in the 1950s—has encouraged the study of the connections between the Jewish people and the Land of Israel.[95] Even the comparison between the Arab regimes and Nazism found in the Kedem Forum brochure reiterates historical assumptions that go back to the 1950s, with the labeling of the Egyptian leader Gamal 'Abd-al-Nasser as a new Hitler.[96] Interestingly, as noted in the chapter dedicated to the digital diasporas, a third element has now been added to the picture: the Christians and other minority groups living in the contemporary Middle East, whose presence allegedly testifies that "what occurred to the Jews is what now occurs to defenseless minorities . . . : the Kurds and the Christians."[97] However, much of the Israeli press and the Kedem Forum—but not only these, since the American JIMENA produced a similar brochure for American Jewish day schools[98]—present a contradictory view of *Mizrahi* Jews as both passive, dispossessed individuals and Zionist activists—an image that resembles the depiction of Holocaust survivors in 1960s Israeli schoolbooks.[99] As a Cairo-born Israeli said to me, with a hint of irony and skepticism, at the

Figure 3.3. The exhibition *Latzet mi-bli lahazor* (Leaving, never to return), Museum of the Land of Israel, Tel Aviv, 2019.
Source: Author.

Eighth World Congress of Jews from Egypt in 2017: "A few more years, and we will all become Holocaust survivors!"[100]

The relevance of the Holocaust and of antisemitism to commemorations of the history of the Jews of the Arab world was also visible in an exhibition held in 2019 at the *MUZA—Muze'on Eretz Israel* of Tel Aviv, entitled *Latzet mi-bli lahazor* (Leaving, never to return) (fig. 3.3). In addition to the many interesting objects put on display by the curator Dana Avrish, mainly thanks to loans by Israelis of *Mizrahi* origin, the exhibition—which occupied a wing of the museum—included two panels for each country of the Middle East and North Africa: one summarized the history and main characteristics of that country's Jewish community, and the other presented a "Timeline of anti-Jewish assaults" from medieval times to the twentieth century.[101]

Here one must ask not whether anti-Jewish violence and sentiments existed in the Middle East and in North Africa, as of course they did, but what happens when a great emphasis is placed on them, at the expense of the rest of the region's Jewish history, and when we make them the main story line of the past. In fact, if both the Holocaust and the mass migration of the Jews of the Arab world reflect difficult and tragic moments in the contemporary history of the Jewish people, they are different events that shed light on much more complicated stories of war, of postwar and postcolonial displacement, and also of nostalgia and friendship.[102] Yet in many of the press articles about the 2014 law and in public declarations by Israeli state officials, *Mizrahim* and *Ashkenazim*, past and present, Nazism and Arab regimes come together to compose quite a confusing and ahistorical memorial landscape. For example, on the occasion of *Yom Ha-Shoah* 2019, in an op-ed in *The Times of Israel*, a journalist of *Mizrahi* origin wrote: "I remember visiting *Yad Vashem* as a teenager and looking for the story of the Iraqi Jews, but I could not find it.... The persecution and suffering of *Mizrahim*, never mind the expulsion of 850,000 *Mizrahim* from the Arab countries of their birth after the creation of Israel, is never recognized with the wail of a siren."[103] But is Yad Vashem, a museum dedicated to the Holocaust and not to Jewish history or to antisemitism more generally, the place where the Jews of Iraq should be commemorated? And must one have a personal or family connection to sense the importance of a historical event like the Holocaust, which nowadays is at the core of Israel's collective identity? Seen from this angle, *Mizrahi* history and the manner in which it is conceived seems to "[be] molded ... more by contemporary political needs than by careful attention to evidence"—producing what more than thirty years ago Mark Cohen had already termed the neo-lachrymose conception of the Arab-Jewish past.[104]

Clearly, the creation of the Jews from Arab Lands and Iran Day reflects the increased presence of the *Mizrahim* in the Israeli public sphere and, in many ways, confirms once more the end of the principle of *mizug galuyiot*, on which early Israeli society was based.[105] It would be unfair not to recognize that the establishment of this commemoration and the cultural initiatives that surround it represent legitimate attempts to deepen the public's knowledge of the Middle Eastern and North African Jewish history. Yet the rationale that underlies this day and the law that regulates it confront it with very Westernized—think of the reference to the Holocaust—and present-oriented eyes, which project the troubled relations between Israel and the Arab world onto a past that, for better or worse, was much more nuanced.

At a larger level, the existence of such a commemoration reveals that categories like migrant and refugee are central in today's political and even everyday lexicon and can be mobilized in different and contrasting manners. In our case, the Jews from the Arab lands at times can be refugees, Zionist pioneers, or simply migrants who resettle in another country—with all the ideological, political, and cultural shiftings that the adoption of one category instead of another implies. A possible solution to this terminological conundrum could be to stop searching for a univocal representation of the Sephardi and *Mizrahi* past, or for one constructed mainly along Western historical paradigms, and to start telling the story of the Jews of the Middle East and North Africa as a multilayered and heterogeneous tale, made of moments of both violence and cohabitation that distinguish it from the stories of the Jews of Europe. Consequently, the juxtaposition between *'aliyah* and migration will need to be revised, so as to consider the Jewish migration to Israel—particularly after 1948—not as a unique case of resettlement but as an experience that, despite having some peculiar characteristics, in many aspects resembles other transnational migrations in the postwar years and during decolonization.[106]

In this way—as even some of the policy makers who contributed to the law on the Jews from Arab Lands and Iran Day admit—the new commemoration could be a more effective point of departure for constructing a historically grounded narrative for the State of Israel and its citizens.[107] The Israel Prize laureate poet of Moroccan origin Erez Biton also seems to suggest a similar point in the preface to the recommendations presented in 2016 by the *Va'adat Biton le-he'atzemet moreshet yahadut-Sfarad ve-ha-mizrah be-ma'arehet ha-hinukh* ("Biton Commission for deepening the heritage of the Sephardi and Eastern Jewries in the educational system") to the then Minister of Education Naftali Bennet, with the aim of improving the presence of Middle Eastern and North African Jewish history and heritage in state-school curriculum. It was not the first time the Israeli Ministry of Education undertook this kind of initiative: think of the largely forgotten Merkaz le-shiluv moreshet yahadut ha-mizrah ("Center for the integration of the heritage of Eastern Jews"), established in 1976 to publish textbooks about the Jews of the Arab world and increase that group's visibility in schools. But notwithstanding the limited results the commission seems to have obtained so far—and the fact that the Jews from Arab Lands and Iran Day has not yet acquired the popularity hoped by its proponents—that of Biton still is an important contribution to the emergence of an Israel more sensible to the voices of the *Mizrahim* than it was some decades ago, in the hope of opening "a real discussion on what it means to be Israeli" that would finally take into account all the Jewish, and even non-Jewish, identities that make up twenty-first-century Israeli society.[108]

JEWS, MUSLIMS, AND EUROPE

The difficulty of crafting univocal and overarching descriptions of the interaction between Jews and their neighbors in North Africa and the Middle East does not emerge only from the Israeli context. It is evident also when we listen to the life stories of many of the Jews who lived in the region and then migrated to Europe or elsewhere. In fact, some of these Jews—depending on their place of birth, their age when they left the country of origin, their migration trajectory, and other factors—maintain positive recollections of premigratory times, whereas others tend to focus on the more painful moments and the final years of the world in which they lived. "[In 1952]," Cairo-born Juliette Glasser explains, "I remember the Muslims going around, saying, 'We are going to kill the Jews, where are the Jews?'"[109] For David Cohen, who was born in Morocco and who later migrated to Canada, one of the most troubling memories of leaving is the sudden departure from his Jewish and Muslim friends: "I never got to say goodbye to any of these kids.... We left, we only had one suitcase each." At a distance of several decades, he realized that he and his family "were attached to something"—that is to say Morocco—"that, without knowing it, we had lost," to the point that the act of leaving became in itself "a defining feature in my life.... It has defined everything."[110] Talking about the attitude of the Libyan Muslim population and its relations with the Jews, Moshe Labi first goes back in time to one of his ancestors, who "in 1492 ... moved [from Spain] to Fès in Morocco, he became a rabbi and he was a Cabbalist and he was famous for one of these *piyutim* [pl. of *piyut*: "liturgical poem"].... He died in 1580, he was buried in a place called Dara and his tomb was revered by the Muslims because they realized he was a great person, a great rabbi." Labi then explains that now the tomb is covered by parking lots, that "all the memories and remnants of the Jewish cemetery are essentially erased by the Arabs."[111] If this harsh judgment probably is true in the Libyan case, one should more carefully assess Egypt, and even more so Morocco. In fact, in that country over the last years more than 160 Jewish cemeteries have been restored thanks to funds bestowed by the Moroccan royal house. While this initiative is due also to touristic and political reasons, it shows a greater awareness of the need to preserve Jewish heritage on the part of state institutions, after years when it was more or less completely neglected and the memory of Jewish Morocco transmitted almost exclusively in the private sphere or, unofficially, at a popular level.[112] This awareness of the country's multicultural identity is confirmed by the inclusion, in 2020, of Judaism and Jewish culture in the Moroccan primary schools' history curriculum.[113]

The quotes with which I opened this section also make us wonder what kind of postmigratory relations can exist today among people from different ethnoreligious backgrounds, Jews and Muslims, who lived together for centuries and who—surely in different ways—continue to do so in the countries to which they immigrated.[114] The topic of postmigratory Jewish-Muslim interaction assumes even greater significance considering the current social and political context and the alleged threat to Europe's identity that, according to some politicians and analysts, Islam and Muslim migrants pose.[115] Therefore, after dealing with the past and present of the history of the Jews of the Middle East and North Africa and with the narration and reconceptualization of these vis-à-vis crucial categories of Jewish history and identity—such as the Holocaust, Zionism, and Israeliness—now I want to look forward to possibilities of Jewish-Muslim interaction in the European future. To do so, I focus on the experience that Jews from Italy and France, especially those who migrated there from the southern shore of the Mediterranean, have with Arab Muslim migrants coming from that same region, and more generally with a European Islam in the making. I try to decipher whether and how the interplay of different historical memories can trigger the birth of new ideas of nationhood and Europeanness, crossing today's ethno-national and religious divides—as well as essentialist and perhaps too-narrow interpretations of what Europe should be—to contribute to a more transcultural future.[116]

By *transcultural future*, I mean one that values experiences of mobility, cultural exchange, hybridity, the cross-fertilization of identities and memories, and any other positive outcome that migration can stimulate.[117] I draw upon the work of the French political theorist and philosopher Etienne Balibar, for whom migrants are part and parcel of European identity and should be included in any public discussion about the future of the continent, as "in all its points, Europe is multiple" and its citizenship should take into consideration "the contribution of all those who are present and active in the social sphere."[118] Actually, Balibar contends that until now "there [has been] something like a 'missing nation' in the middle of Europe, a nation made of several long-established migrant communities with different histories but a similar final destiny, and even some common cultural characters easily seen as threats to European culture."[119]

It is true that in the last decades Judaism has come to be seen as a central facet of the European heritage and—together with Christianity and the legacy of the Enlightenment—a foundational component of the continent's identity and historical memory, both at national and EU level.[120] On the other hand, the acknowledgment of other religious and historical legacies, such as the Islamic one or those of colonialism and migration, as part of Europe's past—and of its postcolonial present—is still lacking. But the barriers between Jews, Muslims, and other Europeans can be more porous than that, like the activities of civil society and the associational world lead us to think. This is the case for the Florentine association Donne per la Pace ("Women for peace"), whose activities I will contextualize vis-à-vis public discussions of migrants among Italian Jews. Then, I will compare the association to similar types of Jewish-Muslim cooperation in France. Since not all the people who take part in these associations—and in Jewish communal discussions on migrants more generally—are Jews who migrated from the Arab world, this will allow us to look at a wider sector of European Jewish society and to gain a deeper understanding of issues as topical as the perception and inclusion of migrants, or lack thereof, in contemporary Europe.

Although migrants from southern Europe or from former colonies already had started to settle mainly in Germany, Belgium, Britain, and France in the 1950s and 1960s, it was only from the 1980s and then especially in the 1990s that Italy saw the arrival of a large number of migrants from the southern shore of the Mediterranean, the Balkans, and eastern Europe. This is partly because of the Italian social and economic history and the fact that more or less until the mid-twentieth century, Italy had been mainly a country of emigration and not of immigration.[121] As of 2022, about 2.6 million Muslims—the majority of whom are among the 5 million foreign residents, whereas only a minority are Italian nationals—live in Italy, especially in the north and center of the country. In most cases they are first-generation migrants born abroad. Unlike other cases in Europe, those who come from former colonies are a minority. This is because the Italian colonial empire was relatively small and made of two main territories: Libya and the Italian East Africa—today's Ethiopia, Eritrea, and Somalia. Most migrants come from Morocco and other countries in North Africa, as well as from Albania and the Middle East. As opposed to the millions of Muslim who live in Italy, the Jews number approximately 35,000. Their largest community is in Rome, followed by those in Milan and then Florence and Turin. The largest Middle Eastern and North African Jewish diaspora in Italy—as I noted already—is that from Libya, but smaller groups of Egyptian, Syrian, Lebanese, and Iranian Jews are also present, mainly in Milan and Rome.[122] On the whole, it has been estimated that between the 1940s and late 1960s about 4,000–5,000 Jews from the Middle East and North Africa, especially Libya and Egypt, settled in Italy.[123] If the figure is quite small considering the total number of Jewish migrants from the region, it nonetheless becomes more relevant juxtaposed with that of the Italian Jewish diaspora.

A focus on Florence, the city where the Jewish-Muslim group Donne per la Pace is based, might seem decentered in relation to both the current migratory flows and the geographic distribution of the Jews of Middle Eastern origin in Italy. At the same time, it should be remembered that Florence has been a focal point for experiences of ecumenism and interreligious dialogue since the postwar period, especially thanks to the work of its Christian Democrat mayor Giorgio La Pira. Among other things, between 1958 and 1964 La Pira organized four *Colloqui mediterranei*, in which representatives of Judaism, Islam, and Christianity discussed themes like world peace, the relations between the south and the north of the world, and intercultural dialogue. This legacy continues to permeate local politics and was explicitly evoked at the beginning of April 2020, when the mayor of Florence Dario Nardella organized in Piazza della Signoria, in the heart of the city's historical center, an interconfessional prayer for the *emergenza Coronavirus*, with the cardinal archbishop of Florence Giuseppe Betori, the imam Izeddin Elzir, and the Florentine chief rabbi Gadi Piperno. On that occasion, Cardinal Betori mentioned La Pira, noting that in the square were present "the representatives of the three Abrahamitic religions, a subject close to the heart of Giorgio La Pira."[124]

With reference to the Florentine Jewish and Islamic communities, if the first existed already in the early modern period and increased significantly in the nineteenth century, mainly thanks to Jewish migration from other parts of Tuscany such as Leghorn and Siena, the Islamic community is much more recent and, at least from an institutional point of view, only dates back to the 1980s. According to the Italian national institute of statistics, Istat, in 2021 approximately 133,000 foreigners officially resided in the province of Florence and more than 59,000 in the city of Florence; of these, around 5,000 were from Muslim-majority countries in North Africa and the Middle East. On the other hand, the Islamic Cultural Centre of Florence estimates that 30,000 Muslims live in the city; this figure, however, includes both people who do not all come from the Arab world and Muslims with Italian nationality.[125] The Florentine Jews number around 1,000 and for the most part are of Italian origin, even though some Egyptians and North Africans arrived in the city between the 1950s and 1960s. So far, the relations between the two communities have been good, thanks to the will of the local chief rabbis and imams. This allowed the construction of "a network of friendship" in a relatively small city, perhaps helped by the fact that the synagogue and the Islamic Cultural Centre—Florence, as of today, does not have a mosque—are located just a few hundred meters from each other in the historical neighborhood of Sant'Ambrogio.[126]

Among the joint projects promoted by the two—with the support of the Florentine City Council—is the educational activity Una sinagoga, una moschea, which has been going on for about fifteen years and is directed toward schoolchildren who, together with teachers, want to know more about the Jewish and Islamic traditions and religious heritage. Specialized guides accompany students and teachers on a tour of the synagogue and the Islamic Cultural Centre, explaining the buildings' architectural features and the principal Jewish and Islamic traditions.[127] The association Donne per la Pace is a much more recent addition to the Florentine panorama of interreligious associationism and dialogue. It was founded in 2015 by three women already active in the lives of their respective religious communities: two of them are Jewish, one Italian and one Israeli, and another is a Muslim who migrated to Italy from Egypt. The aim of the association is to foster reciprocal knowledge between Jews and Muslims living in Florence and, at the same time, highlight the role of women as peace builders and actors in the public sphere, particularly in times of conflict and intercommunal tensions. As of 2017, when I conducted my fieldwork with the group, Donne per la Pace counted around ninety members, even though its informal character and irregular meetings—especially since the outbreak of the COVID-19 pandemic—make it difficult to give an exact figure.[128] According to its founders, Donne per la Pace took inspiration from the Israeli movement Women Wage Peace, which was established after the 2014 war in Gaza and whose main goal is "to prevent the next war and lead to resolution of the conflict that is non-violent, respectable and agreeable to both sides—Israeli and Palestinian, within four years." Since 2014, Women Wage Peace has organized several activities, such as the March of Hope, which in October 2016 saw thousands of women marching "from all four corners of Israel to Jerusalem," demanding peace and justice and the full participation of women in the political process of crafting a future agreement between Israelis and Palestinians.[129]

Among the activities promoted by Donne per la Pace are artistic performances, lectures, city walks, and picnics that gather dozens of women of Jewish, Muslim, and other backgrounds, as well as some men and children. Even though Donne per la Pace does not rely explicitly on the memories of the Jews from the Arab world as its main trigger for intercommunal dialogue, the founders acknowledge that these—and the experience of migration, of belonging to a minority group more generally—can contribute to a rapprochement between Jews and Muslims. The founders Tami and Sanaa explain that their friendship originates in their shared identity as women migrants to Italy: "Being migrants is what united us at the beginning. We felt the same things." Tami adds that "in the last years, in Europe we have seen horrible things happening. And I think that, in some way, today the Muslims in Europe exactly are what we, Jews, were a hundred years ago."[130] Along similar lines, an article in the Turin-based Jewish monthly *Hakeillah* in October 2016 compares the life story of the author's father—a Roman Jew who in the 1930s managed to flee to Argentina and then, after facing many obstacles, escaped from antisemitic persecution—to the situation of today's migrants from Africa and the Arab world: "The frontiers are closed like in the 1930s, and the dreams of freedom and of a better life still have many obstacles before they can be fulfilled."[131] This kind of reasoning also can be found in the Israeli context: in this case, it is the asylum seekers arriving mainly from Sudan and Eritrea whom local human rights activists portray as similar to the Jewish refugees illegally entering British Palestine in the 1940s, by underlining how "many of our grandfathers and grandmothers entered Israel in a way that today is termed as infiltration. . . . We ourselves were refugees only three generations ago; have we already forgotten this lesson?"[132]

But to what extent can today's migrants, and particularly today's Muslim migrants, be compared to what the Jews were? And how should one account for the ongoing presence of antisemitism—sometimes on the part of Muslims—in Europe and elsewhere?[133] It is true that in Italy and other places, political parties from the right increasingly point the finger at Muslims—and not, or at least not as often or in the same ways as in the past, at Jews—as the nation's quintessential outsiders.[134] Nonetheless, antisemitism has not ceased to exist. In the case of France, 45 percent of Jewish respondents to a 2016 poll declared that they had been targets of antisemitic remarks, and 11 percent experienced an antisemitic aggression.[135] In a 2020 poll, the situation was even worse: 70 percent said they had been the victims of antisemitic acts, 64 percent of an antisemitic verbal aggression, and 23 percent of a physical aggression. As for the reasons that made 52 percent of respondents think about leaving France in the near future, 21 percent of respondents indicated a fear for the future of the Jewish community in that country, 12 percent mentioned economic reasons, and 13 percent a fear for the future of France more generally. Moreover, whereas 58 percent of French respondents and 42 percent of French Jews considered traditional anti-Jewish prejudice to be the main cause of today's antisemitism, 45 percent of French Jews—as opposed to 36 percent of the French general public—saw radical Islam as another relevant factor.[136]

Going back to the 2016 poll, 76 percent of the respondents believed that it is difficult to be Jews in today's France, and almost 60 percent believed that being Muslim is equally challenging. In turn, a survey conducted later in the same year by the Paris-based Institut Montaigne around the theme *Un Islam français est possible* discovered that almost 40 percent of Muslim respondents thought that in France "the Muslims are victims of a conspiracy" and that Islamophobia is on the rise.[137] Even without taking these polls at face value, the overall picture bespeaks an increased mistrust between the two groups and between each community and the French state, as well as a decreased interaction between Jews and Muslims in daily life. The shared North African origin of many French Jews and Muslims does not seem to improve the situation, especially when it comes to the younger generations. Misperceptions about past Jewish-Muslim interactions in North Africa are not infrequent among Muslims of Maghrebine origin, who often conflate Jews with Israelis.[138] In fact, a French qualitative inquiry published in 2017, *France: Les Juifs vus par les musulmans*, revealed that even though antisemitic stereotypes can be found among different sectors of the French population, they tend to be more frequent among Muslims.[139] Furthermore, Kimberley Arkin's ethnographic study showed that many French Sephardi adolescents consider habits typical of a shared North African heritage to be inherently Jewish: from the languages spoken in the family to cooking and clothing.[140]

Although these stereotypes also relate to one's socioeconomic status and lack of, or limited, social integration, they confirm the increased *communautarisme* of both Muslims and Jews—which, in the Jewish case, is also a consequence of antisemitic attacks like the March 2012 shooting at the Ozer Hatorah school of Toulouse or the January 2015 attack at the Hypercacher kosher supermarket in Paris and the feelings of insecurity they generated. On a different level, the increase in antisemitism is connected to the spreading of conspiracist ideas and fake news through social media and the internet—media that, here, assume very different characteristics than what we have seen in the case of the Moroccan Jewish website Dafina. In the case of Italy, a 2020 survey of the *Osservatorio antisemitismo* of the Milanese Centro di documentazione ebraica contemporanea showed an increase in recorded cases of antisemitism and the persistence of a number of antisemitic stereotypes, which very often have found in the internet and social media an extraordinary vector for their diffusion.[141]

Clearly, these divisive attitudes do not come out of nowhere and are not just the result of recent episodes of terrorism and antisemitic attacks. They go back at least to the integrationist policies of the 1960s, when—as we have seen—a Jew from Algeria, as a French citizen, had access to a number of services that were not available to the average Algerian Muslim immigrant. Additionally, beneath these attitudes lies the ideological impact that the Arab-Israeli conflict and Western policies toward the Arab world and Israel have on European

Jews and Muslims.[142] From this perspective, the memory—both in its positive and negative aspects—that the Jews of the Arab world have of their country of origin and of the Arab population, instead of being a tool for rapprochement, appears to be a cumbersome past that was gradually wiped out and replaced by intercommunal tension and in some cases by a particularistic feeling of Sephardi Jewishness. Thus, reckoning with a lost Arab, or more generally North African, identity does not stimulate proximity with the Muslim other, but on the contrary underlines one's Jewish ethno-religious identity.

Similarly to Donne per la Pace, the association Amitié Judéo-Musulmane de France (henceforth AJMF), established in 2005, tries to address Muslim antisemitism and Jewish Islamophobia by using the motto *on se ressemble plus qu'il ne semble* ("we are more similar than what it seems"). The association's defining activity is traveling through France on a minibus to "engage Jews and Muslims in dialogue, so that they can reach a better knowledge of their communities, their respective lifestyles and preoccupations."[143] Additionally, the AJMF organizes workshops on antiracism and cooperates with a number of professionals, including teachers and psychologists, and with associations that work in the banlieues. Its founder, Rabbi Michel Serfaty, was born in Marrakech in 1943 and migrated to Strasbourg in the 1960s. Serfaty suffered from an aggression by two young men of Maghrebine origin in 2003, and that, among other things, inspired the foundation of the AJMF. Since then, the rabbi has traveled France, sometimes accompanied by an imam—the two speak of themselves as "brothers in humanity"—but his activities received mixed reactions: he and his minibus at times were welcomed, in other cases criticized. In 2009, he participated in a peace initiative in Gaza together with prominent non-Jewish and Jewish personalities, including the writer Marek Halter. After the *Charlie Hebdo* attacks of January 2015 and the Paris attacks of November 2015, the visibility of the AJMF increased, and Serfaty was the subject of a documentary by the French-German television channel ARTE.[144] Quite surprisingly, in the documentary and in interviews published in French newspapers, television channels, and radio stations, the rabbi never relates his interest for Jewish-Muslim dialogue to his Moroccan background, which is only briefly mentioned and not considered as central. The journalists also talked about his work mostly in the context of the tense interreligious and intercommunal relations between French Jews and Muslims, without taking into much consideration the present legacy of the Middle Eastern and North African past that many share and what this might represent. Serfaty only mentioned his Moroccan past in a few interviews, saying that back in Marrakech his life was "entirely Jewish," his parents advised him never to enter the *casbah* "because there they kill the Jews," and as a result, he got in touch with his Muslim Moroccan peers only as an adolescent, upon enrolling in the scouting movement.[145]

According to Katz, despite the good will of its founder, an association like the AJMF may be limited because it understands the interaction between people of Jewish and Muslim background primarily in religious terms—as highlighted by the fact that the AJMF *tours de l'amitié* are headed by a rabbi and an imam.[146] Different approaches are followed by groups like the Hebrew-Arabic language association Parler en paix, established in 2003, or the Coup de soleil, which was founded in Paris in 1985 to unite "people from the Maghreb and their friends," regardless of their national and ethno-religious origin—and whose main activity in recent years has been the annual book fair Maghreb-Orient des livres.[147] Nonetheless, the fact that both the AJMF and Donne per la Pace are open to people who are neither Jews nor Muslims constitutes a useful step forward in the construction of a more widely shared notion of French and Italian citizenry. The fact that both groups are explicitly apolitical—the AJMF, though ambivalently, also evokes the French notion of *laïcité* as one of its founding principles—further stimulates the participation of a diverse range of people. In the case of Donne per la Pace, this is important because even though the relations between the Florentine Islamic and Jewish communities are quite positive, still there were people from both sides who initially did not see the point of such an initiative: "Listen, people did not know what to think . . . then they saw what we are doing and eventually they came." In the words of Tami, the Israeli founder, "Our strength lies in the fact that the more we grow in numbers, the better it will be for everyone. At the beginning we just invited friends and neighbors." As for the AJMF, Michel Serfaty explains that "to all those who wish to obstacle the friendship between Jews and Muslims, I repeat time and again that I am neither an Israeli, nor a soldier of *Tzahal*. This conflict has nothing to do with us, it is not part of our daily preoccupations."[148]

Going back to Donne per la Pace, the gendered dimension and the role of women as mothers and educators of the children is crucial, insofar as it can be a source of transmission of positive values like peace, coexistence, and justice. Sanaa, the Muslim founder, notes that "we have to start from the mothers, otherwise we will have children that . . . you know . . . it will be difficult. There are people who migrate here and know nothing about this country. . . . There was this religious family, that migrated only a couple of years ago. And the daughter did not want to come [to our activities], but in the end she did and she was happy. . . . Her mother phoned me to tell this. . . . It is not easy for new migrants, they still have ideas [about Jews]." So Donne per la Pace intends to break the barriers between different feelings of national and ethno-religious belonging, in the hope of triggering quotidian acts that will facilitate intercommunal and urban dialogue. This also means digging up unexpected correlations between Jewish and Muslim memories and experiences that have sedimented in the context of immigration and that have become, at least for some people, not so different from one another. Again Sanaa, the Egyptian woman, confesses that "back home, I thought about the Jews and had the impression that they were not like us. . . . But here, since we are in Italy . . . here we are migrants . . . I go and cook at the Jewish Community [Centre] and meet Sandra and Michel, that were born in Egypt . . . and we talk about the Arab singers . . . I could talk to them for hours."[149]

In a similar vein, Albert Bivas—who was born in Egypt in 1941 and migrated first to France and then to the United States—in an interview with the American Sephardi organization JIMENA, recalls how years after the migration he met an unknown colleague in a bar: "He told 'I am a Palestinian' and I said 'I am an Egyptian' . . . I said to him 'Tell me your story' . . . then I said 'Ok, now you told me your story, you can listen to mine.' . . . And from that point on, we were exactly on the same page . . . we just felt sorry for each other, for the situation, for fanaticism and war."[150] Everyday interactions and the immediate telling of personal stories seem to be a most effective catalyst of mutual understanding. In this specific case, a Jewish-Palestinian transcultural heritage emerges in relation to what can be called *everyday multiculturalism*: there, we find selected ethnic elements—like food, music, and the like—perceived to be politically less contentious and more easily accepted by the host society.[151] This is reminiscent of the Egyptian and Algerian Jewish heritage associations, or the novel *Pour l'amour du père* by the Tunisian-born Chochana Boukhobza, which describes North African Jews and Arabs as "fingers of a hand." However, others still feel the urgent need for a shared common ground that includes, yet goes beyond, the everyday dimension and focuses on more general societal and cultural matters. In another article published on the Italian Jewish monthly *Hakeillah*, Gianni Diena admits that "everyone needs points of reference. They can be the most disparate ones, but if the notion of citizen (of France, of Italy, of Europe etc.) still makes sense, the existence of a common ground is essential."[152] But what kind of common ground can be found among Jews, Muslims, and other citizens of Europe, and how can the Jews from the Arab world contribute to its making?

According to Joseph Levi, a strenuous supporter of interreligious dialogue and chief rabbi of Florence at the time of our meeting, "to have migrated from one place to another [in the past], to have been a migrant, does not always mean that today ... in another political context, you are going to be more open to migrants ... the Torah tells thirty-six times to love the stranger ... but when it comes to the level of the individual, well, who knows."[153] To connect the threads of different stories of migration, perhaps one might map the memorial tropes—such as the difficulty of leaving, the integration in a new context, the nostalgia for the homeland or the wish to forget about it, or the importance of preserving one's religious heritage—that bind together people from different backgrounds and relate them to the spaces they live(d) in.

With reference to religion, the international exhibition *Lieux saints partagés*, held at the Musée de Civilisations de l'Europe et de la Méditerranée of Marseille between April and August 2015, is an interesting case. The exhibition aimed at presenting multiple "landscapes of religious entanglement" that can be found on both shores of the Mediterranean, particularly in North Africa and the Near East, and that mainly concern Judaism, Christianity, and Islam.[154] As the title says, it focused on holy places in general: from the Ghriba synagogue of Djerba, Tunisia, to the sanctuary of the House of the Virgin Mary in Ephesus, Turkey, to more informal sites of worship in places as different as the island of Lampedusa, Algiers, and Jerusalem. Unfortunately, the exhibition did not focus much on the presence, or absence, of holy spaces shared by North African and Middle Eastern Muslims and Jews living in contemporary Europe and the ways this continent's memorial landscape might ease or complicate intercommunal dialogue. On the whole, as Michel Wieviorka noted in the exhibition's catalog, *Lieux saints partagés* highlighted that the Mediterranean is an extraordinary laboratory of interaction and conflict, "where the 'bricolage,' to use the expression popularized by Claude Lévi-Strauss, dwells constantly."[155] The focus is on what remains of the past in our time, how this can orient the present and future, and what they look like. A similar approach can be noticed in personal recollections by Jews from the Arab world who, while remembering nostalgically their country of birth as it was before the migration, maintain quite a critical view of almost all that happened after they left and cannot imagine themselves in the future—and in many cases not even in the present—of these places. Thus, the Libyan-born Ivette Journo admits that, even though she is still deeply attached to her native Tripoli, she prefers her life in Rome and cannot see herself in a land that is no longer hers: "Where are my parents? Where are my little sisters? Where is my brother-in-law? Where are they? They are under the asphalt of a hangar. They [i.e., the Libyan Muslims] built a hangar on top of the [Jewish] cemetery."[156]

Even when it comes to today's refugees and migrants from the Middle East, we are confronted with stories that resent divisive approaches between

Jews and Muslims, that mainly refer to the turbulent relations that they have had at least since the 1940s and the foundation of the State of Israel in 1948. Consider, for example, an article published in *Moked*, a magazine supported by the Union of the Italian Jewish Communities, that talked about a group of Syrian refugees who arrived in Milan in 2015. Much of the article focused on the migrants' perception of Israel: "Sitting on green plastic chairs, [for] the Syrian refugees . . . Israel . . . despite all that they saw and suffered from their own people, remains the number one enemy. . . . Adman is curious, he asks questions. . . . But he advises not to disclose to the other refugees that I am Jewish. 'They may react badly,' he warns me."[157] A rosier picture emerges from a charitable initiative by the Jewish Community of Milan, which together with the Catholic association Comunità di Sant'Egidio in 2020 sponsored the arrival of a family of Syrian Muslims from Aleppo. According to the vice president of the Union of the Italian Jewish Communities, Giorgio Mortara, "the malaise of people coming from abroad is a sensitive point for Jews, [since we are] stimulated by a similar historical experience." The Comunità di Sant'Egidio, on its part, underlined that this initiative showed "the sympathetic friendship between communities of believers that come together to create bridges."[158] As in the case of the AJMF, the religious identity of the migrants appears to be the most visible aspect of their identity. But, at the same time, an interesting connection is made here between today's Middle Eastern migrants and Jews, as two groups of people who share experiences of exile, migration, and resettlement. This emerges also from an open letter by the Libyan-born David Gerbi published in *Moked* in January 2021, calling for a greater recognition of the plight of the Middle Eastern and North African Jews in Europe and particularly in Italy: "We are like forgotten refugees, because we did not make enough noise. . . . How would you feel if overnight you were to live in another country? This has been the tragedy of the Jews persecuted and expelled from the Arab world. Perhaps, it is the tragedy of any refugee that suffers in silence."[159]

On the occasion of the 2016 European Day of Jewish Culture, Donne per la Pace organized a performance in the garden of the synagogue of Florence on the theme *Guardare negli occhi: Linguaggi e identità/identità e differenze*, inspired by the work of the renowned artist Marina Abramović (fig. 3.4).

Two lines comprising both women and men—Jews, Muslims, Christians, and others—sat for a few minutes without talking, only looking at one another. The performance asked everyone to "lift the gaze from the cellphone and look at each other in the eyes! Without words, just the eyes. Silent, through a deep visual contact between different souls. When there are no words, prejudices

Figure 3.4. Performance of the association *Donne per la pace* at the Synagogue of Florence, 2016.
Source: Author.

fall too and only people, the hope for empathy and the possibility of finding together a dialogue ... remain."[160] As simple as this suggestion may be, perhaps we should not dismiss it altogether but instead, starting from there, ponder more about Europe and its pasts, its migrant present and future—as if we were all on the edge of a once familiar road that suddenly looks foreign and, at the same time, full of possibilities. But if migration can become a foundational element of a shared European future, why not see it in conjunction with notions of civic solidarity, more than—or in addition to—religion?[161] This does not mean adopting a too-hopeful perspective and ignoring the feelings of antisemitism that some migrants and non-Jewish Europeans have, or the Islamophobia of sectors of the European (Jewish and non-Jewish) society. More simply, it is a call for a more diachronic perspective on these issues that does not impose the contingency of the present on long, if often removed, histories of interreligious and interethnic relations that, in different ways, may be able to continue in the future.

WHERE THE MEDITERRANEAN ENDS

This chapter has looked at how the historical memory in the country of immigration is stimulating the redefinition and inclusion of the North African and Middle Eastern Jewish past and the resulting new ways of dealing with the presence of migrants and refugees in European societies. Then, I discussed different ways of telling the history of proximity and distance between Jews and Arabs across the Mediterranean region. After almost all the Jews left the southern shore of the Mediterranean Sea and resettled in Israel, Europe, or elsewhere, their history in fact continues in—and is reinterpreted through—the present and is not merely something lost in the past. The Holocaust, the Jews from Arab Lands and Iran Day established by the Israeli parliament in 2014, and finally the intersection between the memories of the Jews of the Middle East and North Africa and those of today's Muslim migrants are three possible settings from which original memorializations of the past in the present can be initiated, each performed by different actors and based on different sociopolitical contexts. Whereas the first relates to the work of artists, like Sucary and Albou, and the second to the activities of state institutions, the last one has to do mainly with voluntary associations and civil society.

All this shows how the past of these communities can be evoked and, for better or worse, instrumentalized. I say "for better or worse" because the increased visibility of Sephardi and *Mizrahi* Jews in the public sphere does not automatically imply an increased knowledge and awareness of their history. On the one hand, this increased visibility is a welcome change that finally sheds light on people who have been on the margins of Jewish and Middle Eastern history. But on the other, it often does so in ways that can be quite ambivalent: think, for example, of the Jews from Arab Lands and Iran Day and its ideological background, or even the AJMF's approach to French Jewish-Muslim relations—which refers to the notion of *laïcité* and yet appears to be based on religion more than general feelings of nationhood and civism. In any case, the experience of the Sephardi and *Mizrahi* Jews proves to be a useful template for understanding other histories of migration and displacement, as well as for reconsidering the historical and memorial impact of a traumatic event like the Holocaust.

The interest for the Sephardi and *Mizrahi* past reflects not only the changes that European and Israeli societies have gone through when it comes to the transmission of their historical heritage but also and perhaps principally the diffusion of feelings of communal and individual loss and the urgency of recording a history that—in Israel, Europe, and the US, as well as, for the time being, to a much lesser extent in the Arab world—is perceived as on the verge of disappearance. Time goes by, and, with the passing away of the first generation and under different social and political circumstances, what remains is a history situated on the edge of a sometimes-idealized Mediterranean world that is no more, or perhaps never was. It is a history embedded in a contradictory semantics that conceptualizes Sephardi and *Mizrahi* Jews as Holocaust survivors, refugees, or *ante litteram* migrants to Europe. Certainly, this mirrors the multivocality of the Sephardi and *Mizrahi* Jews and of the Mediterranean region as a space from which their history and memory is constantly recast. It reveals the difficulty of elaborating a shared strategy that addresses the current memorial divides between Israelis and Palestinians, Jews and Muslims, *Ashkenazim* and *Mizrahim*, Europeans and North African migrants.

Sephardi and *Mizrahi* history seems to exist *only* at the borders between Europe, Israel, and the Arab world, at the end of a Mediterranean region that becomes "the stage where the constellation of memories and the conflicting diasporic and nomadic identities" of its protagonists "are constantly revivified."[162] If so—and despite the problematicity of the presentist attitude that many of the memorialization activities portrayed in this chapter embody—this same semantics, when read "along the grain,"[163] is a clue that can help to recover some of the discarded connections and not entirely vanished possibilities of the history of Middle Eastern Jews. It is the case of the Jews of Libya who experienced the Holocaust and nowadays wish to make this known to the public, proposing a deeper reading of this crucial historical event. But also think about the points of contact that undoubtedly exist between the migratory experience of the Maghrebine Jews and Muslims living in contemporary France. If the world of interreligious and interethnic interaction and cohabitation that the Sephardi and *Mizrahi* Jews knew through personal experience—or thanks to the memories of their parents and grandparents—has come to an end and will never return, a more hopeful and less divisive present and future can still be imagined on the basis of unfinished travels of memory across two not-so-distant shores.[164]

NOTES

1. François Hartog, *Régimes d'historicité: Présentisme et expériences du temps* (Paris: Seuil, 2004).

2. Amos Goldberg and Haim Hazan, eds., *Marking Evil: Holocaust Memory in the Global Age* (New York: Berghahn Books, 2015).

3. Christian Jacob, "Introduction: Faire corps, faire lieux," in *Lieux de savoir, t. 1: Espaces et communautés*, ed. Christian Jacob (Paris: Gallimard, 2007),

17–42. On the idea of contemporary memory as a plural construct, see Andreas Huyssen, *Present Pasts: Urban Palimpsests and the Politics of Memory* (Stanford, CA: Stanford University Press, 2003).

4. Here, I draw upon the idea of non-Western—and particularly colonial—history as characterized by multiple possibilities and instabilities vis-à-vis modernity and its outcomes. See Antoinette Burton, "Introduction: The Unfinished Business of Colonial Modernities," in *Gender, Sexuality, and Colonial Modernities*, ed. Antoinette Burton (London: Routledge, 1999), 1–16.

5. Yablonka, *Les Juifs d'Orient*, 31. See also Eric Salerno, *Uccideteli tutti: Libia 1943; gli ebrei nel campo di concentramento fascista di Giado, una storia italiana* (Milan: Il Saggiatore, 2008).

6. Michael Laskier, *The Alliance Israélite Universelle and the Jewish Communities of Morocco, 1862–1962* (Albany: State University of New York Press, 1983), 179.

7. Georges Smadja, "Témoignage de Georges Smadja," in *Les Juifs de Tunisie sous le joug nazi: 9 novembre 1942–8 mai 1943*, ed. Claude Nataf (Paris: Le Manuscrit, 2012), 152–53.

8. Yablonka, *Les Juifs d'Orient*, 30–36; Abitbol, *Les Juifs d'Afrique du Nord*; "Les Juifs d'Orient face au nazisme et à la Shoah," special issue, *Revue d'histoire de la Shoah* 205, no. 2 (2016); "Yehudei Tzfon-'Afriqah be-tqufat ha-Shoah" [The Jews of North Africa during the Holocaust], special issue, *Bishvil ha-zikaron*, no. 30 (2018); Filippo Petrucci, *Gli ebrei in Algeria e Tunisia, 1940–1943* (Florence: Giuntina, 2011); Reeva Spector Simon, *The Jews of the Middle East and North Africa: The Impact of World War Two* (London: Routledge, 2020). The number of North African and Middle Eastern Jews who were deported or who perished in the Holocaust is considerably higher if one includes those who were living in Europe (mainly France but also Italy) when the war broke out. See Jean Laloum, "Des Juifs d'Afrique du Nord au *Pletzl*? Une présence méconnue et des épreuves oubliées (1920–1945)," *Archives Juives* 38, no. 2 (2005): 47–83; Liliana Picciotto, "Ebrei turchi, libici e altri, deportati dall'Italia a Bergen Belsen," *Rassegna Mensile di Israel* 76, no. 3 (2010): 243–59.

9. Krämer, *Jews*, 154–60. More generally, see Jill Edwards, ed., *El Alamein and the Struggle for North Africa* (Cairo: American University in Cairo Press, 2012).

10. Mark Angel, *The Jews of Rhodes: The History of a Sephardic Community* (New York: Sepher Hermon, 1978). See also Esther Fintz Menascé, *Gli ebrei a Rodi: storia di un'antica comunità annientata dai nazisti* (Milan: Guerini e Associati, 1992).

11. Lev Hakak, "The Holocaust in the Hebrew Poetry of Sephardim and Near Eastern Jews," *Shofar*, no. 2 (2005): 89–119.

12. Kobi Oz, *'Avaryan Tza'atzua'* [Petty hoodlum] (Jerusalem: Qeshet, 2002), 136–37.

13. Orly Castel-Bloom, cited in Yochai Oppenheimer, "The Holocaust: A Mizrahi Perspective," *Hebrew Studies*, no. 51 (2010): 295.

14. See Judith Roumani, "Sephardic Literary Responses to the Holocaust," in *Literature of the Holocaust*, ed. Alan Rosen (Cambridge: Cambridge University Press, 2013), 225–37; Tartakowsky, *Les Juifs*, 184–85.

15. Yablonka, *Les Juifs d'Orient*, 221. I also refer to Yvonne Kozlovsky-Golan, *Masakh shel skhehah: 'al-he'adar havayat ha-Shoah shel yehudei-ha-mizrah bamediah u-va-'omanut be-Israel* [Forgotten from the frame: The absence of the Holocaust experience of Mizrahim from the visual arts and media in Israel] (Tel Aviv: Resling, 2017); Kozlovsky-Golan, "Childhood Memories from the Giado Detention Camp in Libya: Fragments from the Oeuvre of Nava T. Barazani," *Shofar: An Interdisciplinary Journal of Jewish Studies* 38, no. 1 (2020): 1–37.

16. Albert Memmi, *La statue de sel* (Paris: Gallimard, 1953).

17. For example, see Jean-Luc Douin, "'Le Chant des Mariées': Rêves d'amour d'une Juive et d'une Musulmane dans une Tunisie sous régime nazi," *Le Monde*, August 16, 2008, http://www.lemonde.fr/cinema/article/2008/12/16/le-chant-des-mariees-reves-d-amour-d-une-juive-et-d-une-musulmane-dans-une-tunisie-sous-regime-nazi_1131561_3476.html#ens_id=1052988; Jeanette Catsoulis, "Bodies in Motion," *New York Times*, October 22, 2009, http://www.nytimes.com/2009/10/23/movies/23wedding.html; Ella Taylor, "The Wedding Song Probes Bond between Two Women," *Village Voice*, October 20, 2009, http://www.villagevoice.com/film/the-wedding-song-probes-bond-between-two-women-6391978.

18. Bahloul, *La maison*.

19. Abdelkrim Allagui, *Juifs et musulmans en Tunisie des origines à nos jours* (Paris: Tallandier, 2016), esp. 84–88.

20. Memmi, *Juifs*, 164.

21. John Esther, "A View of One's Own: Exclusive Interview—Karin Albou," *Jesther Entertainment*, November 6, 2009, http://jestherent.blogspot.it/2009/11/exclusive-interview-karin-albou.html.

22. On Muslim Righteous among the Nations, see Robert Satloff, *Among the Righteous: Lost Stories from the Holocaust's Long Reach into Arab Lands* (New York: Public Affairs, 2006); Ethan Katz, "Did the Paris Mosque Save Jews? A Mystery and Its Memory," *Jewish Quarterly Review* 102, no. 2 (2012): 256–87; Katz, "Secular French Nationhood and Its Discontents: Jews as Muslims and Religion as Race in Occupied France," in *Secularism in Question: Jews and Judaism in Modern Times*, ed. Ari Joskowicz and Ethan Katz (Philadelphia: University of Pennsylvania Press, 2015), 174. The story of the Great Mosque of Paris during the war is also at the center of the French movie *Les hommes libres*, directed by Ismaël Ferroukhi in 2011.

23. Timothy Snyder, *Black Earth: The Holocaust as History and Warning* (New York: Tim Duggan Books, 2015), 316–18.

24. See Kathryn Lachman, "Music and the Gendering of Colonial Space in Karin Albou's *Le chant des mariées*," *Music, Sound, and the Moving Image* 7, no. 1

(2013): 1–18. This is not unique to the Tunisian case but applies more or less to all Jewish communities in the region. On Algeria, see Bahloul, *La maison*. On Morocco, see Emanuela Trevisan Semi and Hanane Sekkat Hatimi, *Mémoire et représentations des Juifs au Maroc: Les voisins absents de Meknès* (Paris: Publisud, 2011). On Egypt, see Miccoli, *Histories*, esp. 110–17.

25. Allociné, "Le chant des mariées," accessed January 4, 2022, http://www.allocine.fr/film/fichefilm-131759/secrets-tournage/.

26. Esther, "A View of One's Own."

27. Michael Laskier, *North African Jewry in the Twentieth Century: The Jews of Morocco, Tunisia, and Algeria* (New York: New York University Press, 1994), 76.

28. Maurice Roumani, "First, Libya's Jews Were Deported. Then the SS Stepped in," *Ha-'Aretz*, February 8, 2020, https://www.haaretz.com/world-news/.premium.MAGAZINE-first-libya-s-jews-were-deported-then-the-s-s-stepped-in-1.8504840.

29. Robert Watson, "Coproducing Nostalgia across the Mediterranean: Visions of the Jewish-Muslim Past in French-Tunisian Cinema," *Politics-Rivista di Studi Politici* 5, no. 1 (2016): 105–23. The TV movie *Villa Jasmin* is based on the autobiographical novel of the same name by Serge Moati, published in France in 2003.

30. I base my opinion on a public lecture by Yossi Sucary, held on November 14, 2016, at the Center for Jewish History in New York, in which I participated.

31. Hanna Yablonka, "Oriental Jewry and the Holocaust: A Tri-generational Perspective," *Israel Studies* 14, no. 1 (2009): 109.

32. See also Yvonne Kozlovsky-Golan, "Site of Amnesia: The Absence of North African Jewry in Visual Depictions of the Experience of World War II," *Jewish Film & New Media: An International Journal* 2, no. 2 (2014): 153–80.

33. See the website of the New York–based theater company *La Mama*, available at http://lamama.org/benghazi/.

34. See Rachel Simon, "Les Juifs de Libye au seuil de la Shoah," *Revue d'histoire de la Shoah* 205, no. 2 (2016): 221–62.

35. Yossi Sucary, *Benghazi Bergen-Belsen* (Tel Aviv: Am Oved, 2013), 18.

36. See, for example, "Ricordi di Tripoli," Levluv/Germogli, Sivan 5767/June 2007, 30, YBZ VI 330.3.

37. Staff of the Libyan Jewish Heritage Centre, interview by the author, Or Yehudah, May 24, 2018. See Piera Rossetto, "Displaying Relational Memory: Notes on Museums and Heritage Centres of the Libyan Jewish Community," *Memory and Ethnicity: Ethnic Museums in Israel and the Diaspora* (Newcastle: Cambridge Scholars, 2013), 77–95.

38. Sucary, *Benghazi*, 37.

39. Sucary, *Benghazi*, 80.

40. Sucary, *Benghazi*, 299. See Batya Shimony, "Lihiyot mizrahi, laga'at ba-shoah, lihiyot Isra'eli" [Being a Mizrahi Jew, an Israeli and touching the

Holocaust], *Ha-Oketz*, April 2014, http://www.haokets.org/2014/04/28/תויהל-ילארשי-תויהל-האושב-תעגל-יחרזמ-/.

41. See Katherine E. Fleming, "The Stereotyped 'Greek Jew' from Auschwitz-Birkenau to Israeli Popular Culture," *Journal of Modern Greek Studies*, no. 25 (2007): 17–40.

42. Jennifer Lipman, "The Unspoken Holocaust: Interview with Yossi Sucary," *Jewish Chronicle*, July 7, 2016, https://www.thejc.com/lifestyle/features/the-unspoken-holocaust-1.60277. Oral evidence suggests that, in those years, many Israelis of Libyan origin—both schoolchildren and adults—shared similar experiences.

43. I refer particularly to Shalom-Chetrit, *Intra-Jewish Conflict*, 1–15.

44. Sucary, *Benghazi*, 235.

45. Sucary, *Benghazi*, 186.

46. Sucary, *Benghazi*, 283.

47. Sucary, *Benghazi*, 301.

48. "La comunità tripolina in Israele," Levluv/Germogli, Nissan 5771/April 2011, 30, YBZ VI 330.3.

49. Harvey Goldberg, "The Notion of 'Libyan Jewry' and Its Cultural-Historical Complexity," in *La bienvenue et l'adieu: Migrants juifs et musulmans au Maghreb (XVe–XXe siècle)*, ed. Frédéric Abécassis, Karima Dirèche, and Rita Aouad (Casablanca: La Croisée des Chemins, 2012), 2:121–34.

50. Yablonka, *Les Juifs d'Orient*, 98.

51. Yablonka, *Les Juifs d'Orient*, 270.

52. Batya Shimony, "Holocaust Envy: Globalization of the Holocaust in the Israeli Discourse," in *Marking Evil*, ed. Amos Goldberg and Haim Hazan (New York: Berghahn, 2015), 311.

53. See Goldberg, "Notion of 'Libyan Jewry'"; Jacques Roumani, David Meghnagi, and Judith Roumani, eds., *Jewish Libya: Memory and Identity in Text and Image* (Syracuse, NY: Syracuse University Press, 2018).

54. See Idith Zertal, *Israel's Holocaust and the Politics of Nationhood* (Cambridge: Cambridge University Press, 2005). On the Holocaust as *the* global memorial template, see Patrizia Violi, *Paesaggi della memoria: Il trauma, lo spazio, la storia* (Milan: Bompiani, 2014), esp. 113–14.

55. Huyssen, *Present Pasts*, 14. See also Stein and Boum, eds., *Holocaust and North Africa*.

56. Régine Azria, cited in Tartakowsky, *Les Juifs*, 184.

57. Alessandra Di Castro (director of the Jewish Museum of Rome), email message to author, January 22, 2016; Olga Melasecchi (curator of the Jewish Museum of Rome), email message to author, January 24, 2016; Pamela Priori (public affairs assistant, Embassy of the State of Israel in Rome), telephone interview by the author, January 20, 2016.

58. "The Jewish Refugees from Arab Countries," *Israeli Ministry of Foreign Affairs*, November 30, 2014, http://mfa.gov.il/MFA/AboutIsrael/Spotlight/Pages/The-Jewish-Refugees-from-Arab-Countries.aspx.

59. See, for example, Charles S. Liebman and Eliezer Don-Yihya, *Civil Religion in Israel: Traditional Judaism and Political Culture in the Jewish State* (Berkeley: University of California Press, 1983); Don Handelmann and Elihu Katz, "State Ceremonies of Israel: Remembrance Day and Independence Day," in *Israeli Judaism: The Sociology of Religion in Israel*, ed. Shlomo Deshen, Charles S. Liebman, and Moshe Shokeid (New Brunswick: Transaction, 1995), 75–86.

60. Emanuela Trevisan Semi, "The 'Symbolic Homeland' in the Jewish Italian Diaspora: The Celebration of Civil Israeli Religion in Italy," *Journal of Modern Jewish Studies* 5, no. 1 (2006): 95–108.

61. Levana Zamir (president of the *Hitahdut 'oley-Mitzrayim be-Israel* [Union of Egyptian migrants in Israel]), interview by the author, Tel Aviv, December 12, 2015.

62. Shimon Ohayon, cited in Haviv Rettig Gur, "Jewish 'Refugee' Day Proposal Advances in Knesset," *Times of Israel*, February 4, 2014, http://www.timesofisrael.com/jewish-refugee-day-proposal-advances-in-knesset/.

63. Article 1, section 'Alef, "Hoq yom le-tziyun ha-yetziah ve-ha-gerush shel ha-yehudim me-'artzot 'arav u-me-'Iran, Hatasha'd-2014," *Reshumot—Sefer ha-hoqim* [Registers—Book of laws], Heh Tammuz 5776/3 July 2014, 585.

64. Handelmann and Katz, "State Ceremonies."

65. Lucette Valensi, "From Sacred History to Historical Memory and Back: The Jewish Past," *History and Anthropology* 2, no. 2 (1986): 283–305.

66. Lyn Julius, "Why Jewish Refugees Must Be Remembered on 30 November," *Huffington Post*, November 23, 2015, http://www.huffingtonpost.com/lyn-julius/why-jewish-refugees-must-_b_8622742.html.

67. Nancy Reynolds, *A City Consumed: Urban Commerce, the Cairo Fire, and the Politics of Decolonization in Egypt* (Stanford, CA: Stanford University Press, 2012).

68. Rachel Simon, "Zionism," in *The Jews of the Middle East and North Africa in Modern Times*, ed. Reeva Spector Simon, Michael Laskier, and Sara Reguer (New York: Columbia University Press, 2002), 177, table 9.1.

69. Article 1, section 'Alef, paragraph 3, "Hoq yom," 585.

70. Raphael Patai, "The Jewish 'Refugees' in the Middle East," *Journal of International Affairs* 7, no. 1 (1953): 51.

71. "Text of the 1951 Geneva Convention Relating to the Status of Refugees," UNHCR, 14, http://www.unhcr.org/protect/PROTECTION/3b66c2aa10.pdf. See also Susan M. Akram, "Myths and Realities of the Palestinian Refugee Problem: Reframing the Right of Return," in *International Law and the Israeli-Palestinian Conflict: A Rights-Based Approach to Middle East Peace*, ed. Susan M.

Akram, Michael Dumper, Michael Lynk, and Iain Scobbie (London: Routledge, 2011), 33–34.

72. Shepard, *Invention*, 170–73.

73. Shenhav, *Arab Jews*, 142–46. See also Baussant, "Travail de la mémoire," esp. 130–36; Carole Basri, "The Jewish Refugees from Arab Countries: An Examination of Legal Rights—a Case Study of Human Rights Violations of Iraqi Jews," *Fordham International Law Journal* 26, no. 3 (2002): 656–720.

74. "JIMENA's Mission and History," JIMENA: Jews Indigenous to the Middle East and North Africa, accessed January 4, 2022, http://www.jimena.org/about-jimena/mission-statement-and-organizational-history/.

75. "JJAC Mission Statement," JJAC: Justice for Jews from Arab Countries, accessed January 4, 2022, http://www.justiceforjews.com/mission.html. See Shayna Zamkanei, "Justice for Jews from Arab Countries and the Rebranding of the Jewish Refugee," *International Journal of Middle East Studies* 48, no. 3 (2016): 511–30.

76. "Pe'ilut memshelet-Israel" [The activity of the Israeli government], in *Higadta le-binkha: Moreshet qehillot Yahadut-'arav ve-'Iran* [And you shall tell your children: The heritage of the Jewish communities of the Arab lands and Iran] (Jerusalem: Minister for Senior Citizens, n.d.), 17.

77. Yisrael Yeshayahu, cited in Shenhav, *Arab Jews*, 158.

78. Ofer Aderet, "Israel to Compensate Iraqi, Moroccan, Algerian Jews for Holocaust-Era Persecution," *Ha-'Aretz*, December 4, 2015, http://www.haaretz.com/israel-news/.premium-1.690077.

79. Ronit Matalon, *Qol tze'adenu* [The sound of our steps] (Tel Aviv: Am Oved, 2008), 27–28.

80. From the letter of an unnamed Moroccan migrant, cited in Bryan K. Roby, *The Mizrahi Era of Rebellion: Israel's Forgotten Civil Rights Struggle, 1948–1966* (Syracuse, NY: Syracuse University Press, 2015), 148.

81. Abdelmalek Sayad, *La double absence: des illusions de l'émigré aux souffrances de l'immigré* (Paris: Seuil, 1999). See also Shayna Zamkanei, "The Politics of Defining Jews from Arab Countries," *Israel Studies* 21, no. 2 (2016): 1–26.

82. Eddy Cohen, "Jewish Nakba Can No Longer Be Ignored," *Yediot 'Aharonot*, November 30, 2015, http://www.ynetnews.com/articles/0,7340, L-4732793,00.html.

83. Ofer Aderet, "Jews from Arab Lands: Israel Commemorates Flight of 850,000 Jews from Arab, Muslim Countries," *Ha-'Aretz*, November 30, 2015, http://www.haaretz.com/israel-news/.premium-1.689085.

84. Mati Tuchfeld, "For First Time, Israel to Honor Jews Expelled from Arab States," *Israel Ha-yom*, November 13, 2015, http://www.israelhayom.com/site/newsletter_article.php?id=29673.

85. Ilanit Chernick, "Global Kaddish Planned for Neglected Exile of North African Jewry," *Jerusalem Post*, November 29, 2019, https://www.jpost.com/israel-news/global-kaddish-planned-for-neglected-exile-of-arab-north-african-jewry-609281.

86. *Eretz Tzion ve-Yerushalayim* [Land of Israel and Jerusalem], accessed January 4, 2022, https://www.30november2020.com/en.

87. Orly Harari, "'Ahavah, shutafut-goral ve-solidariyut hevratit: yom ha-yetziah ve-ha-gerush shel yehudei-'artzot 'Arav ve-'Iran" [Love, a shared destiny and social solidarity: The day marking the exit and expulsion of the Jews from arab lands and Iran], *'Arutz 7*, November 30, 2021, accessed January 4, 2022, https://www.inn.co.il/news/533299.

88. Shenhav, *Arab Jews*, 200.

89. See Michael Rothberg, *Multidirectional Memory: Remembering the Holocaust in the Age of Decolonization* (Stanford, CA: Stanford University Press, 2009), 18.

90. See Jeffrey C. Blutinger, "Yad Vashem and the State of Holocaust Education in Israeli Schools in the 1960s," *Jewish Social Studies* 21, no. 1 (2015): 123–50.

91. "About Us," *Kedem Forum for Israeli Public Diplomacy*, accessed April 30, 2021, http://www.forumkedem.org.il/english/about-us. My analysis is based on the brochures and website of the Kedem Forum, as well as on my own participant observation during a one-day workshop held in Tel Aviv in December 2015, in which members of the forum and about fifty Israeli high school teachers participated.

92. Eddy Cohen and Golan Barhum, *Hoveret 'iyun ve-hadrakhah la-moreh: Ha-plitim ha-yehudim me-'artzot 'Arav* [Study booklet for teachers: The Jewish refugees from the Arab lands] (Tel Aviv: no publisher, 2015).

93. Adi Hashmonay, "Hatza'at hoq: hakarah la-nitzolim u-la-nirtzahim be-pogrom ha-Farhud" [Law proposal: Recognize the survivors and victims of the Farhud pogrom], *Yisrael ha-yom*, December 7, 2020, https://www.israelhayom.co.il/article/827157. Earlier than that, in 2015, June 1 had been declared International Farhud Day with a public commemoration held at an event streamed by the United Nations and supported by the Israeli Ministry of Foreign Affairs. See https://mfa.gov.il/MFA/AboutIsrael/History/Pages/June-1-declared-International-Farhud-Day-Jun-2015.aspx.

94. Cohen and Barhum, *Hoveret 'iyun*. On Israeli ethnic museums and heritage centers, see Emanuela Trevisan Semi, Dario Miccoli, and Tudor Parfitt, eds., *Memory and Ethnicity: Ethnic Museums in Israel and the Diaspora* (Newcastle: Cambridge Scholars, 2013).

95. Yael Zerubavel, *Recovered Roots: Collective Memory and the Making of Israeli National Tradition* (Chicago: University of Chicago Press, 1995), esp. 81–82.

96. Zertal, *Israel's Holocaust*. I discussed this topic in relation to the Egyptian Jewish case in Miccoli, *Histories*, 157–67.

97. Cohen and Barhum, *Hoveret 'iyun*.

98. See Adam Eilath, "Mizrahi Remembrance Month Student Curriculum Framework," *JIMENA*, accessed January 4, 2022, http://www.jimena.org/wp-content/uploads/2015/11/MRM-Student-Curriculum-Framework.pdf.

99. Blutinger, "Yad Vashem," 139.

100. Attendee of the Eighth World Congress of Jews from Egypt, conversation with the author, Tiberias, May 8–9, 2017.

101. See "Latzet mi-bli lahazor" [Leaving, never to return], *MUZA—Muze'on Eretz Israel*, 2019, https://www.eretzmuseum.org.il/731.

102. Rothberg, *Multidirectional Memory*. On the pedagogical implications of teaching and comparing the Holocaust, see Antonio Brusa, "La terra di nessuno fra storia, memoria e insegnamento della storia. Didattica e non-didattica della Shoah," in *Pop Shoah? Immaginari del genocidio ebraico*, ed. Francesca R. Recchia Luciani and Claudio Vercelli (Genoa: Il melangolo, 2016), 30–45.

103. Hen Mazzig, "Why Does Holocaust Remembrance Day Ignore Middle Eastern Jews?," *Times of Israel*, May 2, 2019, https://blogs.timesofisrael.com/why-does-holocaust-remembrance-day-ignore-middle-eastern-jews/.

104. Cohen, "Neo-Lachrymose Conception," 60.

105. See Eliezer Ben-Rafael and Yochanan Peres, *Is Israel One? Religion, Nationalism, and Multiculturalism Confounded* (Leiden: Brill, 2005); Eliezer Ben-Rafael, *The Emergence of Ethnicity: Cultural Groups and Social Conflict in Israel* (London: Greenwood, 1982); Alex Weingrod, ed., *Studies in Israeli Ethnicity: After the Ingathering* (New York: Gordon and Breach Science, 1985).

106. Gur Alroey, *An Unpromising Land: Jewish Migration to Palestine in the Early Twentieth Century* (Stanford, CA: Stanford University Press, 2014), 1–32.

107. Xenia Svetlova (member of the Israeli Parliament), interview by the author and Michèle Baussant, Jerusalem, June 13, 2016.

108. See Erez Biton, "Dvar Yoshev-rosh" [Foreword of the president], in *Duah va'adat Biton le-he'atzemet moreshet yahadut-Sfarad ve-ha-mizrah be-ma'arehet ha-hinukh* [Proceedings of the Biton Commission for deepening the heritage of the Sephardic and Eastern Jewries in the educational system] (Jerusalem: Ministry of Education, 2016), 5. On the *Merkaz le-shiluv moreshet yahadut ha-mizrah*, see Avi Picard, "Like a Phoenix: The Renaissance of Sephardic/Mizrahi Identity in Israel in the 1970s and 1980s," *Israel Studies* 22, no. 2 (2017): 6–8; Yaron Tsur, "Ha-historiografiah ha-'israelit ve-ha-be'aiah ha-'edatit" [The Israeli historiography and the ethnic problem], *Pe'amim*, no. 94–95 (2003): 1–47. For the first assessment of the results of the *Va'adat Biton* two years after the publication of its recommendations, see Ruti Suarez, "'Avru shnatayim: mi zokher 'et-va'adat Biton?" [Two years have passed: Who remembers the Biton

Commission?], *Ha-maqom*, July 3, 2018, https://www.ha-makom.co.il/post/ruti-bitton-report.

109. Juliette Glasser, interview, *Sephardi Voices*, 2016, accessed January 4, 2022, https://vimeo.com/155175561.

110. David Cohen, interview, *Sephardi Voices*, 2016, accessed January 4, 2022, https://vimeo.com/156927565.

111. Moshe Labi, interview, *Sephardi Voices*, 2016, accessed January 4, 2022, https://vimeo.com/155176203.

112. See Emanuela Trevisan Semi, "Entre lieux de mémoire et lieux de l'oubli au Maroc: quelle politique et quels acteurs pour la mémoire juive?," *Ethnologies* 39, no. 2 (2017): 69–80. On the ambivalence of the Moroccan state toward the Moroccan Jewish heritage, see Aomar Boum, "The Plastic Eye: The Politics for Jewish Representation in Moroccan Museums," *Ethnos* 75, no. 1 (2010): 49–77.

113. Jonathan Shamir, "Moroccan Schools Teach Jewish History in Groundbreaking First," *Ha-'Aretz*, December 10, 2020, https://www.haaretz.com/middle-east-news/.premium-moroccan-schools-teach-jewish-history-in-groundbreaking-first-1.9360358.

114. Consider the original studies by Mandel, *Muslims and Jews*; Katz, *Burdens*; Arkin, *Rhinestones*. Also consider the research that concentrated on the void that the departure of Jews left in the Arab Muslim world, particularly in Morocco: Boum, *Memories of Absence*; Emanuela Trevisan Semi and Hanane Sekkat-Hatimi, *Mémoire et représentations des Juifs au Maroc: les voisins absents de Meknès* (Paris: Publisud, 2011).

115. Dan Stone, "On Neighbours and Those Knocking at the Door: Holocaust Memory and Europe's Refugee Crisis," *Patterns of Prejudices* 52, no. 2–3 (2018): 231–43.

116. See Lucy Bond and Jessica Rapson, eds., *The Transcultural Turn: Interrogating Memory between and beyond Borders* (Berlin: De Gruyter, 2014); Bo Strath, "A European Identity: To the Historical Limits of a Concept," *European Journal of Social Theory* 5, no. 4 (2002): 387–401.

117. Ulrike Meinhof and Anna Triandafyllidou, "Transcultural Europe: An Introduction to Cultural Policy in a Changing Europe," in *Transcultural Europe: Cultural Policy in a Changing Europe* ed. Ulrike Meinhof and Anna Triandafyllidou (London: Palgrave, 2006), 3–22.

118. Etienne Balibar, *We, the People of Europe? Reflections on Transnational Citizenship* (Princeton, NJ: Princeton University Press, 2003), 5, 50.

119. Balibar, "At the Borders of Europe: From Cosmopolitanism to Cosmopolitics," *Translation*, Spring 2014, 100.

120. Jonathan Chaplin, "Conclusion: Christianity and the 'Souls' of Europe," in *God and the EU: Faith in the European Project*, ed. Jonathan Chaplin and Gary Wilton (London: Routledge, 2016), 267–75. Consider also Philip Schlesinger

and François Foret, "Political Roof and Sacred Canopy? Religion and the EU Constitution," *European Journal of Social Theory* 9, no. 1 (2006): 59–81.

121. For an overview, see Klaus J. Bade, *Migration in European History* (Oxford: Blackwell, 2003), esp. 217–74. On Italy's migration history, see at least Choate, *Emigrant Nation*.

122. The estimated number of Muslims is provided by Fabrizio Ciocca, *L'Islam italiano* (Rome: Meltemi, 2019), which combined figures from the *Annuario statistico italiano 2019* (Rome: Istituto Nazionale di Statistica, 2019) and other figures elaborated in 2021 by *ISMU—Iniziative e Studi sulla Multietnicità*, accessed January 4, 2022, https://www.ismu.org/wp-content/uploads/2021/06/Lappartenenza-religiosa-degli-stranieri-residenti-in-Italia.-Prime-ipotesi-al-1°-gennaio-2021.pdf. The figures for Italian Jews are taken from Campelli, *Comunità va cercando*. See also Ugo G. Pacifici Noja and Giorgio Pacifici, *Ebreo chi? Sociologia degli ebrei italiani oggi* (Milan: Jaca Book, 2017).

123. It is still worth going back to the pioneering work by Sergio Della Pergola, *Anatomia dell'ebraismo italiano* (Rome: Carucci, 1976), esp. 55–56.

124. See the video of the ceremony: "Firenze, in Piazza della Signoria, le religioni pregano per il Coronavirus," *YouTube*, April 3, 2020, https://www.youtube.com/watch?time_continue=432&v=Kky5-ew5Ju8&feature=emb_title.

125. See Istat, "Statistiche demografiche 2021," http://demo.istat.it/strasa2021/index.html; "Cittadini stranieri Firenze 2019," *Tuttitalia*, accessed January 4, 2022, https://www.tuttitalia.it/toscana/77-firenze/statistiche/cittadini-stranieri-2019/. The number of Muslims living in Florence is an estimation provided by the Florentine Islamic Cultural Centre.

126. Joseph Levi (former chief rabbi of the Jewish Community of Florence), interview by the author, Florence, December 9, 2016.

127. Assessorato all'Educazione del Comune di Firenze/Comunità Ebraica di Firenze/Comunità Islamica di Firenze e Toscana, *Una sinagoga, una moschea* (Florence: Tipografia Comune di Firenze, 2011).

128. Tami Eyal and Sanaa Ahmed, Donne per la Pace, interview by the author, Florence, October 5, 2016.

129. "Mission Statement," Women Wage Peace, accessed January 4, 2016, http://womenwagepeace.org.il/en/mission-statement/.

130. Eyal and Ahmed, Donne per la Pace, interview by the author.

131. Anna Bises and Bruno Montesano, "La difficoltà di emigrare: Un ebreo a Ventimiglia nel 1939 e i migranti oggi," *Hakeillah*, October 2016, 14. On the memorial entanglements between Italian Jews, migrants, and today's Italy, see Derek Duncan, "'Il clandestino è l'ebreo di oggi': Imprints of the Shoah on Migration to Italy," *Quest—Issues in Contemporary Jewish History*, no. 10 (2016), 60–88; Anna Chiara Cimoli and Stefano Pasta, "Il ciclo di vita della memoria: i profughi al Memoriale della Shoah di Milano," *Roots & Routes* 5, no. 20 (2015/2016), http://www.roots-routes.org/?p=16228.

132. Itamar Mann, cited in Moriel Ram and Haim Yacobi, "African Asylum Seekers and the Changing Politics of Memory in Israel," in *History, Memory and Migration*, ed. Olaf J. Kleist and Irial Glynn (London: Palgrave Macmillan, 2012), 154. More specifically, on the possible philosophical interplay between the *Jewish question* and the contemporary *Muslim question*, see Sara R. Farris, "From the Jewish Question to the Muslim Question: Republican Rigorism, Culturalist Differentialism and Antinomies of Enforced Emancipation," *Constellations* 21, no. 2 (2014): 296–307.

133. Amikam Nachmani, "The Past as a Yardstick: Europeans, Muslim Migrants and the Onus of European-Jewish Histories," *Israel Affairs* 22, no. 2 (2016): 318–54.

134. Emanuela Trevisan Semi, "From Judeophobia to Islamophobia in the Italian Media, with a Special Focus on the Northern League Party Media," in *Jews, Muslims, and Mass Media: Mediating the 'Other,'* ed. Yulia Egorova and Tudor Parfitt (London: Routledge, 2004), 48–54.

135. Bordes-Benayoun et al., *Perceptions et attentes*.

136. Dominique Reynié and Simone Rodan-Benzaquen, *Radiographie de l'antisémitisme en France* (Paris: Fondation pour l'innovation politique, 2020).

137. Bordes-Benayoun et al., *Perceptions et attentes*, 45, 60–62; Hakim El Karoui, *Un Islam français est possible* (Paris: Institut Montaigne, 2016), 33.

138. Gunther Jikeli, *European Muslim Antisemitism* (Bloomington: Indiana University Press, 2015), 156.

139. Mehdi Ghouirgate, Iannis Roder, and Dominique Schnapper, eds., *France: les Juifs vus par les musulmans; Entre stéréotypes et méconnaissances* (Paris: Fondation pour l'innovation politique, 2017).

140. Arkin, *Rhinestones*, 212, *passim*.

141. "Antisemitismo in Italia 2019," *Relazione annuale 2020 a cura dell'Osservatorio antisemitismo della Fondazione CDEC*, February 26, 2020, https://osservatorioantisemi-c02.kxcdn.com/wp-content/uploads/2020/03/Annuale_Antisemitismo_Giornalisti_28feb2020.pdf.

142. See Amelia H. Lyons, *The Civilizing Mission in the Metropole: Algerian Families and the French Welfare during Decolonization* (Stanford, CA: Stanford University Press, 2013); Mandel, *Muslims and Jews*.

143. "Qui sommes-nous?," *Amitié judéo-musulmane de France*, accessed January 4, 2022, https://ajmfparis1.com/qui-sommes-nous/.

144. See Thomas Dandois and Alexandra Kagan, *Un rabbin dans les cités: sur la route avec l'amitié judéo-musulmane de France*, television documentary, *ARTE*, September 26, 2015; Laetitia Saavedra, "Un rabbin dans la cité," radio interview, *France Inter*, March 15, 2015, https://www.franceinter.fr/emissions/interception/interception-15-mars-2015; Loïc de la Mornais, "Gaza, initiative pour la paix de Marek Alter," *France2*, March 19, 2009, http://www.ina.fr/video/3862679001026/gaza-initiative-pour-la-paix-de-marek-alter-video.html.

145. Catherine Coroller, "Yahoud," *Libération*, December 10, 2003, 40.
146. Katz, *Burdens*, 316–18.
147. See "Coup de Soleil: À la rencontre du Maghreb," *Coup de Soleil*, http://coupdesoleil.net/agenda-culturel/; *Parler en paix*, accessed January 4, 2022, http://www.parlerenpaix.org/.
148. Michel Serfaty, cited in Sarah Diffalah, "Dans le quartiers, la haine du Juif ne disparaîtra pas par miracle," *Le Nouvel Observateur*, January 31, 2015.
149. Similar remarks emerge from interviews conducted among Londoners of South Asian background living in the (formerly Jewish) London East End. See Samuel Everett and Ben Gidey, "Getting Away from the Noise: Jewish-Muslim Interactions and Narratives in E1/Barbès," *Francosphères* 7, no. 2 (2018): 193.
150. Albert Bivas, interview, JIMENA, https://www.youtube.com/watch?v=PZXUUJDOzUk.
151. Camille Schmoll and Giovanni Semi, "Shadow Circuits: Urban Spaces and Mobilities across the Mediterranean," *Identities* 20, no. 4 (2013): 388.
152. Gianni Diena, "Integrazione, assimilazione e comunitarismo," *Hakeillah*, March 2016, 7. See Akbar Ahmed and Edward Kessler, "Constructive Dialogue: A Muslim and Jewish Perspective on Dialogue between Islam and Judaism," in *The Routledge Handbook of Muslim-Jewish Relations*, ed. Josef Meri (London: Routledge, 2016), 253–70.
153. Levi, interview by the author.
154. Dionigi Albera, "Chemins de traverse entre les monothéismes," in *Lieux saints partagés* (Arles: MUCEM/Actes Sud, 2015), 18.
155. Michel Wieviorka, "Faut-il parler de multiculturalisme à propos de la Méditerranée?," in *Lieux saints partagés* (Arles: MUCEM/Actes Sud, 2015), 194.
156. Ivette Journo, interview by Livia Genah and Miriam Haiun, *Banca della Memoria Ebraica*, Jewish Community of Rome, March 7, 2011, https://www.youtube.com/watch?v=lHaLlhdkfgY.
157. Rossella Tercatin, "A Milano tra i rifugiati siriani. 'Il nostro nemica resta Israele,'" *Moked*, September 13, 2015, http://moked.it/blog/2015/09/13/a-milano-tra-i-rifugiati-siriani-il-nostro-nemico-resta-israele/.
158. "Famiglia siriana accolta a Milano grazie alle comunità ebraiche," *Shalom*, January 28, 2020, https://www.shalom.it/blog/news-in-italia-bc171-eliminato/famiglia-siriana-accolta-a-milano-grazie-alle-comunita-ebraiche-b723751.
159. David Gerbi, "Ebrei di Libia, facciamoci sentire," *Moked*, January 4, 2021, https://moked.it/blog/2021/01/04/ebrei-di-libia-facciamoci-sentire/. Gerbi is a psychologist and the author of the memoirs *Refugee-rifugiato: Io ebreo, libico, italiano* (2013) and *Costruttori di pace* (2003).
160. From the brochure of the performance "Guardare negli occhi," Donne per la Pace, Synagogue of Florence, September 19, 2016.

161. Emilia Salvanou, "Migration and the Shaping of Transcultural Memory at the Margins of Europe," *EuropeNow*, no. 6 (2017), http://www.europenowjournal.org/2017/04/03/migration-and-the-shaping-of-transcultural-memory-at-the-margins-of-europe/. Interesting reflections on these issues also can be found in Shaul Bassi, *Essere qualcun altro: Ebrei postmoderni e postcoloniali* (Venice: Cafoscarina, 2011), esp. 193–206.

162. Gaia Giuliani, "Afterword: The Mediterranean as a Stage; Borders, Memories, Bodies," in *Decolonising the Mediterranean: European Colonial Heritages in North Africa and the Middle East*, ed. Gabriele Proglio (Newcastle: Cambridge Scholars, 2016), 96.

163. Ann Laura Stoler, *Along the Archival Grain: Epistemic Anxieties and Colonial Common Sense* (Princeton, NJ: Princeton University Press, 2010).

164. Erll, "Travelling Memory."

CONCLUSION

Afterlives of Exile

"IF WE DO EFFECTIVELY POSSESS the capacity to experience the past in the truest sense of the word," as after all we still want to believe, "it is the feeling of nostalgia that bears the clearest sign of such experience and is likely to be the most suitable point of departure for discovering the nature of that experience."[1] These words from the historian Frank Ankersmit describe well one of the assumptions that guided me in the writing of *A Sephardi Sea*: the idea that the Jews of the southern Mediterranean shore, and their descendants, in different but interwoven ways cherish—or, in some cases, mourn—a space and time that can never return but that nonetheless still exists in their life. The investigation of their memories and heritage can therefore help us experience a lost Jewish world, understand better what its present and future look like, and—finally—assess the legacy of similar histories of displacement and migration across the Mediterranean region, in Europe and Israel. In this respect, literary production, and the autobiographical texts that I took into consideration in the first chapter, proved to be particularly valuable sources, as did the activities of North African and Egyptian Jewish migrant associations and museums, and many other—public and private—memory- and heritage-related practices detected in places as different as Paris, Florence, and Tel Aviv.

But what kind of past is rooted in an often-controversial nostalgic sentiment, and, no less important, what kind of present and future does it produce? How can the North African and Egyptian Jews long for a time perceived as traumatic and sometimes negative? How can their children and grandchildren strive for a place that most of them have never seen? An answer could be that these "ordinary exiles" have become "artists of their lives" and therefore have been able to transform their "inability to return home in both a personal tragedy and an enabling future."[2] Thus, in the case of the Jews of the M'zab—a desertic region in southern Algeria that long remained on the edge of the Algerian Jewish history and that took part only marginally in the process of Frenchification that characterized the history of this community[3]—remembering the time before the migration to France and Israel could imply continuing to write and recite *baqqashot* (lit. "supplications, liturgical prayers") that glorify the Promised Land. The *baqqashot* had the double goal of underlining their belonging to the Jewish people while, at the same time, expressing hope for the future, since "suffering can only be temporary."[4] From the perspective of 1960s Alsace, where many of them resettled, the Land of Israel and the M'zab blended together to compose a magnified longing for an imaginary *là-bas*, where the difficulties of life in the desert were forgotten in light of the hardship of the new existence in France.

On the other hand, the poet Moiz Benarroch—who was born in the Moroccan city of Tetouan in the 1960s and migrated with his family to Israel in the 1970s—writes about the postmigratory life on the basis of a complex, but not religion-oriented, mixture of diasporic and national motifs. Just like any other migrant in today's world, he owns

> a suitcase
> I always take it with me
> ... and the suitcase is full of toys
> no child ever played with
> full of memories
> of people without a past.[5]

The Algerian *baqqashot* and Benarroch's suitcase reflect the existence of a both sacred and profane Jewish imaginary that looks back to ancient times but also forward to an unknown yet possibly hopeful future that is waiting to be written. It is an imaginary based on feelings of loss that goes beyond history and its spatiotemporal reality but that is close to the heart of many: the afterlife of an exile that, eventually, becomes a permanent present for these Jewish diasporas.

As Lucette Valensi and Yosef Haim Yerushalmi noted, the Jewish people, once dispersed, did not share a history anymore and therefore had to preserve a common memory of the exile.[6] In 1948, and even previously after the rise of modern Jewish historiography in the nineteenth century, the situation certainly changed. Nevertheless, the memory of the past and of the centuries of exile still is one of the keys that allows one to grasp the *shibboleth* of Sephardi and *Mizrahi* Jewishness in and beyond the Mediterranean. Despite the religious, emotional, and national ties to *Eretz Israel*, the colonial influence of countries like France or Italy and the attachments Jews have developed for them in the course of years, the act of leaving North Africa and Egypt for these three countries in most cases did not result in a homecoming or repatriation, as it has sometimes been reimagined and understood. As a consequence of the national contexts and ideologies that these Jewish migrants had to confront, it was conceived more as an exile, or better to say an *exilic homecoming* that—for many—has continued up to today: "We left with a suitcase," recalls the president of the Israeli-based Algerian Jewish heritage association Moriel, "and now we cannot go back. *C'est fini*.... It was a wonderful land, fertile soil... the streets, the school, the *lycée*. In Algeria everything was better."[7] "When we left, it felt like mourning," adds a Tunisian Jewish woman interviewed for the 2016 television documentary *Tunisie: Une mémoire juive*.[8] An ancient Jewish world that existed for centuries in places like Tangiers and Cairo, even after changing profoundly during late Ottoman and colonial times and surviving more or less up to the mid-twentieth century, was lost forever. That said, this book demonstrates that, from the perspective of the new homelands where the North African and Middle Eastern Jews are living, there is still a possibility—if not to resurrect this Mediterranean world, which in any case should never be idealized or looked at only through the lens of nostalgia—at least to imagine it in a way that would allow Jews, Arabs, and others to all have a place and live together.

This new Mediterranean will be different from the one in which they lived and that many like to remember. In fact, its geographic and imaginative boundaries have changed. To retrieve the lost Sephardi worlds that once thrived in cities like Casablanca, Tunis, Cairo, and Benghazi, today we need to search for them in places as different as the suburbs of Paris, in Tel Aviv and Ashdod, Florence, Milan, Marseille, or New York. However, the Jewish mnemonic and identity reference to exile still appears to be central, even more so considering that the Sephardi geography has shifted throughout the centuries—since the expulsion from the Iberian Peninsula in the fifteenth century. The Jewish migrations from the Arab world here lose much of their alleged exceptionality and become part of a longer history of mobility and displacement.[9] If the Sephardi diasporic consciousness was born—as some scholars contend—after the *gerush* from Spain, the contemporary Sephardi and *Mizrahi* Jewish identities then would be the result of the post-1948 and postcolonial migrations to Israel, Europe, and other countries.[10]

These migrations determined new—and often more tense—intercommunal and interreligious relations between Jews and (Muslim) Arabs, North Africans and Europeans. They also led to the birth of Jewish identities and diasporic communities that, as we have seen, do not always correspond to those that existed before the 1950s and 1960s. In many cases, the arrival of the Jews from the southern Mediterranean shore provoked profound changes in the country of immigration, as regards Jewish demography and society: think of the consequences of the migrations for the primarily Ashkenazi Israel of the 1950s, or consider the impact of the arrival of hundreds of thousands of Algerian, Moroccan, Egyptian, and Tunisian Jews in post-Holocaust France. These Jewish migrations, either to Israel or to elsewhere, marked the end of diasporas—which in some cases dated back hundreds or even thousands of years and which in others were more recent constructs—only to create new diasporas both inside and outside the Mediterranean region. Out of the original context, the North African and Middle Eastern Jewish heritage and identity have survived by adapting to new ideological and cultural realities. For example, it is through the adoption of a Zionist perspective that an American-born woman in her forties now living in Israel explained to me that for her making 'aliyah was a way of "closing the circle" after centuries of diasporic life and a way to better keep record of her family's past. That said, she also admitted that sometimes she has the impression of being almost "the only one of my generation" to be interested in the Egyptian heritage of her mother's family, which nowadays is "spread around the globe."[11]

One of the main challenges that the Sephardi and *Mizrahi* diasporas are facing and that this book also tried to address is how to transmit their heritage in the future and to the younger generations, who are not always keen on knowing more about an increasingly faraway past. The internet surely is helping to preserve it in new ways, not only through the founding of an association or the publication of a memoir. That said, both the Sephardi Mediterranean recalled on a Facebook group and the one portrayed in the novel *E venne la notte* of the Libyan Victor Magiar are inevitably going to refer to a world that does not exist as such. Even though memories and postmemories of it proliferate, what is at stake is not only—and not so much—what this world looked like but why its history and memory are so frequently reimagined and evoked today. From this perspective, literary writings and even more spaces like the North African Jewish rooms in the *Mémorial de la Shoah* of Paris or the Israeli memorial day known as Jews from Arab Lands and Iran Day reveal the degree and kind of integration, or lack thereof, of these Jewries in new national contexts. Even groups like the Italian Donne per la pace and the French AJMF, while looking back to the Jewish and Arab Muslim pasts, mainly depend on contemporary societal dynamics and, from there, try to reconfigure the future relations between

Jews and Muslims at times of interethnic and interreligious tension, as well as of increased mobility and displacement.

Over the last years, thousands of migrants moved from the south to the north of the world, passing through and often dying in the Mediterranean Sea, seeking a better life and escaping terror, persecution, and poverty. Some come from countries torn by conflict, like Libya, Syria, or Yemen, or from places like Egypt, where—despite the regime change that followed the so-called Arab Spring—freedom and democracy are still lacking. Despite the great difference that exists between these migrants and the Sephardi and *Mizrahi* Jews, perhaps the history of the latter may help us decipher some of the problems that today's migrants from that same region have to face and the kinds of challenge and opportunity they represent for the countries that are asked to host and take care of them. Thus, the history of the Jews of the southern Mediterranean shore also reminds us of the unresolved ambiguities that characterize Europe and North Africa, Jews and Arabs. *We Sephardis*, one could say, paraphrasing the title of Arendt's famous essay "We Refugees," which in 1943 talked about the (European) Jewish war refugee "as 'vanguard', as 'conscious pariah' bravely leading the way towards new developments and ideas."[12]

Even if the North African and Egyptian Jewish past—and the ways in which it is remembered—does not mirror centuries of innate and perennial harmony in the region, perhaps it still signals possibilities of mutual coexistence and reciprocity: think of the friendship between the Jewish Myriam and the Muslim Nour as portrayed in Albou's movie *Le chant des mariées*, set in 1940s Tunis. Furthermore, the study of the North African and Middle Eastern Jewish experience sheds light on other paradigms of Jewish history that go beyond the Western one and that in turn dictate alternative identity and memorial options.[13] Looking back at this past and its efforts to be commemorated and relived out of its original space and time may constitute a way of "mending an injury"[14] and contribute to the composition of a more nuanced history of the Mediterranean region at large.

As *A Sephardi Sea* has tried to show, literature, the arts, and different forms of heritagization are acting as an arena where unresolved political and identity tensions can be discussed, and sometimes mitigated. In relation to this, the perpetual quest—one generation after the other—for a homeland, *from afar* and at a distance of several decades, suggests that for migrants and children of migrants like the Jews of North Africa and the Middle East, "home is a moving target, home and abroad often appear as mirror images of one another."[15] If the father of the protagonist of Boukhobza's *Pour l'amour du père* identified Tunis with today's Israel, in a similar vein Albert Bensoussan, thinking of the many

Algerian Jews now populating the streets of Netanya and Ashdod, writes that "all those faces that I meet, those of my family and friends, I recognize them, I find them again, I make them part of this landscape—in place of a depopulated Algeria."[16] The country of emigration and that of immigration, together with other places that these people have encountered during their diasporic voyage, construct a multidimensional landscape that cuts across the Mediterranean region.

What for sure seems attenuated is the connection with the country of origin not as it looked when the Jews left it—which, on the contrary, remains a crucial reference point—but as it is today. In some cases it is very difficult or impossible, for personal or political reasons, to reconnect to the physical territory of the motherland and construct there a new North African and Middle Eastern Jewish affective geography. Today's Mediterranean, perhaps more profoundly than in previous centuries, is a region of fragments and divisions that cannot be rejoined easily. That said, it is also true that not all Jewish migrants are eager to reconnect to a land that brings to the surface a sorrowful and traumatic history, and some prefer to reimagine it on the basis of their memory instead of going back to confront the actual reality. This is what occurs in the novel *Ha-roman ha-mitzri* by Orly Castel-Bloom, which tells a surreal tale of rebellious Egyptian *kibbutznikim* and Sephardi pig farmers and illustrates the extent to which "one of the most pleasant freedoms of the literary migrant [is] to be able to choose [the] parents" and reinvent a family story that best reflects the needs of the characters.[17]

Although it has not been the focus of *A Sephardi Sea*, I should mention that in recent years a number of Jewish-related heritage initiatives have emerged in places like Morocco and Egypt: think of the restoration of the *mellah* of Meknès and Marrakech, or the interest shown—at least at an official level—by the Egyptian government for the preservation of the Cairo and Alexandria synagogues. The peace agreements signed in 2020 between Israel and some Arab countries (such as the United Arab Emirates and Bahrein), and even more so the strengthening of diplomatic relations between Israel and Morocco, will probably help to change the picture in the near future. Already today, it is undeniable that the memory of the bygone days when Arabs, Jews, and others lived together in the Middle East, not always harmoniously but still in ways that seem inconceivable, is more and more often evoked in movies, documentaries, and books published in the Arab world: from the Egyptian television series *Harat al-yahud* (2015) to novels such as *The Tobacco Keeper* (2008) by the Iraqi Ali Badr and *Le dernier juif de Tamentit* (2012) by the Algerian Amin Zaoui.[18] The reasons underlying this revival—ambivalent as it might be—are multiple, but they all point to absence and loss as defining categories of the current Arab-Jewish (missed) encounter: absence from the motherland; loss of contact in the new countries of immigration with people who once were friends and neighbors; absence from a country's national conscience and—until recently—also from the mainstream Jewish historical narratives; and more generally a lack of interaction between most Jews and Arabs living in the same country.[19]

But then, can there be such a thing as the Sephardi Mediterranean? Is it still here, among us? My hope is that *A Sephardi Sea* has demonstrated that this world—rooted in a past that has been eradicated from its original setting and that is nowadays largely imagined in the shape of everyday objects, books, familiar faces, and contrasting emotions—continues to flow across the southern and northern shores of the Mediterranean Sea, and even beyond it. As long as someone continues to remember the many stories and people that populated this "liquid continent,"[20] it will be possible to follow the connections that continue to exist between and unite Europe, North Africa, and Israel, Jews and Arabs. At such a time of rising nationalism, xenophobia, and global uncertainty as the one we are living in, remembering and sometimes even longing for a vanished past asks us to be more attentive to the present and, most of all, the future of a Great Sea—*ha-yam ha-gadol*—that we continue to inhabit and traverse.

NOTES

1. Frank Ankersmit, *History and Tropology: The Rise and Fall of the Metaphor* (Berkeley: University of California Press, 1994), 196.
2. Svetlana Boym, *The Future of Nostalgia* (New York: Basic Books, 2001), 252.
3. Stein, *Saharan Jews*.
4. Freddy Raphaël, "La mémoire blessée des Juifs du M'zab," in *Communautés Juives des marges du Maghreb*, ed. Michel Abitbol (Jerusalem: Ben-Tzvi Institute, 1982), 143.
5. Moiz Benarrosh, *Bilingual Poems/Shirim du-lashonim* (Jerusalem: Moben, 2005).
6. Valensi, "From Sacred"; Yerushalmi, *Zakhor*.
7. Jean-Charles Bénichou (president of Moriel), interview by the author, Netanya, May 17, 2017.
8. Fatma Cherif, "Tunisie: une mémoire juive," *TV5Monde*, 2016, http://www.tv5monde.com/programmes/en/programme-tv-tunisie-une-memoire-juive/20135/.
9. Abravanel, "L'historicité en milieu sépharade."

10. Ray, *After Expulsion*.

11. Michelle Brocco, interview by the author, Jerusalem, May 12, 2017.

12. Cindy Horst and Odin Lysaker, "Miracles in Dark Times: Hannah Arendt and Refugees as 'Vanguard,'" *Journal of Refugee Studies*, 2019, 1–18.

13. Here I follow the approach proposed in Bashkin, *New Babylonians*, 233.

14. Pierre Assouline, *Retour à Séfarad* (Paris: Gallimard, 2018), 16.

15. Boym, *Future*, 288.

16. Albert Bensoussan, "L'Algérie Juive pour mémoire," *JudaicAlgeria*, October 20, 2015, https://www.judaicalgeria.com/pages/l-algerie-juive-pour-memoire.html.

17. Salman Rushdie, cited in Bryan Cheyette, *Diasporas of the Mind: Jewish and Postcolonial Writing and the Nightmare of History* (New Haven, CT: Yale University Press, 2013), 26.

18. On the Egyptian case, see Yaron Shemer, "From Chahine's *al-Iskandariyya . . . leh* to *Salata baladi* and *'An Yahud Masr*: Rethinking Egyptian Jews' Cosmopolitanism, Belonging and Nostalgia in Cinema," *Middle East Journal of Culture and Communication* 7, no. 3 (2014): 351–75. However, I should mention that during the month of Ramadan 2020, the Egyptian sci-fi TV series *Al-nihaya* [The end] opted for a different path, predicting the destruction of Israel and the return of the Jews to Europe, without mentioning those who came instead from the Middle East and North Africa. See: TOI Staff, "Israel Decries Egyptian TV Show Predicting Its Destruction, Breakup of the US," *Times of Israel*, April 26, 2020, https://www.timesofisrael.com/israel-decries-egyptian-tv-show-predicting-its-destruction/.

19. Constance de Gourcy, "L'institution de l'absence en Méditerranée," *Revue des mondes musulmans et de la Méditerranée*, no. 144 (2018), https://journals.openedition.org/remmm/11649.

20. Gabriel Audisio, *Jeunesse de la Méditerranée* (Paris: Gallimard, 1935), 15.

REFERENCES

Archives
Archive and Library of the Yad Ben-Tzvi Institute, Jerusalem.

Newspapers and periodicals
Bney Ha-Ye'or—Hitahdut 'oley-Mitzrayim be-Israel.
Goshen—'Alon yahadut-Mitzrayim/Bulletin des Juifs d'Egypte en Israël.
Levluv/Germogli—Organizzazione mondiale Ebrei di Libia.
Morial—Mémoires et Traditions des Juifs d'Algérie.
Yetziat-Mitzrayim shelanu—Ktav-'et le-moreshet yahadut-Mitzrayim.

Interviews
Aharoni, Ada, writer and researcher, Haifa, May 26, 2014.
Bénichou, Jean-Charles, president of Moriel—Moreshet yehudei 'Algeriah, Netanya, May 17, 2017.
Brocco, Michelle, heritage activist, Jerusalem, May 12, 2017.
Carsiente, Ariel, independent researcher and member of Moriel—Moreshet yehudei 'Algeriah, Jerusalem, June 17, 2016.
Chekroun Cohen, Ruth, webmaster of the website *Yahadut Algeria* and member of Moriel—Moreshet yehudei 'Algeriah, telephone interview, July 19, 2016.
Cohen, André, secretary of the Association pour la sauvegarde du patrimoine culturel des Juifs d'Egypte, telephone interview, November 19, 2012.
Di Castro, Alessandra, director of the Jewish Museum of Rome, email interview, January 22, 2016.
Eyal, Tami, and Sanaa Ahmed, Donne per la Pace, Florence, October 5, 2016.
Levi, Joseph, chief rabbi of the Jewish Community of Florence, Florence, December 9, 2016.

Melasecchi, Olga, curator of the Jewish Museum of Rome, email interview, January 24, 2016.
Nebot, Didier, president of Morial—Mémoires et Traditions des Juifs d'Algérie, Paris, March 23, 2016.
Priori, Pamela, public affairs assistant for the Embassy of the State of Israel in Rome, telephone interview, January 20, 2016.
Staff of the Libyan Jewish Heritage Centre, interview with Michèle Baussant, Or Yehudah, May 24, 2018.
Svetlova, Xenia, member of the Israeli Parliament, interview with Michèle Baussant, Jerusalem, June 13, 2016.
Zamir, Levana, president of the Hitahdut 'oley-Mitzrayim be-Israel, Tel Aviv, December 12, 2015.

Movies and documentaries

Albou, Karin. *Le chant des mariées*, 2008.
Cherif, Fatma. *Tunisie: une mémoire juive*, 2016.
Dandois, Thomas, and Alexandra Kagan. *Un rabbin dans les cités: sur la route avec l'amitié judéo-musulmane de France*, 2015.
Qarmel, Marco. *She'elah shel zman* [A question of time], 2005.

Websites

Amitié Judéo-Musulmane de France, http://rouen.deciplex.com/alexandra.
AMUSSEF—Les Amis du Musée du monde sépharade, https://amussef.org.
Association pour la sauvegarde du patrimoine culturel des Juifs d'Egypte, http://aspcje.free.fr.
Banca della Memoria Ebraica, http://www.memoriebraiche.it.
Dafina, http://www.dafina.net.
EFJA (Association Nationale Exode des Français Juifs d'Algérie), http://www.efja.org.
JIMENA (Jews Indigenous to the Middle East and North Africa), http://www.jimena.org.
JJAC (Justice for Jews from Arab Countries), http://justiceforjews.com.
Kedem Forum for Israeli Public Diplomacy, http://www.forumkedem.org.il.
Les enfants des Juifs d'Alexandrie et d'Egypte, https://www.facebook.com/groups/176948023247.
Mémorial de la Shoah, http://www.memorialdelashoah.org.
Morial, http://www.morial.fr.
Musée d'Art et d'Histoire du Judaïsme, https://www.mahj.org.
Museo Ebraico di Roma, https://www.museoebraico.roma.it.
Sephardi Voices, http://sephardivoices.com.

Books, articles, and papers

Abitbol, Michel. "La mémoire occultée et retrouvée: Juifs d'Orient et de Méditerranée en Israel." In *Milieux et mémoire*, edited by Frank Alvarez-Péreyre, 41–49. Jerusalem: CRFJ, 1993.

———. *Les Juifs d'Afrique du Nord sous Vichy*. Paris: Riveneuve, 2008.

Abramovich, Dvir. "Conjuring Egypt in Israeli Literature: Yitzhak Gormezano Goren's *Blanche*." *Australian Journal of Jewish Studies*, no. 22 (2008): 5–25.

Abravanel, Nicole. "L'historicité en milieu sépharade ou le primat de la spatialité." *Vingtième siècle* 117, no. 1 (2013): 183–97.

Abulafia, David. *The Great Sea: A Human History of the Mediterranean*. Oxford: Oxford University Press, 2011.

Aciman, André. *Out of Egypt*. New York: Picador, 1994.

Aderet, Ofer. "Israel to Compensate Iraqi, Moroccan, Algerian Jews for Holocaust-Era Persecution." *Ha-'Aretz*, December 4, 2015. http://www.haaretz.com/israel-news/.premium-1.690077.

———. "Jews of Arab Lands: Israel Commemorates Flight of 850,000 Jews from Arab, Muslim Countries." *Ha-'Aretz*, November 30, 2015. http://www.haaretz.com/israel-news/.premium-1.689085.

Admon, Thelma. "'Ha-roman ha-mitzri': 'otobiografiah le-lo' sentimentaliyut u-le-lo' patos" ["The Egyptian novel": An autobiography without sentimentalism and pathos]. *Ma'ariv*, January 22, 2015. http://www.maariv.co.il/culture/literature/Article-460728.

Agnon, Shmuel Yosef. *Tehillah*. Tel Aviv: Shocken, 1977.

Aharoni, Ada et Alii. *'Idan ha-zahav shel-Yehudei-Mitzrayim: 'Aqirah ve-tqumah be-'Israel* [The golden age of Jews from Egypt: Uprooting and revival in Israel]. Holon: Orion, 2014.

Ahmed, Akbar, and Edward Kessler. "Constructive Dialogue: A Muslim and Jewish Perspective on Dialogue between Islam and Judaism." In *The Routledge Handbook of Muslim-Jewish Relations*, edited by Josef Meri, 253–70. London: Routledge, 2016.

Akram, Susan M. "Myths and Realities of the Palestinian Refugee Problem: Reframing the Right of Return." In *International Law and the Israeli-Palestinian Conflict: A Rights-Based Approach to Middle East Peace*, edited by Susan M. Akram, Michael Dumper, Michael Lynk, and Iain Scobbie, 183–98. London: Routledge, 2011.

Albera, Dionigi. "Chemins de traverse entre les monothéismes." In *Lieux saints partagés*, 10–30. Arles: MUCEM/Actes Sud, 2015.

Aldrich, Robert. *Vestiges of Colonial Empire in France*. London: Palgrave, 2005.

Alhadeff, Gini. *The Sun at Midday: Tales of a Mediterranean Family*. New York: Anchor Books, 1997.

Aliberti, Davide. *Sefarad: una comunidad imaginada (1924–2015)*. Madrid: Marcial Pons, 2018.
Allagui, Abdelkrim. *Juifs et musulmans en Tunisie des origines à nos jours*. Paris: Tallandier, 2016.
Allociné. "Le chant des mariées." http://www.allocine.fr/film/fichefilm-131759/secrets-tournage/.
Allouche-Benayoun, Joëlle. "Les Juifs d'Algérie: du dhimmi au citoyen français." In *Les Juifs d'Algérie, une histoire de ruptures*, edited by Joëlle Allouche-Benayoun and Geneviève Dermenjian, 27–42. Aix-en-Provence: Presses Universitaires de Provence, 2015.
Allouche-Benayoun, Joëlle, and Doris Bensimon, eds. *Juifs d'Algérie, hier et aujourd'hui: Mémoires et identités*. Toulouse: Privat, 1989.
Alroey, Gur. *An Unpromising Land: Jewish Migration to Palestine in the Early Twentieth Century*. Stanford, CA: Stanford University Press, 2014.
Angel, Mark. *The Jews of Rhodes: The History of a Sephardic Community*. New York: Sepher Hermon, 1978.
Ankersmit, Frank. *History and Tropology: The Rise and Fall of the Metaphor*. Berkeley: University of California Press, 1994.
Arendt, Hannah. *The Jewish Writings*. New York: Shocken, 2008.
Arkin, Kimberley. *Rhinestones, Religion, and the Republic: Fashioning Jewishness in France*. Stanford, CA: Stanford University Press, 2014.
Assan, Valérie, and Yolande Cohen, eds. "Circulations and migrations des Juifs du Maghreb en France, de la veille de la Première Guerre Mondiale aux années 1960." Special issue, *Archives Juives* 53, no. 1 (2020).
Assessorato all'Educazione del Comune di Firenze/Comunità Ebraica di Firenze/Comunità Islamica di Firenze e Toscana. *Una sinagoga, una moschea*. Florence: Tipografia Comune di Firenze, 2011.
Assouline, Pierre. *Retour à Séfarad*. Paris: Gallimard, 2018.
Audenino, Patrizia, ed. *Fuggitivi e rimpatriati: L'Italia dei profughi tra guerra e decolonizzazione*. Viterbo: Archivio Storico dell'emigrazione italiana, 2018.
———. *La casa perduta: La memoria dei profughi nell'Europa del Novecento*. Rome: Carocci, 2015.
Audisio, Gabriel. *Jeunesse de la Méditerranée*. Paris: Gallimard, 1935.
Augé, Marc. *Les formes de l'oubli*. Paris: Payot, 1998.
Bade, Klaus J. *Migration in European History*. Oxford: Blackwell, 2003.
Bahloul, Joëlle. *La maison de mémoire*. Paris: Metailié, 1992.
———. *Le culte de la table dressée: rites et traditions de la table juive algérienne*. Paris: Metailié, 1983.
Balibar, Etienne. "At the Borders of Europe: From Cosmopolitanism to Cosmopolitics." *Translation*, Spring 2014, 83–103.
———. *We, the People of Europe? Reflections on Transnational Citizenship*. Princeton, NJ: Princeton University Press, 2003.

Ballas, Shimon. "Iya." In *Keys to the Garden: New Israeli Writing*, edited by Ammiel Alcalay, 69–99. San Francisco: City Lights Books, 1996.

Baratieri, Daniela. *Memories and Silences Haunted by Fascism: Italian Colonialism MCMXXX–MCMLX*. Bern: Peter Lang, 2010.

Barile, Laura. *Il resto manca: Storie mediterranee*. Turin: Aragno, 2003.

Bashkin, Orit. *New Babylonians: A History of Jews in Modern Iraq*. Stanford, CA: Stanford University Press, 2012.

Basri, Carole. "The Jewish Refugees from Arab Countries: An Examination of Legal Rights—a Case Study of Human Rights Violations of Iraqi Jews." *Fordham International Law Journal* 26, no. 3 (2002): 656–720.

Bassi, Shaul. *Essere qualcun altro: ebrei postmoderni e postcoloniali*. Venice: Cafoscarina, 2011.

Baussant, Michèle. "Heritage and Memory: The Example of an Egyptian Jewish Association." *International Social Science Journal*, no. 203–4 (2011): 45–56.

———. *Pieds-noirs: mémoires d'exil*. Paris: Stock, 2002.

———. "Travail de la mémoire et usage public du passé: l'exemple des Juifs d'Egypte." In *Mémoire des migrations, temps de l'histoire*, edited by Marianne Amar, Hélène Bertheleu, and Laure Teulières, 123–38. Tours: Presses Universitaires François Rabelais, 2015.

———. "'Who Gave You the Right to Abandon Your Prophets?' Jewish Sites of Ruins and Memory in Egypt." *Quest—Issues in Contemporary Jewish History*, no. 16 (2019): 45–71.

Bédard, Jean-Luc. "Mouvances identitaires et restructuration de soi et des autres parmi des Judéo-marocains à Montréal." In *Identités sépharades et modernité*, edited by Jean-Claude Lasry, Joseph Lévy, and Yolande Cohen, 175–90. Levis: Les Presses de l'Université Laval, 2007.

Behar, Moshe. "What's in a Name? Socio-terminological Formations and the Case for Arabised Jews." *Social Identities* 15, no. 6 (2009): 747–71.

Beinin, Joel. *The Dispersion of Egyptian Jewry: Culture, Politics and the Formation of a Modern Diaspora*. Berkeley: University of California Press, 1998.

Bellentani, Federico, and Mario Panico. "The Meanings of Monuments and Memorials: A Semiotic Approach." *Punctum* 2, no. 1 (2016): 28–46.

Ben-Ari, Eyal. "Saint's Sanctuaries in Israeli Development Towns: On a Mechanism of Urban Transformation." *Urban Anthropology* 16, no. 2 (1987): 243–72.

Ben-Ari, Eyal, and Yoram Bilu. "Modernity and Charisma in Contemporary Israel: The Case of Baba Sali and Baba Baruch." *Israel Affairs* 1, no. 3 (1995): 224–36.

Benarrosh, Moiz. *Bilingual Poems/Shirim du-lashonim*. Jerusalem: Moben, 2005.

Benbassa, Esther. Preface to *Itinéraires sépharades: Complexité et diversité des identités*, edited by Esther Benbassa. Paris: PUPS, 2010.

Benbassa, Esther, and Aron Rodrigue. *Sephardi Jewry: A History of the Judeo-Spanish Communities 14th–20th Centuries*. Berkeley: University of California Press, 2000.

Ben-Rafael, Eliezer. *The Emergence of Ethnicity: Cultural Groups and Social Conflict in Israel*. London: Greenwood, 1982.
Ben-Rafael, Eliezer, and Miriam Ben-Rafael. *Sociologie et sociolinguistique des francophonies israéliennes*. Bern: Peter Lang, 2013.
Ben-Rafael, Eliezer, and Yochanan Peres. *Is Israel One? Religion, Nationalism, and Multiculturalism Confounded*. Leiden: Brill, 2005.
Ben Simon, Daniel. *Ha-maroqa'im* [The Moroccans]. Jerusalem: Carmel, 2016.
Bensimon-Donath, Doris. *L'intégration des Juifs nord-africains en France*. Paris: Mouton, 1971.
Bensoussan, Albert. "L'Algérie Juive pour mémoire." *JudaicAlgeria*. October 20, 2015. https://www.judaicalgeria.com/pages/l-algerie-juive-pour-memoire.html.
Bensoussan, Georges. *Jews in Arab Countries: The Great Uprooting*. Bloomington: Indiana University Press, 2019.
Ben-Ur, Aviva. *Sephardi Jews in America*. New York: New York University Press, 2009.
Bernal, Victoria. "Diaspora, Cyberspace and Political Imagination: The Eritrean Diaspora Online." *Global Networks* 6, no. 2 (2006): 161–79.
Bernard, Anna. *Rhetorics of Belonging: Nation, Narration, and Israel/Palestine*. Liverpool: Liverpool University Press, 2013.
Bertrand, Romain. *Mémoires d'empire: La controverse autour du 'fait colonial.'* Broissieux: Editions du Croquant, 2006.
Bevilacqua, Piero, Andreina Clementi, and Emilio Franzina, eds. *Storia dell'emigrazione italiana*. Rome: Donzelli, 2001.
Bicchi, Federica, and Richard Gillespie, eds. *The Union for the Mediterranean*. London: Routledge, 2012.
Bin-Nun, Yigal. "La négociation de l'évacuation en masse des Juifs du Maroc." In *La fin du Judaisme en terres d'Islam*, edited by Shmuel Trigano, 303–58. Paris: Denoel, 2009.
Bises, Anna, and Bruno Montesano. "La difficoltà di emigrare: Un ebreo a Ventimiglia nel 1939 e i migranti oggi." *Hakeillah*, October 2016, 14.
Blévis, Laure. "Les avatars de la citoyenneté en Algérie coloniale ou les paradoxes d'une catégorisation." *Droit et Société* 48, no. 2 (2001): 557–81.
Blutinger, Jeffrey C. "Yad Vashem and the State of Holocaust Education in Israeli Schools in the 1960s." *Jewish Social Studies* 21, no. 1 (2015): 123–50.
Bond, Lucy, and Jessica Rapson, eds. *The Transcultural Turn: Interrogating Memory between and beyond Borders*. Berlin: De Gruyter, 2014.
Bordes-Benayoun, Chantal. "Unité et dispersion des choix identitaires des Juifs originaires du Maghreb en France contemporaine." In *La bienvenue et l'adieu: Migrants Juifs et musulmans au Maghreb, XV-XX siècle*, edited by Frédéric Abécassis, Karima Dirèche, and Rita Aouad, 23–36. Casablanca: Centre Jacques-Berque, 2012.

Bordes-Benayoun, Chantal, Dominique Schnapper, Brice Teinturier, and Etienne Mercier. *Perceptions et attentes de la population juive: le rapport à l'autre et aux minorités*. Paris: Fondation du Judaïsme Français/IPSOS, 2016.
Borschel-Dan, Amanda. "Worshipers Fete 'Very Emotional' Shabbat in Refurbished Alexandria Synagogue." *Times of Israel*, February 16, 2020. https://www.timesofisrael.com/over-180-jews-gather-in-alexandria-to-celebrate-shabbat-in-refurbished-synagogue/.
Bortolotto, Chiara. "From Objects to Processes: UNESCO's Intangible Cultural Heritage." *Journal of Museum Ethnography* 19, no. 21 (2007): 21–33.
Boukhobza, Chochana. *Pour l'amour du père*. Paris: Seuil, 1996.
———. *Un été à Jérusalem*. Paris: Balland, 1986.
Boum, Aomar. *Memories of Absence: How Muslims Remember Jews in Morocco*. Stanford, CA: Stanford University Press, 2013.
———. "The Plastic Eye: The Politics for Jewish Representation in Moroccan Museums." *Ethnos* 75, no. 1 (2010): 49–77.
Boyarin, Daniel. *A Traveling Homeland: The Babylonian Talmud as Diaspora*. Philadelphia: University of Pennsylvania Press, 2015.
Boym, Svetlana. *The Future of Nostalgia*. New York: Basic Books, 2001.
Braudel, Fernand, ed. *La Méditerranée: L'espace et l'histoire*. Paris: Flammarion, 1985.
———. *La Méditerranée et le monde méditerranéen à l'époque de Philippe II*. Paris: Armand Colin, 1949.
Bregoli, Francesca. "Hebrew Printing and Communication Networks between Livorno and North Africa, 1740–1789." In *Report of the Oxford Centre for Hebrew and Jewish Studies 2007–2008*, 51–59. Oxford: Oxford University Press, 2009.
———. *Mediterranean Enlightenment: Livornese Jews, Tuscan Culture, and Eighteenth-Century Reform*. Stanford: Stanford University Press, 2014.
Brinkerhoff, Jennifer M. *Digital Diasporas: Identity and Transnational Engagement*. Cambridge: Cambridge University Press, 2009.
Brusa, Antonio. "La terra di nessuno fra storia, memoria e insegnamento della storia. Didattica e non-didattica della Shoah." In *Pop Shoah? Immaginari del genocidio ebraico*, edited by Francesca R. Recchia Luciani and Claudio Vercelli, 30–45. Genoa: Il melangolo, 2016.
Buettner, Elizabeth. *Europe after Empire: Decolonization, Society, and Culture*. Cambridge: Cambridge University Press, 2016.
Burton, Antoinette. "Introduction: The Unfinished Business of Colonial Modernities." In *Gender, Sexuality, and Colonial Modernities*, edited by Antoinette Burton, 1–16. London: Routledge, 1999.
Cabasso, Gilbert. *A la rencontre des Juifs d'Egypte*. Paris: Nahar Misraim, 1978.
———, ed. *Juifs d'Egypte: Images et textes*. Paris: Editions su Scribe, 1984.
Cahen, Claude. "Dhimma." In *Encylopédie de l'Islam*, edited by Bernard Lewis, Charles Pellat, Joseph Schacht, and Charles E. Bosworth, 2:234–38. Leiden: Brill, 1977.

Calchi Novati, Giampaolo. "Mediterraneo e questione araba nella politica estera italiana." In *Storia dell'Italia repubblicana*, edited by Francesco Barbagallo, 2:197–263. Turin: Einaudi, 2005.

Cameron, Fiona, and Sarak Kenderdine. *Theorizing Digital Cultural Heritage: A Critical Approach*. Boston: MIT Press, 2007.

Campelli, Enzo. *Comunità va cercando ch'è sì cara ... Sociologia dell'Italia ebraica*. Milan: Franco Angeli, 2013.

Carman, John, and Marie Louise Stig Sorensen. "Heritage Studies: An Outline." In *Heritage Studies: Methods and Approaches*, edited by John Carman and Marie Louise Stig Sorensen, 11–28. London: Routledge, 2009.

Castel-Bloom, Orly. *Ha-roman ha-mitzri* [The Egyptian novel]. Tel Aviv: Hakibbutz ha-meuhad, 2015.

Catsoulis, Jeanette. "Bodies in Motion." *New York Times*, October 22, 2009. http://www.nytimes.com/2009/10/23/movies/23wedding.html.

Chambers, Iain. *Mediterranean Crossings: The Politics of an Interrupted Modernity*. Durham, NC: Duke University Press.

Chaplin, Jonathan. "Conclusion: Christianity and the 'Souls' of Europe." In *God and the EU: Faith in the European Project*, edited by Jonathan Chaplin and Gary Wilton, 267–75. London: Routledge, 2016.

Charbit, Denis. "L'historiographie du décret Crémieux: Le retour du refoulé." In *Les Juifs d'Algérie, une histoire de ruptures*, edited by Joëlle Allouche-Benayoun and Geneviève Dermenjian, 43–61. Aix-en-Provence: Presses Universitaires de Provence, 2015.

Chartier, Roger. *Au bord de la falaise: L'histoire entre certitudes et inquiétude*. Paris: Albin Michel, 1998.

Chernick, Ilanit. "Global Kaddish Planned for Neglected Exile of North African Jewry." *Jerusalem Post*, November 29, 2019. https://www.jpost.com/israel-news/global-kaddish-planned-for-neglected-exile-of-arab-north-african-jewry-609281.

Cheyette, Bryan. *Diasporas of the Mind: Jewish and Postcolonial Writing and the Nightmare of History*. New Haven, CT: Yale University Press, 2013.

Choate, Mark. *Emigrant Nation: The Making of Italy Abroad*. Cambridge, MA: Harvard University Press, 2008.

Choay, Françoise. *L'allégorie du patrimoine*. Paris: Seuil, 1992.

Cimoli, Anna Chiara, and Stefano Pasta. "Il ciclo di vita della memoria: i profughi al Memoriale della Shoah di Milano." *Roots & Routes* 5, no. 20 (2015/2016). http://www.roots-routes.org/?p=16228.

Cixous, Hélène. "The Names of Oran." In *Algeria in Others' Languages*, edited by Anne-Emmanuelle Berger, 185–86. Ithaca, NY: Cornell University Press, 2002.

Clancy-Smith, Julia. *Mediterraneans: North Africa and Europe in an Age of Migration, c. 1800–1900*. Berkeley: University of California Press, 2011.

———. "Twentieth-Century Historians and Historiography of the Middle East: Women, Gender, and Empire." In *Middle East Historiographies: Narrating the Twentieth Century*, edited by Israel Gershoni, Amy Singer, and Yusuf Hakan Erdem, 70–100. Seattle: University of Washington Press, 2006.
Cloarec, Glenn. "Eric Zemmour, 'son' Judaïsme, 'son' identité française et toutes ses polémiques." *The Times of Israel*, December 5, 2021, https://fr.timesofisrael.com/eric-zemmour-son-judaisme-son-identite-francaise-et-toutes-ses-polemiques/.
Cohen, Daniel J., and Roy Rosenzweig. *Digital History: A Guide to Gathering, Preserving, and Presenting the Past on the Web*. Philadelphia: University of Pennsylvania Press, 2003.
Cohen, Eddy. "Jewish Nakba Can No Longer Be Ignored." *Yediot 'Aharonot*, November 30, 2015. http://www.ynetnews.com/articles/0,7340,L-4732793,00.html.
Cohen, Erik H. *The Jews of France at the Turn of the Third Millennium: A Sociological and Cultural Analysis*. Ramat Gan: Rappaport Center of Bar Ilan University, 2009.
———. *The Jews of France Today: Identity and Values*. Leiden: Brill, 2011.
Cohen, Mark R. "The Neo-lachrymose Conception of Arab-Jewish History." *Tikkun* 6, no. 3 (1991): 60–64.
Cohen, Uri. *Liqro' 'et-Orly Castel-Bloom* [Reading Orly Castel-Bloom]. Tel Aviv: Ahuzat Bayit, 2011.
Cole, Juan. "Constantine before the Riots of August 1934: Civil Status, Anti-Semitism, and the Politics of Assimilation in Interwar French Algeria." *Journal of North African Studies* 17, no. 5 (2012): 839–61.
Comberiati, Daniele. "'Province minori' di un 'impero minore': Narrazioni italo-ebraiche dalla Libia e dal Dodecaneso." In *Fuori centro: Percorsi postcoloniali nella letteratura italiana*, edited by Roberto Derobertis, 95–110. Rome: Aracne, 2010.
Confino, Alon. "Collective Memory and Cultural History: Problems of Method." *American Historical Review* 102, no. 5 (1997): 1386–403.
———. "Miracles and Snow in Palestine and Israel: Tantura, a History of 1948." *Israel Studies* 17, no. 2 (2012): 25–60.
———. "The Warm Sand of the Coast of Tantura: History and Memory in Israel after 1948." *History & Memory* 27, no. 1 (2015): 43–82.
Coroller, Catherine. "Yahoud." *Libération*, December 10, 2003, 40.
Cremisi, Teresa. *La Triomphante*. Milan: Adelphi, 2016.
Crivello, Maryline. "Les arts de la mémoire en Méditerranée." In *Les échelles de la mémoire en Méditerranée (XIXe-XXIe siècle)*, edited by Maryline Crivello, 12–31. Arles: Actes Sud, 2010.
Dahan, Momi. "Ha-'im kor ha-hitukh hitzliah ba-sadeh ha-kalkali?" [Did the melting pot succeed in the economic field?]. Israel Democracy Institute Working Paper, Jerusalem, October 2013, 1–50.

Dammond, Liliane S. *The Lost World of the Egyptian Jews: First-Person Accounts from Egypt's Jewish Community in the Twentieth Century*. With Yvette M. Raby. New York: iUniverse, 2007.

David, Eyal. "Hayey-ha-yomyom shel ha-yehudim bney-ha-ma'amad ha-beyinoni-gavoah ba'ir Tripoli be-Luv (1951–1967)" [The everyday life of upper-middle-class Jews in the city of Tripoli, Libya (1951–1967)]. MA diss., Hebrew University of Jerusalem, 2015.

De Felice, Renzo. *Ebrei in un paese arabo: Gli ebrei nella Libia contemporanea tra colonialismo, nazionalismo arabo e sionismo (1835–1970)*. Bologna: il Mulino, 1987.

De Gourcy, Constance. "L'institution de l'absence en Méditerranée." *Revue des mondes musulmans et de la Méditerranée*, no. 144 (2018). https://journals.openedition.org/remmm/11649.

DeKoven Ezrahi, Sidra. *Booking Passage: Exile and Homecoming in the Modern Jewish Imagination*. Berkeley: University of California Press, 2000.

Del Boca, Angelo. "The Myths, Suppressions, Denials and Defaults of Italian Colonialism." In *A Place in the Sun: Africa in Italian Colonial Culture from Post-Unification to the Present*, edited by Patrizia Palumbo, 17–36. Berkeley: University of California Press, 2003.

Della Pergola, Sergio. *Anatomia dell'ebraismo italiano*. Rome: Carucci, 1976.

———. "Ha-demografiah" [The demography]. In *Mitzrayim* [Egypt], edited by Nahem Ilan, 33–48. Jerusalem: Yad Ben-Tzvi, 2008.

Deringil, Selim. *The Well-Protected Domains: Ideology and the Legitimation of Power in the Ottoman Empire*. London: IB Tauris, 1998.

Dermenjian, Geneviève. *La crise anti-juive oranaise 1895–1905: l'anti-sémitisme dans l'Algérie coloniale*. Paris: L'Harmattan, 1986.

———. "Les Juifs d'Algérie entre deux hostilités." In *Les Juifs d'Algérie, une histoire de ruptures*, edited by Joëlle Allouche-Benayoun and Geneviève Dermenjian, 135–52. Aix-en-Provence: Presses Universitaires de Provence, 2015.

Derrida, Jacques. *Le monolinguisme de l'autre*. Paris: Galilée, 1996.

Devir, Nathan P. "Midrashic Bodies: Prostitution as Revolt in Chochana Boukhobza's *Un été à Jérusalem*." *Nashim*, no. 23 (2012): 129–44.

Diena, Gianni. "Integrazione, assimilazione e comunitarismo." *Hakeillah*, March 2016, 7.

Diffalah, Sarah. "Dans le quartiers, la haine du Juif ne disparaîtra pas par miracle." *Le Nouvel Observateur*, January 31, 2015.

Diminescu, Dana, and Benjamin Loveluck. "Traces of Dispersion: Online Media and Diasporic Identities." *Crossings: Journal of Migration and Culture* 5, no. 1 (2014): 23–39.

Dobie, Madeleine. "For and Against the Mediterranean: Francophone Perspectives." *Comparative Studies of South Asia, Africa and the Middle East* 34, no. 2 (2014): 389–404.

Douin, Jean-Luc. "'Le Chant des Mariées': rêves d'amour d'une Juive et d'une Musulmane dans une Tunisie sous régime nazi." *Le Monde*, August 16, 2008. http://www.lemonde.fr/cinema/article/2008/12/16/le-chant-des-mariees-reves-d-amour-d-une-juive-et-d-une-musulmane-dans-une-tunisie-sous-regime-nazi_1131561_3476.html#ens_id=1052988.

Duah va'adat Biton le-he'atzemet moreshet yahadut-Sfarad ve-ha-mizrah be-ma'arehet ha-hinukh [Proceedings of the Biton Commission for deepening the heritage of the Sephardic and Eastern Jewries in the educational system]. Jerusalem: Ministry of Education, 2016.

Duncan, Derek. "'Il clandestino è l'ebreo di oggi': Imprints of the Shoah on Migration to Italy." *Quest—Issues in Contemporary Jewish History*, no. 10 (2016): 60–88.

Edwards, Jill, ed. *El Alamein and the Struggle for North Africa*. Cairo: American University in Cairo Press, 2012.

Elbaz, Mikhael. "Ethnicité et générations en Amérique du Nord. Le cas de la seconde génération des Juifs sépharades à Montréal." *Revue internationale d'action communautaire*, no. 31 (1994): 63–77.

Eldridge, Claire. "Remembering the Other: Postcolonial Perspectives on Relationships between Jews and Muslims in French Algeria." *Journal of Modern Jewish Studies* 11, no. 3 (2012): 1–19.

El Houssi, Leila. "Italians in Tunisia: Between Regional Organisation, Cultural Adaptation and Political Division, 1869s–1940s." *European Review of History/Revue Européenne d'Histoire* 19, no. 1 (2012): 163–81.

———. "The Qrana Italian Jewish Community of Tunisia between XVIII–XIX Century: An Example of Transnational Dimension." *Studi Emigrazione*, no. 186 (April–June 2012): 361–69.

El Karoui, Hakim. *Un Islam français est possible*. Paris: Institut Montaigne, 2016.

Erll, Astrid. "Travelling Memory." *Parallax* 17, no. 4 (2011): 4–18.

Esther, John. "A View of One's Own: Exclusive Interview—Karin Albou." *Jesther Entertainment*. November 6, 2009. http://jestherent.blogspot.it/2009/11/exclusive-interview-karin-albou.html.

Everett, Anna. *Digital Diaspora: A Race for Cyberspace*. Albany: State University of New York Press, 2009.

Everett, Samuel, and Ben Gidey. "Getting Away from the Noise: Jewish-Muslim Interactions and Narratives in E1/Barbès." *Francosphères* 7, no. 2 (2018): 174–96.

Farris, Sara R. "From the Jewish Question to the Muslim Question: Republican Rigorism, Culturalist Differentialism and Antinomies of Enforced Emancipation." *Constellations* 21, no. 2 (2014): 296–307.

Figuière-Cagnac, V. "Dolly City ou la jungle de la vie." *Zafon*, no. 33–34 (1998): 55–65.

Fintz Menascé, Esther. *Gli ebrei a Rodi: storia di un'antica comunità annientata dai nazisti*. Milan: Guerini e Associati, 1992.

Fischbach, Michael R. *Jewish Property Claims against Arab Countries*. New York: Columbia University Press, 2008.
Fleming, Katherine E. "The Stereotyped 'Greek Jew' from Auschwitz-Birkenau to Israeli Popular Culture." *Journal of Modern Greek Studies*, no. 25 (2007): 17–40.
Fogu, Claudio. "From Mare Nostrum to Mare Aliorum: Mediterranean Theory and Mediterraneism in Contemporary Italian Thought." *California Italian Studies* 1, no. 1 (2010). http://escholarship.org/uc/item/7vp210p4#page-13.
Fortunati, Leopoldina. *Migration, Diaspora and Information Technology in Global Societies*. With Raul Pertierra and Jane Vincent. London: Routledge, 2011.
Fourcade, Marie Blanche. "La mise en ligne des mémoires du génocide arménien." *Ethnologie française* 37, no. 3 (2007): 525–31.
Fraenkel, Jonathan. *The Damascus Affaire, "Ritual Murder," Politics, and the Jews in 1840*. Cambridge: Cambridge University Press, 1997.
Fuller, Mia. *Moderns Abroad: Architecture, Cities and Italian Imperialism*. London: Routledge, 2007.
Gabaccia, Donna. *Italy's Many Diasporas*. Seattle: University of Washington Press, 2000.
Gerber, Jane S. "History of the Jews in the Middle East and North Africa from the Rise of Islam until 1700." In *The Jews of the Middle East and North Africa in Modern Times*, edited by Reeva Spector Simon, Michael Laskier, and Sara Reguer, 3–18. New York: Columbia University Press, 2002.
Gerbi, David. "Ebrei di Libia, facciamoci sentire." *Moked*, January 4, 2021, https://moked.it/blog/2021/01/04/ebrei-di-libia-facciamoci-sentire.
Gershoni, Israel, and James P. Jankowski. *Egypt, Islam, and the Arabs: The Search for an Egyptian Nationhood, 1900–1930*. Oxford: Oxford University Press, 1986.
Ghouirgate, Mehdi, Iannis Roder, and Dominique Schnapper, eds. *France: les Juifs vus par les musulmans: Entre stéréotypes et méconnaissances*. Paris: Fondation pour l'innovation politique, 2017.
Giaccardi, Elisa. "Introduction: Reframing Heritage in a Participatory Culture." In *Heritage and Social Media: Understanding Heritage in a Participatory Culture*, edited by Elisa Giaccardi, 1–10. London: Routledge, 2012.
Ginat, Rami. *A History of Egyptian Communism: Jews and Their Compatriots in Quest of Revolution*. Boulder: Lynne Rienner, 2011.
Ginzburg, Carlo. *Il filo e le tracce: Vero, falso, finto*. Milan: Feltrinelli, 2006.
———. "Just One Witness." In *Probing the Limits of Representation: Nazism and the "Final Solution,"* edited by Saul Friedländer, 82–96. Cambridge, MA: Harvard University Press, 1992.
Giuliani, Gaia. "Afterword: The Mediterranean as a Stage; Borders, Memories, Bodies." In *Decolonising the Mediterranean: European Colonial Heritages in North Africa and the Middle East*, edited by Gabriele Proglio, 91–103. Newcastle: Cambridge Scholars, 2016.

Goitein, Shlomo D. *Jews and Arabs*. New York: Shocken, 1955.

———. *A Mediterranean Society: The Jewish Communities of the Arab World as Portrayed in the Cairo Geniza*. 5 vols. Berkeley: University of California Press, 1967–88.

Goldberg, Amos, and Haim Hazan, eds. *Marking Evil: Holocaust Memory in the Global Age*. New York: Berghahn Books, 2015.

Goldberg, Harvey. "From Sephardi to Mizrahi and Back Again: Changing Meanings of 'Sephardi' in Its Social Environment." *Jewish Social Studies* 15, no. 1 (2008): 165–88.

———. *Jewish Life in Muslim Libya: Rivals and Relatives*. Chicago: University of Chicago Press, 1990.

———. "The Notion of 'Libyan Jewry' and Its Cultural-Historical Complexity." In *La bienvenue et l'adieu: Migrants juifs et musulmans au Maghreb (XVe–XXe siècle)*, edited by Frédéric Abécassis, Karima Dirèche, and Rita Aouad, 2:121–34. Casablanca: La Croisée des Chemins, 2012.

Gormezano Goren, Yitzhaq. *Ba-derekh la-'itztadion* [The path to the stadium]. Tel Aviv: Bimat Qedem, 2003.

Gottreich, Emily. "Historicizing the Concept of Arab Jew in the Maghrib." *Jewish Quarterly Review* 98, no. 4 (2008): 433–51.

———. *The Mellah of Marrakesh: Jewish and Muslim Space in Morocco's Red City*. Bloomington: Indiana University Press, 2006.

Grange, Daniel. *L'Italie et la Méditerranée: Les fondements d'une politique étrangère*. Rome: Ecole française de Rome, 1994.

Gribetz, Jonathan M. *Defining Neighbors: Religion, Race and the Early Arab-Zionist Encounter*. Princeton, NJ: Princeton University Press, 2014.

Grosfoguel, Ramon, Yvon Le Bot, and Alexandra Poli. "Intégrer les musées dans les approches sur l'immigration: Vers de nouvelles perspectives de recherche." *Hommes & Migration*, no. 1293 (2011): 6–11.

Grumberg, Karen. *Place and Ideology in Contemporary Hebrew Literature*. Syracuse, NY: Syracuse University Press, 2011.

Haberfeld, Yitzhaq, and Yinnon Cohen. "Ha-hagirah ha-yehudit le-Isra'el: shinuim be-ramot haskalah, sheker ve-hishtalvut kalkalim, 1948–2000" [Jewish immigration to Israel: Changes in the level of education, income, and economic integration]. *Megamot*, no. 48 (2012): 504–34.

Hakak, Lev. "The Holocaust in the Hebrew Poetry of Sephardim and Near Eastern Jews." *Shofar*, no. 2 (2005): 89–119.

Halbwachs, Maurice. *On Collective Memory*. Chicago: University of Chicago Press, 1992.

Handelmann, Don, and Elihu Katz. "State Ceremonies of Israel: Remembrance Day and Independence Day." In *Israeli Judaism: The Sociology of Religion in Israel*, edited by Shlomo Deshen, Charles S. Liebman, and Moshe Shokeid, 75–86. New Brunswick: Transaction.

Harari, Orly. "'Ahavah, shutafut-goral ve-solidariyut hevratit: yom ha-yetziah ve-ha-gerush shel yehudei-'artzot 'Arav ve-'Iran" [Love, a shared destiny and social solidarity: the day marking the exit and expulsion of the Jews from Arab Lands and Iran]. *'Arutz 7*, November 30, 2021, https://www.inn.co.il/news/533299.

Hartog, François. *Régimes d'historicité: présentisme et expériences du temps*. Paris: Seuil, 2004.

Hashmonay, Adi. "Hatza'at hoq: hakarah la-nitzolim u-la-nirtzahim be-pogrom ha-Farhud" [Law proposal: Recognize the survivors and victims of the Farhud pogrom]. *Yisrael ha-yom*, December 7, 2020, https://www.israelhayom.co.il/article/827157.

Hassoun, Jacques. *Histoire des Juifs du Nil*. Paris: Minerve, 1990.

Hever, Hannan. *'El-ha-hof ha-mequveh* [To the yearned shore]. Jerusalem: Ha-kibbutz ha-meuhad, 2007.

———. "We Have Not Arrived from the Sea: A Mizrahi Literary Geography." *Social Identities* 10, no. 1 (2004): 31–51.

Higadta le-binkha: Moreshet qehillot Yahadut-'arav ve-'Iran [And you shall tell your children: The heritage of the Jewish communities of the Arab lands and Iran]. Jerusalem: Minister for Senior Citizens, n.d.

Hine, Christine. *Virtual Ethnography*. London: Sage, 2000.

Hirsch, Marianne, and Leo Spitzer. *Ghosts of Home: The Afterlife of Czernowitz in Jewish Memory*. Berkeley: University of California Press, 2010.

Hoffmann, Adina, and Peter Cole. *Sacred Trash: The Lost and Found World of the Cairo Genizah*. New York: Shocken Books, 2011.

Horden, Peregrine, and Nicholas Purcell. *The Corrupting Sea: A Study of Mediterranean History*. London: Blackwell, 2000.

Horst, Cindy, and Odin Lysaker. "Miracles in Dark Times: Hannah Arendt and Refugees as 'Vanguard.'" *Journal of Refugee Studies*, 2019, 1–18.

Hovanessian, Martine. "Diasporas et identités collectives." *Hommes et Migrations*, no. 1265 (2007): 8–21.

Huyssen, Andreas. *Present Pasts: Urban Palimpsests and the Politics of Memory*. Stanford, CA: Stanford University Press, 2003.

Isabella, Maurizio, and Konstantina Zanou, eds. *Mediterranean Diasporas: Politics and Ideas in the Long 19th Century*. London: Bloomsbury, 2015.

Israel-Pelletier, Aimée. *On the Mediterranean and the Nile: The Jews of Egypt*. Bloomington: Indiana University Press, 2018.

Jablonka, Ivan. *L'histoire est une littérature contemporaine*. Paris: Seuil, 2014.

Jacob, Christian. "Introduction: Faire corps, faire lieux." In *Lieux de savoir, t. 1: Espaces et communautés*, edited by Christian Jacob, 17–42. Paris: Gallimard, 2007.

Jikeli, Gunther. *European Muslim Antisemitism*. Bloomington: Indiana University Press, 2015.

Jordi, Jean-Jacques, and Emile Temime, eds. *Marseille et le choc des décolonisations: Les rapatriements, 1954–1964*. Aix-en-Provence: Edisud, 1996.

Julius, Lyn. "Why Jewish Refugees Must Be Remembered on 30 November." *Huffington Post*, November 23, 2015. http://www.huffingtonpost.com/lyn-julius/why-jewish-refugees-must-_b_8622742.html.

Jurgenson, Nathan. "The IRL Fetish." *New Inquiry*, June 28, 2012. http://thenewinquiry.com/essays/the-irl-fetish/.

Kaspi, André, ed. *Histoire de l'Alliance Israélite Universelle de 1860 à nos jours*. Paris: Armand Colin, 2010.

Katriel, Tamar. "Homeland and Diaspora in Israeli Vernacular Museums." In *Memory and Ethnicity: Ethnic Museums in Israel and the Diaspora*, edited by Emanuela Trevisan Semi, Dario Miccoli, and Tudor Parfitt, 1–19. Newcastle: Cambridge Scholars, 2013.

Katz, Ethan. *The Burdens of Brotherhood: Jews and Muslims from North Africa to France*. Cambridge, MA: Harvard University Press, 2015.

———. "Did the Paris Mosque Save Jews? A Mystery and Its Memory." *Jewish Quarterly Review* 102, no. 2 (2012): 256–87.

———. "Entre émancipation et antijudaisme: la mémoire collective des Juifs d'Algérie dans la longue durée (1930–1970)." In *Les Juifs d'Algérie, une histoire de ruptures*, edited by Joëlle Allouche-Benayoun and Geneviève Dermenjian, 197–224. Aix-en-Provence: Presses Universitaires de Provence, 2015.

———. "Secular French Nationhood and Its Discontents: Jews as Muslims and Religion as Race in Occupied France." In *Secularism in Question: Jews and Judaism in Modern Times*, edited by Ari Joskowicz and Ethan Katz, 168–87. Philadelphia: University of Pennsylvania Press, 2015.

Katz, Ethan, Lisa Leff, and Maud Mandel, eds. *Colonialism and the Jews*. Bloomington: Indiana University Press, 2017.

Kelner, Shaul. *Tours That Bind: Diaspora, Pilgrimage, and Israeli Birthright Tourism*. New York: New York University Press, 2010.

Khazzoom, Aziza. "Did the Israeli State Engineer Segregation? On the Placement of Jewish Immigrants in Development Towns in the 1950s." *Social Forces* 84, no. 1 (2005): 115–34.

Kozinets, Robert V. *Netnography: Doing Ethnographic Research Online*. London: Sage, 2010.

Kozlovsky-Golan, Yvonne. "Childhood Memories from the Giado Detention Camp in Libya: Fragments from the Oeuvre of Nava T. Barazani." *Shofar: An Interdisciplinary Journal of Jewish Studies* 38, no. 1 (2020): 1–37.

———. *Masakh shel skhehah: 'al-he'adar havayat ha-Shoah shel yehudei-ha-mizrah ba-mediah u-va-'omanut be-Israel* [Forgotten from the frame: The absence of the Holocaust experience of Mizrahim from the visual arts and media in Israel]. Tel Aviv: Resling, 2017.

———. "Site of Amnesia: The Absence of North African Jewry in Visual Depictions of the Experience of World War II." *Jewish Film & New Media: An International Journal* 2, no. 2 (2014): 153–80.

Krämer, Gudrun. *The Jews of Modern Egypt, 1914–1952*. London: IB Tauris, 1989.

Lachman, Kathryn. "Music and the Gendering of Colonial Space in Karin Albou's *Le chant des mariées*." *Music, Sound, and the Moving Image* 7, no. 1 (2013): 1–18.

Lagnado, Lucette. *The Man in the White Sharkskin Suit*. New York: HarperCollins, 2007.

Laguerre, Michel S. "Digital Diasporas. Definition and Methods." In *Diasporas in the New Media Age: Identity, Politics and Community*, edited by Alonso Andoni and Pedro J. Oiarzabal, 49–64. Reno: University of Nevada Press, 2010.

———. *Global Neighborhoods: Jewish Quarters in Paris, London, and Berlin*. Albany: State University of New York Press, 2008.

Laloum, Jean. "Des Juifs d'Afrique du Nord au *Pletzl*? Une présence méconnue et des épreuves oubliées (1920–1945)." *Archives Juives* 38, no. 2 (2005): 47–83.

Landau, Jacob. *Jews in Nineteenth-Century Egypt*. New York: New York University Press, 1969.

———. "Ritual Murder Accusations in Nineteenth-Century Egypt." In *Middle Eastern Themes: Papers in History and Politics*, edited by Jacob Landau, 99–142. London: Frank Cass, 1973.

Landes, David S. *Bankers and Pashas: International Finance and Economic Imperialism in Egypt*. Cambridge, MA: Harvard University Press, 1958.

Laqueur, Walter. *The History of Zionism*. London: IB Tauris, 2003.

Laskier, Michael. *The Alliance Israélite Universelle and the Jewish Communities of Morocco, 1862–1962*. Albany: State University of New York Press, 1983.

———. "Aspects of the Activities of the Alliance Israélite Universelle in the Jewish Communities of the Middle East and North Africa: 1860–1918." *Modern Judaism* 3, no. 2 (1983): 147–71.

———. "The Evolution of Zionist Activity in the Jewish Communities of Morocco, Tunisia and Algeria: 1897–1947." *Studies in Zionism* 4, no. 2 (1983): 205–36.

———. *The Jews of Egypt, 1920–1970: In the Midst of Zionism, Anti-Semitism, and the Middle East Conflict*. New York: New York University Press, 1992.

———. *North African Jewry in the Twentieth Century: The Jews of Morocco, Tunisia, and Algeria*. New York: New York University Press, 1994.

Lavabre, Marie-Claire. "La 'mémoire collective' entre sociologie de la mémoire et sociologie des souvenirs?" June 27, 2016. https://halshs.archives-ouvertes.fr/halshs-01337854.

Lear, Jonathan. *Freud*. London: Routledge, 2005.

Le Foll Luciani, Pierre-Jean. *Les juifs algériens dans la lutte anticoloniale: Trajectoires dissidentes (1934–1965)*. Rennes: Presses universitaires de Rennes, 2016.

Lehmann, Matthias B. "A Livornese 'Port Jew' and the Sephardim of the Ottoman Empire." *Jewish Social Studies* 11, no. 2 (2005): 51–76.

Leibler, Anat. "Disciplining Ethnicity: Social Sorting Intersects with Political Demography in Israel's Pre-state Period." *Social Studies of Science* 44, no. 2 (2014): 271–92.

Lejeune, Philippe. *Le pacte autobiographique.* Paris: Seuil, 1975.

"Les Juifs d'Orient face au nazisme et à la Shoah." Special issue, *Revue d'histoire de la Shoah* 205, no. 2 (2016).

Levy, André. *Return to Casablanca: Jews, Muslims, and an Israeli Anthropologist.* Chicago: University of Chicago Press, 2015.

Lévy, André. *Il était une fois les Juifs marocains.* Paris: L'Harmattan, 1995.

Levy, Daniel, and Natan Sznaider, eds. *The Holocaust and Memory in the Global Age.* Philadelphia: Temple University Press, 2006.

Levy, Lital. "Mihu yehudi-'aravi? 'Iyun meshaveh be-toldot ha-she'elah, 1880–2010" [Who is an Arab Jew? A comparative historical analysis of the question, 1880–2010]. *Te'oriah u-viqoret*, no. 38–39 (2011): 101–35.

Lewis, Bernard. *The Jews of Islam.* Princeton, NJ: Princeton University Press, 1978.

Lichtenstein, Nina B. "North Africa, France, and Israel: Sephardic Identities in the Works of Chochana Boukhobza." *Sephardic Horizons* 3, no. 2 (2013). http://www.sephardichorizons.org/Volume3/Issue2/Identities.html.

Liebman, Charles S., and Eliezer Don-Yihya. *Civil Religion in Israel: Traditional Judaism and Political Culture in the Jewish State.* Berkeley: University of California Press, 1983.

Linhard, Tabea Alexa. *Jewish Spain: A Mediterranean Memory.* Stanford, CA: Stanford University Press, 2015.

Lipman, Jennifer. "The Unspoken Holocaust: Interview with Yossi Sucary." *Jewish Chronicle*, July 7, 2016. https://www.thejc.com/lifestyle/features/the-unspoken-holocaust-1.60277.

Logan, William, and Reeves Keir. "Introduction: Remembering Places of Pain and Shame." In *Places of Pain and Shame: Dealing with "Difficult Heritage,"* edited by William Logan and Keir Reeves, 1–14. London: Routledge, 2009.

Lorcin, Patricia M. E., and Todd Shepard, eds. *French Mediterraneans: Transnational and Imperial Histories.* Lincoln: University of Nebraska Press, 2016.

Louis, W. Roger, and Louis Owen. *Suez 1956: The Crisis and Its Consequences.* Oxford: Clarendon, 1989.

Lowenthal, David. *The Past Is a Foreign Country.* Cambridge: Cambridge University Press, 1985.

Luzon, Raphael. *Tramonto libico: Storia di un ebreo arabo.* Florence: Giuntina, 2015.

Lyons, Amelia H. *The Civilizing Mission in the Metropole: Algerian Families and the French Welfare during Decolonization.* Stanford, CA: Stanford University Press, 2013.

MacDonald, Sharon. *Difficult Heritage: Negotiating the Nazi Past in Nuremberg and Beyond.* London: Routledge, 2009.

———. "Migrating Heritage, Networks and Networking: Europe and Islamic Heritage." In *Migrating Heritage: Experiences of Cultural Networks and*

Cultural Dialogue in Europe, edited by Perla Innocenzi, 53–64. London: Ashgate, 2014.

Magiar, Victor. *E venne la notte: Ebrei in un paese arabo*. Florence: Giuntina, 2003.

Mandel, Maud. *Muslims and Jews in France: History of A Conflict*. Princeton, NJ: Princeton University Press, 2014.

Mantran, Robert. *Histoire de l'empire ottoman*. Paris: Fayard, 1989.

Marglin, Jessica M. "Mediterranean Modernity through Jewish Eyes: The Transimperial Life of Abraham Ankawa." *Jewish Social Studies* 20, no. 2 (2014): 34–68.

Matalon, Ronit. *Qol tze'adenu* [The sound of our steps]. Tel Aviv: Am Oved, 2008.

Mazzig, Hen. "Why Does Holocaust Remembrance Day Ignore Middle Eastern Jews?" *Times of Israel*, May 2, 2019. https://blogs.timesofisrael.com/why-does-holocaust-remembrance-day-ignore-middle-eastern-jews/.

Meinhof, Ulrike, and Anna Triandafyllidou. "Transcultural Europe: An Introduction to Cultural Policy in a Changing Europe." In *Transcultural Europe: Cultural Policy in a Changing Europe*, edited by Ulrike Meinhof and Anna Triandafyllidou, 3–22. London: Palgrave, 2006.

Melfa, Daniela. *Migrando a Sud: Coloni italiani in Tunisia (1881–1939)*. Rome: Aracne, 2008.

Memmi, Albert. *Juifs et arabes*. Paris: Gallimard, 1974.

Mezzadra, Sandro, and Brett Neilson. *Border as Method, or, The Multiplication of Labor*. Durham, NC: Duke University Press, 2013.

Miccoli, Dario. "Another History: Family, Nation and the Remembrance of the Egyptian Jewish Past in Contemporary Israeli Literature." *Journal of Modern Jewish Studies* 13, no. 3 (2014): 321–39.

———. "A Fragile Cradle: Writing Jewishness, Nationhood and Modernity in Cairo, 1920–1940." *Jewish Social Studies* 21, no. 3 (2016): 1–29.

———. *Histories of the Jews of Egypt: An Imagined Bourgeoisie, 1880s–1950s*. London: Routledge, 2015.

———. "The Jews of the Middle East and North Africa: A Historiographic Debate." *Middle Eastern Studies* 56, no. 3 (2020): 511–20.

———. *La letteratura israeliana mizrahi: narrazioni, identità, memorie degli ebrei del Medio Oriente e Nord Africa*. Florence: Giuntina, 2016.

———. "Moses and Faruq: The Jews and the Study of History in Interwar Egypt, 1920s–1940s." *Quest—Issues in Contemporary Jewish History*, no. 4 (2012): 165–80.

Miège, Jean-Louis, and Colette Dubois, eds. *L'Europe retrouvée: Les migrations de la décolonisation*. Paris: L'Harmattan, 1994.

Miller Gilson, Susan. "Sensitive Ruins: On the Preservation of Jewish Religious Sites in the Muslim World." In *Synagogues of the Islamic World: Architecture, Design, and Identity*, edited by Mohammed Gharipour. Edinburgh: Edinburgh University Press, 2017.

Minuti, Rolando, ed. *Il web e gli studi storici: Guida critica all'uso della rete*. Rome: Carocci, 2015.

———. *Internet et le métier d'historien: Réflexions sur les incertitudes d'une mutation*. Paris: PUF, 2001.

Molho, Anthony. "Ebrei e marrani fra Italia e Levante ottomano." In *Storia d'Italia, Annali 11*, edited by Corrado Vivanti, 1011–43. Turin: Einaudi, 1997.

Moreno, Aviad. "Moroccan Jewish Emigration to Latin America: The State of Research and New Directions." *Hésperis-Tamuda*, no. 2 (2016): 123–40.

Moya, Jose C. "Immigrants and Associations: A Global and Historical Perspective." *Journal of Ethnic and Migration Studies* 31, no. 5 (2005): 833–64.

Naar, Devin A. "From the 'Jerusalem of the Balkans' to the Goldene Medina: Jewish Immigration from Salonika to the United States." *American Jewish History* 93, no. 4 (2007): 435–73.

Nabil, Maikel. "Egypt's Christians, Facing the Fate of Egyptian Jews." *Times of Israel*, September 28, 2012. http://blogs.timesofisrael.com/egypts-christians-facing-the-fate-of-egyptian-jews/.

Nachmani, Amikam. "The Past as a Yardstick: Europeans, Muslim Migrants and the Onus of European-Jewish Histories." *Israel Affairs* 22, no. 2 (2016): 318–54.

Naggar, Jean. *Sipping from the Nile: My Exodus from Egypt*. Las Vegas: AmazonEncore, 2008.

Naguib, Nefissa. "The Fragile Tale of Egyptian Jewish Cuisine: Food Memoirs of Claudia Rosen and Colette Rossant." *Food and Foodways* 14, no. 1 (2006): 35–53.

Nahum, André. "L'exil des Juifs de Tunisie: L'échec d'une continuité." *Pardès* 34, no. 1 (2003): 233–46.

Nebot, Didier. *Mémoire d'un dhimmi: Cinq siècles d'histoire juive en Algérie*. Sèvres: Les Editions des Rosiers, 2012.

Nicolaidis, Kalypso, and Berny Sèbe, eds. *Echoes of Colonialism: The Present of Europe's Past*. London: IB Tauris, 2015.

Noiret, Serge. "'Public History' e 'Storia pubblica' nella rete." *Ricerche storiche* 39, no. 2–3 (2009): 275–327.

Noiriel, Gérard. *Le creuset français: histoire de l'immigration (XIXe–XXe siècle)*. Paris: Seuil, 1988.

Nolden, Thomas. *In Lieu of Memory: Contemporary Jewish Writing in France*. Syracuse, NY: Syracuse University Press, 2006.

Nora, Pierre. "La génération." In *Les lieux de mémoire*, edited by Pierre Nora, vol. 3, t. 1. Paris: Gallimard, 1992.

Oomen, Johan, and Lora Aroyo. "Crowdsourcing in the Cultural Heritage Domain: Opportunities and Challenges." In *Communities and Technology '11: Proceedings of the Fifth International Conference*, 138–49. New York: ACM, 2011.

Oppenheimer, Yochai. "Be-shem ha-'av: 'edipaliyiut ba-sipporet ha-mizrahit shel ha-dor ha-sheni" [In the name of the father: Oedipal themes in second-generation *mizrahi* literature]. *Te'oriah u-viqoret*, no. 40 (2012): 161–84.

———. "The Holocaust: A Mizrahi Perspective." *Hebrew Studies*, no. 51 (2010): 303–28.
Osservatorio antisemitismo. *Relazione annuale 2020 a cura dell'Osservatorio antisemitismo della Fondazione CDEC*. February 26, 2020. https://osservatorioantisemi-c02.kxcdn.com/wp-content/uploads/2020/03/Annuale_Antisemitismo_Giornalisti_28feb2020.pdf.
Oz, Kobi. *'Avaryan Tza'atzua'* [Petty hoodlum]. Jerusalem: Qeshet, 2002.
Pacifici Noja, Ugo G., and Giorgio Pacifici. *Ebreo chi? Sociologia degli ebrei italiani oggi*. Milan: Jaca Book, 2017.
Panebianco, Stefania. "The Euro-Mediterranean Partnership in Perspective: The Political and Institutional Context." In *A New Euro-Mediterranean Cultural Identity*, edited by Stefania Panebianco, 23–46. London: Frank Cass, 2003.
Patai, Raphael. "The Jewish 'Refugees' in the Middle East." *Journal of International Affairs* 7, no. 1 (1953): 51–56.
Peleg, Yaron. *Israeli Culture between the Two Intifadas: A Brief Romance*. Austin: University of Texas Press, 2008.
Pendola, Marinette. *La riva lontana*. Palermo: Sellerio, 2000.
Petrucci, Filippo. *Gli ebrei in Algeria e Tunisia, 1940–1943*. Florence: Giuntina, 2011.
Philips, Kendall R., and G. Mitchell Reyes. "Introduction: Surveying Global Memoryscapes; The Shifting Terrain of Public Memory Studies." In *Global Memoryscapes: Contesting Remembrance in a Transnational Age*, edited by Kendall R. Phillips and G. Mitchell Reyes, 1–26. Tuscaloosa: University of Alabama Press, 2011.
Picard, Avi. "Like a Phoenix: The Renaissance of Sephardic/Mizrahi Identity in Israel in the 1970s and 1980s." *Israel Studies* 22, no. 2 (2017): 1–25.
Picciotto, Liliana. "Ebrei turchi, libici e altri, deportati dall'Italia a Bergen Belsen." *Rassegna Mensile di Israel* 76, no. 3 (2010): 243–59.
Plapp, Laurel. *Zionism and Revolution in European-Jewish Literature*. London: Routledge, 2008.
Podselver, Laurence. "L'alya des Juifs de France: De la communauté à la nation, premiers éléments d'une recherche." In *Socio-anthropologie des judaïsmes contemporains*, edited by Chantal Bordes-Benayoun, 335–46. Paris: Honoré Champion, 2015.
———. "Le pélerinage tunisien de Sarcelles: De la tradition à l'hédonisme contemporain." *Socio-anthropologie*, no. 10 (2001). https://socio-anthropologie.revues.org/157.
Ponzanesi, Sandra, and Koen Leurs. "On Digital Crossings in Europe." *Crossings: Journal of Migration and Culture* 5, no. 1 (2014): 3–22.
Pratt, Mary Louise. "Thoughts on Intangibility and Transmission." In *Anthropological Perspectives on Intangible Cultural Heritage*, edited by Lourdes Arizpe and Cristina Amescua, 79–82. London: Springer, 2013.

Ram, Moriel, and Haim Yacobi. "African Asylum Seekers and the Changing Politics of Memory in Israel." In *History, Memory and Migration*, edited by Olaf J. Kleist and Irial Glynn, 154–70. London: Palgrave Macmillan, 2012.

Raphaël, Freddy. "La mémoire blessée des Juifs du M'zab." In *Communautés Juives des marges du Maghreb*, edited by Michel Abitbol, 137–52. Jerusalem: Ben-Tzvi Institute, 1982.

Ray, Jonathan. *After Expulsion: 1492 and the Making of Sephardic Jewry*. New York: New York University Press, 2013.

Reid, Donald M. "Nationalizing the Pharaonic Past: Egyptology, Imperialism, and Egyptian Nationalism, 1922–1952." In *Rethinking Nationalism in the Arab Middle East*, edited by James P. Jankowski and Israel Gershoni, 127–49. New York: Columbia University Press, 1997.

———. *Whose Pharaohs? Archaeology, Museums, and Egyptian National Identity from Napoleon to World War One*. Berkeley: University of California Press, 2002.

Rettig Gur, Haviv. "Jewish 'Refugee' Day Proposal Advances in Knesset." *Times of Israel*, February 4, 2014. http://www.timesofisrael.com/jewish-refugee-day-proposal-advances-in-knesset/.

Reynié, Dominique, and Simone Rodan-Benzaquen. *Radiographie de l'antisémitisme en France*. Paris: Fondation pour l'innovation politique, 2020.

Reynolds, Nancy. *A City Consumed: Urban Commerce, the Cairo Fire, and the Politics of Decolonization in Egypt*. Stanford, CA: Stanford University Press, 2012.

Ricoeur, Paul. *Memory, History, Forgetting*. Chicago: University of Chicago Press, 2004.

Rieder, Bernard, and Theo Roehle. "Digital Methods: Five Challenges." In *Understanding Digital Humanities*, edited by David M. Berry, 67–84. New York: Palgrave Macmillan, 2012.

Roby, Bryan K. *The Mizrahi Era of Rebellion: Israel's Forgotten Civil Rights Struggle, 1948–1966*. Syracuse, NY: Syracuse University Press, 2015.

Rodrigue, Aron. *Images of Sephardi and Eastern Jewries in Transition: The Teachers of the Alliance Israélite Universelle*. Portland: University of Washington Press, 2003.

———. "L'exportation du paradigme révolutionnaire: Son influence sur le judaïsme sépharade et oriental." In *Histoire politique des Juifs de France*, edited by Pierre Birnbaum, 221–43. Paris: Presses de Sciences Po, 1990.

Rosen-Lapidot, Efrat, and Harvey Goldberg. "The Triple Loci of Jewish-Maghrebi Ethnicity: Voluntary Associations in Israel and in France." *Journal of North African Studies* 18, no. 1 (2013): 112–30.

Rossant, Colette. *Apricots on the Nile: A Memoir with Recipes*. New York: Washington Square, 1999.

Rossetto, Piera. "Displaying Relational Memory: Notes on Museums and Heritage Centres of the Libyan Jewish Community." In *Memory and Ethnicity: Ethnic*

Museums in Israel and the Diaspora, edited by Emanuela Trevisan Semi, Dario Miccoli, and Tudor Parfitt, 77–95. Newcastle: Cambridge Scholars, 2013.

———. "Mémoires de diaspora, diaspora de mémoires: Juifs de Libye entre Israël et l'Italie, de 1948 à nos jours." PhD diss., EHESS Toulouse/Ca' Foscari University, 2015.

———. "Note ai margini di una migrazione: donne ebree dalla Libia tra Israele e Italia." In *Il genere nella ricerca storica*, edited by Saveria Chemotti and Maria Cristina La Rocca, 190–200. Padua: Il Poligrafo, 2015.

———. "'We Were All Italians!' The Construction of a Sense of Italianness among Jews from Libya (1920s–1960s)." *History & Anthropology*, January 14, 2021. https://www.tandfonline.com/doi/full/10.1080/02757206.2020.1848821.

Rothberg, Michael. "Introduction: Between Memory and Memory: From Lieux de Mémoire to Noeuds de Mémoire." *Yale French Studies*, no. 118–19 (2010): 3–12.

———. *Multidirectional Memory: Remembering the Holocaust in the Age of Decolonization*. Stanford, CA: Stanford University Press, 2009.

———. "Remembering Back: Cultural Memory, Colonial Legacies, and Postcolonial Studies." In *The Oxford Handbook of Postcolonial Studies*, edited by Graham Duggan, 359–79. Oxford: Oxford University Press, 2013.

Roumani, Jacques, David Meghnagi, and Judith Roumani, eds. *Jewish Libya: Memory and Identity in Text and Image*. Syracuse, NY: Syracuse University Press, 2018.

Roumani, Judith. "Sephardic Literary Responses to the Holocaust." In *Literature of the Holocaust*, edited by Alan Rosen, 225–37. Cambridge: Cambridge University Press, 2013.

Roumani, Maurice. "First, Libya's Jews Were Deported. Then the SS Stepped in." *Ha-'Aretz*, February 8, 2020. https://www.haaretz.com/world-news/.premium.MAGAZINE-first-libya-s-jews-were-deported-then-the-s-s-stepped-in-1.8504840.

———. *Gli ebrei di Libia: dalla coesistenza all'esodo*. Rome: Castelvecchi, 2015.

Rustow, Marina. *The Lost Archive: Traces of a Caliphate in a Cairo Synagogue*. Princeton, NJ: Princeton University Press, 2020.

Sadun, Haim. "Ha-tziyonut" [Zionism]. In *Algeriah* [Algeria], edited by Haim Sadun, 193–212. Jerusalem: Yad Ben-Tzvi, 2011.

Safran, William. "The Jewish Diaspora in a Comparative and Theoretical Perspective." *Israel Studies* 10, no. 1(2005): 36–60.

Salerno, Eric. *Uccideteli tutti: Libia 1943: Gli ebrei nel campo di concentramento fascista di Giado, una storia italiana*. Milan: Il Saggiatore, 2008.

Salvanou, Emilia. "Migration and the Shaping of Transcultural Memory at the Margins of Europe." *EuropeNow*, no. 6 (2017). http://www.europenowjournal.org/2017/04/03/migration-and-the-shaping-of-transcultural-memory-at-the-margins-of-europe/.

Sanyal, Debarati. *Memory and Complicity: Migrations of Holocaust Remembrance.* New York: Fordham University Press, 2015.
Saou-Dufrêne, Bernadette N. "Les musées du Maghreb à l'ère numérique: le futur à la rencontre du passé." In *Patrimoines du Maghreb à l'ère numérique*, edited by Bernadette N. Saou-Dufrêne, 77–113. Paris: L'Harmattan, 2014.
Sarfatti, Michele. *Gli ebrei nell'Italia fascista.* Turin: Einaudi, 2000.
Satloff, Robert. *Among the Righteous: Lost Stories from the Holocaust's Long Reach into Arab Lands.* New York: Public Affairs, 2006.
Saul, Mahir, and José Ignacio Hualde, eds. *Sepharad as Imagined Community: Language, History and Religion from the Early Modern Period to the 21st Century.* New York: Peter Lang, 2017.
Sayad, Abdelmalek. *La double absence: des illusions de l'émigré aux souffrances de l'immigré.* Paris: Seuil, 1999.
Schely-Newman, Esther. *Our Lives Are but Stories: Narratives of Tunisian-Israeli Women.* Detroit: Wayne State University Press, 2002.
Scherini, Marianna. "The Image of Israel and Israelis in the French, British and Italian Press during the 1982 Lebanon War." In *Global Antisemitism: A Crisis of Modernity*, edited by Charles Asher Small, 187–202. Leiden: Brill, 2013.
Schlesinger, Philip, and François Foret. "Political Roof and Sacred Canopy? Religion and the EU Constitution." *European Journal of Social Theory* 9, no. 1 (2006): 59–81.
Schmoll, Camille, and Giovanni Semi. "Shadow Circuits: Urban Spaces and Mobilities across the Mediterranean." *Identities* 20, no. 4 (2013): 377–92.
Schorsch, Jonathan. "Disappearing Origins: Sephardi Autobiography Today." *Prooftexts*, no. 27 (2007): 82–150.
Schreier, Joshua. *Arabs of the Jewish Faith: The Civilizing Mission in Colonial Algeria.* New Brunswick: Rutgers University Press, 2010.
Schroeter, Daniel. "A Different Road to Modernity: Jewish Identity in the Arab World." In *Diasporas and Exiles: Varieties of Jewish Identity*, edited by Howard Wettstein, 150–63. Berkeley: University of California Press, 2002.
Schumacher, Tobias. "Introduction: The Study of Euro-Mediterranean Cultural and Social Co-operation in Perspective." In *Conceptualizing Cultural and Social Dialogue in the Euro-Mediterranean Area*, edited by Michelle Pace and Tobias Schumacher, 3–12. London: Routledge, 2007.
Schwartz, Seth. *Were the Jews a Mediterranean Society? Reciprocity and Solidarity in Ancient Judaism.* Princeton, NJ: Princeton University Press, 2010.
Schwartz, Stephanie Tara. "The Concept of Double Diaspora in Sami Michael's *Refuge* and Naim Kattan's *Farewell, Babylon*." *Comparative Studies of South Asia, Africa and the Middle East* 30, no. 1 (2010): 92–100.
Schwarz, Guri. *Ritrovare se stessi: Gli ebrei nell'Italia postfascista.* Rome: Laterza, 2004.

Scioldo-Zürcher, Yann. *Devenir métropolitain, parcours et politique d'intégration de rapatriés d'Algérie à la métropole, de 1954 au début du XXIe siècle*. Paris: Éditions de l'École des hautes études en sciences sociales, 2010.
Scott, Joan. *The Politics of the Veil*. Princeton, NJ: Princeton University Press, 2007.
Sebag, Paul. *Histoire des Juifs de Tunisie: Des origines à nos jours*. Paris: L'Harmattan, 1991.
Sebbar, Leila, ed. *Une enfance juive en Méditerranée musulmane*. Saint-Pourçain-sur-Sioule: Bleu autour, 2012.
Shalom-Chetrit, Sami. *Intra-Jewish Conflict in Israel: White Jews, Black Jews*. London: Routledge, 2010.
Sharkey, Heather. *A History of Muslims, Christians, and Jews in the Middle East*. Cambridge: Cambridge University Press, 2017.
Shemer, Yaron. "From Chahine's *al-Iskandariyya . . . leh* to *Salata baladi* and *'An Yahud Masr*: Rethinking Egyptian Jews' Cosmopolitanism, Belonging and Nostalgia in Cinema." *Middle East Journal of Culture and Communication* 7, no. 3 (2014): 351–75.
Shenhav, Yehudah. *The Arab Jews: A Postcolonial Reading of Nationalism, Religion, and Ethnicity*. Stanford, CA: Stanford University Press, 2006.
Shepard, Todd. "Algerian Nationalism, Zionism, and French Laïcité: A History of Ethnoreligious Nationalisms and Decolonization." *International Journal of Middle East Studies*, no. 45 (2013): 445–67.
———. *The Invention of Decolonization: The Algerian War and the Remaking of France*. Ithaca, NY: Cornell University Press, 2006.
Shimony, Batya. "Holocaust Envy: Globalization of the Holocaust in the Israeli Discourse." In *Marking Evil: Holocaust Memory in the Global Age*, edited by Amos Goldberg and Haim Hazan, 296–317. New York: Berghahn, 2015.
———. "Lihiyot mizrahi, laga'at ba-shoah, lihiyot Isra'eli" [Being a Mizrahi Jew, an Israeli and touching the Holocaust]. *Ha-Oketz*, April 2014. http://www.haokets.org/2014/04/28/ילארשי-תויהל-האושב-תעגל-יחרזמ-תויהל/.
Shohat, Ella. "By the Bitstream of Babylon: Cyberfrontiers and Diasporic Vistas." In *Drifting: Architecture and Migrancy*, edited by Stephen Cairns, 271–87. London: Routledge, 2004.
———. "The Invention of the Mizrahim." *Journal of Palestine Studies* 29, no. 1 (1999): 5–20.
———. "Rupture and Return: Zionist Discourse and the Study of Arab Jews." *Social Text* 21, no. 2 (2003): 49–74.
———. "Sephardim in Israel: Zionism from the Standpoint of Its Jewish Victims." *Social Text*, no. 19–20 (1988): 1–35.
Shuval, Judith. *Immigrants on the Threshold*. New Brunswick: Aldine Transaction, 1963.

Shveymer, Yotam. "'Ha-roman ha-mitzri': Biqoret noqevet u-mushlemet" ["The Egyptian novel": A profound and excellent critique]. *Yedi'ot 'Aharonot*, January 20, 2015. http://www.ynet.co.il/articles/0,7340,L-4617053,00.html.
Silberstein, Laurence J. *The Postzionism Debates: Knowledge and Power in Israeli Culture*. London: Routledge, 1999.
Simon, Patrick, and Claude Tapia. *Le Belleville des Juifs tunisiens*. Paris: Autrement, 1998.
Simon, Rachel. "Between the Family and the Outside World: Jewish Girls in the Modern Middle East and North Africa." *Jewish Social Studies* 7, no. 1 (2000): 81–108.
———. "Les Juifs de Libye au seuil de la Shoah." *Revue d'histoire de la Shoah* 205, no. 2 (2016): 221–62.
———. "Zionism." In *The Jews of the Middle East and North Africa in Modern Times*, edited by Reeva Spector Simon, Michael Laskier, and Sara Reguer, 165–79. New York: Columbia University Press, 2002.
Simon, Reeva Spector. "Europe in the Middle East." In *The Jews of the Middle East and North Africa in Modern Times*, edited by Reeva Simon, Michael Laskier, and Sara Reguer, 19–28. New York: Columbia University Press, 2003.
———. *The Jews of the Middle East and North Africa: The Impact of World War Two*. London: Routledge, 2020.
Siney-Lange, Charlotte. "Grandes et petites misères du grande exode des Juifs nord-africains vers la France." *Le mouvement social* 197, no. 4 (2001): 29–55.
Slyomovics, Susan. "Geographies of Jewish Tlemcen." *Journal of North African Studies* 5, no. 4 (2000): 81–96.
Smadja, Georges. "Témoignage de Georges Smadja." In *Les Juifs de Tunisie sous le joug nazi: 9 novembre 1942–8 mai 1943*, edited by Claude Nataf, 152–53. Paris: Le Manuscrit, 2012.
Smith, Andrea. *Colonial Memory and Postcolonial Europe: Maltese Settlers in Algeria and France*. Bloomington: Indiana University Press, 2006.
Snir, Re'uven. "'A Carbon Copy of Ibn al-Balad'? The Participation of Egyptian Jews in Modern Arab Culture." *Archiv Orientální*, no. 74 (2006): 37–64.
Snyder, Timothy. *Black Earth: The Holocaust as History and Warning*. New York: Tim Duggan Books, 2015.
Spadaro, Barbara. *Una colonia italiana: Incontri, memorie e rappresentazioni tra Italia e Libia*. Florence: Le Monnier, 2013.
Spilerman, Seymour, and Jack Habib. "Development Towns in Israel: The Role of Community in Creating Ethnic Disparities in Labor Force Characteristics." *American Journal of Sociology* 81, no. 4 (1976): 781–812.
Starr, Deborah. *Remembering Cosmopolitan Egypt: Literature, Culture, and Empire*. London: Routledge, 2009.
———. "Reterritorializing the Dream: Orly Castel Bloom's Remapping of Israeli Identity." In *Mapping Jewish Identities*, edited by Lawrence Silberstein, 220–49. New York: New York University Press, 2000.

Stein, Sarah A. "Citizens of a Fictional Nation: Ottoman-Born Jews in France during the First World War." *Past and Present* 226, no. 1 (2015): 227–54.

———. *Saharan Jews and the Fate of French Algeria*. Chicago: University of Chicago Press, 2014.

Stein, Sarah A., and Aomar Boum, eds. *The Holocaust and North Africa*. Stanford, CA: Stanford University Press, 2018.

Stoler, Ann Laura. *Along the Archival Grain: Epistemic Anxieties and Colonial Common Sense*. Princeton, NJ: Princeton University Press, 2010.

Stone, Dan. "On Neighbours and Those Knocking at the Door: Holocaust Memory and Europe's Refugee Crisis." *Patterns of Prejudices* 52, no. 2–3 (2018): 231–43.

Stora, Benjamin. *Histoire de la guerre d'Algérie*. Paris: La Découverte, 1993.

———. *La gangrène et l'oubli: La mémoire de la guerre d'Algérie*. Paris: La Découverte, 2005.

———. *Les trois exils: Juifs d'Algérie*. Paris: Stock, 2006.

———. "L'impossible neutralité des Juifs d'Algérie." In *La guerre d'Algérie 1954–2004: la fin de l'amnèsie*, edited by Mohammed Harbi and Benjamin Stora, 287–315. Paris: Laffont, 2004.

Stora, Benjamin, Nala Aoudat, Elodie Bouffard, and Hana Boghanim, eds. *Juifs d'Orient: une histoire plurimillénaire*. Paris: Gallimard, 2021.

Strath, Bo. "A European Identity: To the Historical Limits of a Concept." *European Journal of Social Theory* 5, no. 4 (2002): 387–401.

Stroumsa, Guy G. "Religious Memory, between Orality and Writing." *Memory Studies* 9, no. 3 (2016): 332–40.

Suarez, Ruti. "'Avru shnatayim: mi zokher 'et-va'adat Biton?" [Two years have passed: Who remembers the Biton Commission?]. *Ha-maqom*, July 3, 2018. https://www.ha-makom.co.il/post/ruti-bitton-report.

Sucary, Yossi. *Benghazi Bergen-Belsen*. Tel Aviv: Am Oved, 2013.

Swenson, Astrid. *The Rise of Heritage: Preserving the Past in France, Germany and England, 1789–1914*. Cambridge: Cambridge University Press, 2013.

Tartakowsky, Ewa. *Les Juifs et le Maghreb: Fonctiones sociales d'une littérature d'exil*. Tours: Presses Universitaires François Rabelais, 2016.

Taylor, Ella. "The Wedding Song Probes Bond between Two Women." *Village Voice*, October 20, 2009. http://www.villagevoice.com/film/the-wedding-song-probes-bond-between-two-women-6391978.

Tercatin, Rossella. "A Milano tra i rifugiati siriani. 'Il nostro nemica resta Israele.'" *Moked*, September 13, 2015. http://moked.it/blog/2015/09/13/a-milano-tra-i-rifugiati-siriani-il-nostro-nemico-resta-israele/.

Terras, Melissa. "Digital Curiosities: Resource Creation via Amateur Digitisation." *Literary and Linguistic Computing* 25, no. 4 (2010): 425–38.

Thomas, Dominic. "Museums in Postcolonial Europe: An Introduction." *African and Black Diaspora: An International Journal* 2, no. 2 (2009): 125–35.

Tignor, Robert L. "The Economic Activities of Foreigners in Egypt, 1920–1950: From Millet to Haute Bourgeoisie." *Comparative Studies in Society and History* 22, no. 3 (1980): 416–49.

———. *Modernization and British Colonial Rule in Egypt, 1882–1914*. Princeton, NJ: Princeton University Press, 1966.

Tironi, Stefano. "La comunità ebraica tripolina tra la Libia e Roma." MA diss., Ca' Foscari University, 2002.

Tölölyan, Kachig. "The Contemporary Discourse of Diaspora Studies." *Comparative Studies of South Asia, Africa and the Middle East* 27, no. 3 (2007): 647–55.

Torre, Angelo. "Public History e Patrimoine: due casi di storia applicata." *Quaderni Storici*, no. 3 (2015): 629–59.

Trevisan Semi, Emanuela. "Entre le contexte oublié et l'hégémonisation du 'fait juif': Quelques réflexions à partir du narratif sioniste." In *Socio-anthropologie des judaïsmes contemporains*, edited by Chantal Bordes-Benayoun, 101–9. Paris: Honoré Champion, 2015.

———. "Entre lieux de mémoire et lieux de l'oubli au Maroc: quelle politique et quels acteurs pour la mémoire juive?" *Ethnologies* 39, no. 2 (2017): 69–80.

———. "From Egypt to Israel: The Birth of a Karaite Edah in Israel." In *Karaite Judaism: A Guide to Its History and Literary Sources*, edited by Meira Pollack, 431–51. Leiden: Brill, 2003.

———. "From Judeophobia to Islamophobia in the Italian Media, with a Special Focus on the Northern League Party Media." In *Jews, Muslims, and Mass Media: Mediating the "Other,"* edited by Yulia Egorova and Tudor Parfitt, 48–54. London: Routledge, 2004.

———. "L'année prochaine à ... Ouazzan: des usages socio-politiques d'un culte d'un saint juif." In *Visions du monde et modernités religieuses: Regards croisés*, edited by Noureddine Harrami and Imed Meliti, 219–26. Paris: Publisud, 2011.

———. "Lifewriting between Israel, the Diaspora and Morocco: Revisiting the Homeland through Locations and Objects of Identity." In *Contemporary Sephardic and Mizrahi Literature: A Diaspora*, edited by Dario Miccoli, 84–97. London: Routledge, 2017.

———. "The 'Symbolic Homeland' in the Jewish Italian Diaspora: The Celebration of Civil Israeli Religion in Italy." *Journal of Modern Jewish Studies* 5, no. 1 (2006): 95–108.

Trevisan Semi, Emanuela, Dario Miccoli, and Tudor Parfitt, eds. *Memory and Ethnicity: Ethnic Museums in Israel and the Diaspora*. Newcastle: Cambridge Scholars, 2013.

Trevisan Semi, Emanuela, and Hanane Sekkat Hatimi. *Mémoire et représentations des Juifs au Maroc: les voisins absents de Meknès*. Paris: Publisud, 2011.

Trinchese, Stefano, ed. *Mare nostrum: percezione ottomana e mito mediterraneo in Italia all'alba del '900*. Milan: Guerini, 2005.

Trivellato, Francesca. *The Familiarity of Strangers: The Sephardic Diaspora, Livorno, and Cross-cultural Trade in the Early Modern Period*. New Haven, CT: Yale University Press, 2009.

Tsur, Yaron. "Ha-historiografiah ha-'israelit ve-ha-be'aiah ha-'edatit" [The Israeli historiography and the ethnic problem]. *Pe'amim*, no. 94–95 (2003): 1–47.

———. *Qehillah qru'ah: Yehudei-Maroqo ve-ha-le'umiyut 1943–1954* [A torn community: The Jews of Morocco and nationalism 1943–1954]. Tel Aviv: Am Oved, 2001.

Tuchfeld, Mati. "For First Time, Israel to Honor Jews Expelled from Arab States." *Israel Ha-yom*, November 13, 2015. http://www.israelhayom.com/site/newsletter_article.php?id=29673.

Valensi, Lucette. "From Sacred History to Historical Memory and Back: The Jewish Past." *History and Anthropology* 2, no. 2 (1986): 283–305.

Valensi, Lucette, and Abraham Udovitch. *The Last Arab Jews: The Communities of Djerba, Tunisia*. New York: Harwood Academic, 1984.

Vatikiotis, Panayotis J. *The History of Modern Egypt from Muhammad Ali to Mubarak*. London: Weidenfeld and Nicholson, 1991.

Vaughn Findley, Carter. "The Tanzimat." In *The Cambridge History of Turkey*, edited by Resat Kasaba, 4:11–37. Cambridge: Cambridge University Press, 2008.

Violi, Patrizia. *Paesaggi della memoria: Il trauma, lo spazio, la storia*. Milan: Bompiani, 2014.

Vitali, Stefano. *Passato digitale: Le fonti dello storico nell'era del computer*. Milan: Bruno Mondadori, 2004.

Wacks, David. *Double Diaspora in Sephardic Literature: Jewish Cultural Production before and after 1492*. Bloomington: Indiana University Press, 2015.

Watenpaugh, Keith D. *Being Modern in the Middle East: Revolution, Nationalism, Colonialism, and the Arab Middle Class*. Princeton, NJ: Princeton University Press, 2006.

Watson, Robert. "Between Liberation(s) and Occupation(s): Reconsidering the Emergence of Maghrebi Jewish Communism, 1942–1945." *Journal of Modern Jewish Studies* 13, no. 3 (2014): 381–98.

———. "Coproducing Nostalgia across the Mediterranean: Visions of the Jewish-Muslim Past in French-Tunisian Cinema." *Politics-Rivista di Studi Politici* 5, no. 1 (2016): 105–23.

———. "Memories (Out) of Place: Franco-Judeo-Algerian Autobiographical Writing, 1995–2010." *Journal of North African Studies* 17, no. 1 (2013): 1–22.

Weingrod, Alex. "Introduction." In *Studies in Israeli Ethnicity: After the Ingathering*, edited by Alex Weingrod, IX–XIX. New York: Gordon and Breach Science, 1985.

———, ed. *Studies in Israeli Ethnicity: After the Ingathering*. New York: Gordon and Breach Science, 1985.

Wieviorka, Michel. "Faut-il parler de multiculturalisme à propos de la Méditerranée?" In *Lieux saints partagés*, 186–95. Arles: MUCEM/Actes Sud, 2015.

Yablonka, Hanna. *Les Juifs d'Orient, Israël et la Shoah*. Paris: Calmann-Lévy, 2016.
———. "Oriental Jewry and the Holocaust: A Tri-generational Perspective." *Israel Studies* 14, no. 1 (2009): 94–122.
Yardeni, Navah Sarah. *Yehudei-Tunisiah be-Israel: 'Edot ve-te'ud*. [Tunisian Jews in Israel: Testimony and documentation]. Lod: Orot Yahadut Maghreb, 2009.
Yerushalmi, Yosef Haim. *Zakhor: Jewish History and Jewish Memory*. Seattle: University of Washington Press, 1992.
Yiftahel, Oren, and Eretz Tzfadia. "Between Periphery and 'Third Space': Identity of Mizrahim in Israel's Development Towns." In *Israelis in Conflict*, edited by Adriana Kemp, David Newman, Uri Ram and Oren Yiftahel, 203–35. Eastbourne: Sussex Academic, 2004.
Zafrani, Haim. *Deux mille ans de vie juive au Maroc*. Paris: Maisonneuve & Larose, 1998.
Zamir, Levana. *Mi-ta'amei Mitzrayim* [The flavors of Egypt]. Tel Aviv: Beit Alim, n.d.
———. *Trumot ve-hishgeyhem shel-yotzei-Mitzrayim be-Isra'el be-50 shanot ha-medinah 1948–1998* [Achievements and constributions of Egyptian Jews in Israel in its first fifty years]. Tel Aviv: Hitahdut 'olei-Mitzrayim be-Isra'el, 2003.
Zamkanei, Shayna. "Justice for Jews from Arab Countries and the Rebranding of the Jewish Refugee." *International Journal of Middle East Studies* 48, no. 3 (2016): 511–30.
———. "The Politics of Defining Jews from Arab Countries." *Israel Studies* 21, no. 2 (2016): 1–26.
Zertal, Idith. *Israel's Holocaust and the Politics of Nationhood*. Cambridge: Cambridge University Press, 2005.
Zerubavel, Yael. *Recovered Roots: Collective Memory and the Making of Israeli National Tradition*. Chicago: University of Chicago Press, 1995.
Zohar, Nissim. *Ha-molokhiyah shel 'ima'* [Mother's molokhiyah]. Tel Aviv: Yediot Aharonot, 2006.
Zytnicki, Colette. "Du rapatrié au séfarade: L'intégration des Juifs d'Afrique du Nord dans la société française: essai de bilan." *Archives Juives* 38, no. 2 (2005): 84–102.
———. *Les Juifs du Maghreb: Naissance d'une historiographie coloniale*. Paris: PUPS, 2011.

INDEX

Note: Page numbers in italics indicate figures.

'Abd-al-Nasser, Gamal, 144
absence: and the Holocaust, 122; from the motherland, 182
Aciman, André, 47
Africa, 5, 150. *See also* North Africa
Agnon, Shmuel Yosef, 3, 28
Aharoni, Ada, 72, 73
AJMF (Amitié Judéo-Musulmane de France), 155, 156, 179–80
Albou, Karin, 125, 127, 128
Alexandria, 9, 10, 23, 45, 51, 70, 72, 102
Algeria, 9, 10, 12, 25, 77–82, 89, 90; exile from, 178; Juifs d'Algérie exhibition, 83–84; Mémorial de la Shoah, 86; M'zab, 177; relationship with France, 91; in Second World War, 87, 123
Algerian Jews. *See* Jews of Algeria
Algerian Muslims, 79–80
Algerian War, 78, 91, 104
Alhadeff, Gini, 23
'aliyah, 6, 26, 48, 147
Alliance Israélite Universelle, 11, 126
'Alon moreshet yahadut-Mitzrayim, 71
American Jewish Committee, 101
ancestry, Sephardi, 53
anti-Jewish incidents, 10, 124, 135
antisemitic stereotypes, 10
antisemitism, 10, 54, 91, 97, 139, 145, 155; in France, 26, 104, 153, 154

Arab-Berber society, 25, 78, 80
Arab heritage, 131–32
Arabic language, 32–33, 132
Arab-Israeli conflict, 3, 7, 12, 35, 76, 139, 154–55; Libya, 37, 42
Arab-Jewish relations, 7, 11, 53, 178–79, 182; in Libya, 35, 36; in Tunisia, 128
Arab Jews, 8–9, 41–42
Arab nationalism, 126, 127, 140
Arabness, 7, 42, 91
Artom, Elia Samuele, 43
Ashkenazi Jews, 9, 68, 132
assimilationist ideology, 11
associational culture, 68–77, 95
Association des ex-victimes des persecutions anti-juives en Egypte, 68–70, 71, 72
Association des Juifs Originaires d'Algérie (AJOA), 79
Association Nationale Exode des Français Juifs d'Algérie (EFJA), 88, 89
Association Nebi Daniel, 76, 101
Association pour la sauvegarde du patrimoine culturel des Juifs d'Egypte (ASPCJE), 98–99, 103
Auschwitz-Birkenau, 124

Baba Sali, 91
Baghdad, 41; *farhud,* 124, 141, 144
Balbo, Italo, 37

215

Ballas, Shimon, 41
baqqashot, 177
Barazani, Nava, 125
Beer-Sheva, 28
Beirut, 9
Belleville, 31–32, 33
belonging, 9, 81–82, 93, 177
Bénabou, Marcel, 125
Benarroch, Moiz, 177
Benghazi, 40, 41, 43, 130, 141
Benghazi Bergen-Belsen (Sucary), 125, 129–34, 135
Bensoussan, Albert, 180–81
Bergen-Belsen, 130, 132, 133–34
Betori, Cardinal, 151
Biton, Erez, 147
Biton Commission, 147
blood libel accusation, 10
Bnei Brit, 11
Bnei ha-Ye'or, 74–75
Boukhobza, Chochana, 23, 26–34, 35, 52, 54, 157
Busi, Dudu, 134

Cairo, 1, 11, 44, 50, 101, 139; anti-Jewish riots, 1948, 124; *genizah*, 65
Camp David Summit, 140
Carmel, Marco, 129
Castel-Bloom, Orly, 23, 46, 48, 49–52, 53–54, 124, 181
Castelbolognesi, Gustavo, 43
Center for the integration of the heritage of Eastern Jews, 147
Centro di documentazione ebraica contemporanea, 154
cinema, and memory, 13
collective identities, 9, 95, 146
Colloqui mediterranei, 151
colonialism, 10, 15, 34, 53, 54, 126; and Algeria, 66; Libya, 36; role in separating Jews from Muslims, 127
colonial studies, 25
colonization, 82, 89, 91
communautarisme, 88, 154
Comunità di Sant'Egidio, 159
concentration camps, 12, 123, 124, 132
connected migrants, 103

conversion, 12
conversos, 49
cookery, 75
Corfu, 10
country of origin, 31, 77, 140, 148, 155; connection with, 181; and identity, 52–53; nostalgia for, 54
Coup de soleil, 156
Crémieux Decree, 10, 78, 82, 87
Cremisi, Teresa, 51
crise anti-juive, Oran, 10
Cyrenaica, 34

Dafina, 94–98, 103, 104
Damascus affair, 10
Dawan, Daniela, 35, 39–40
decolonization, 3, 5, 42, 140, 147
Derrida, Jacques, 81
dhimma/dhimmi, 7, 82, 91, 136
dhimmitude, 54
Diaspora, 8, 13, 17, 34, 68, 138; creating new, 179; digital, 92–93, 96–97; Egyptian Jewish, 46; Libyan Jewish, 43; Tunisian, 26
difficult heritage, 77, 78, 84, 91
digital diaspora, 92–104
digital technologies, 67, 92
Djerba, 26
Dodecanese islands, 5
Dolly City (Castel-Bloom), 45
Donne per la Pace, 150, 152–53, 156–57, 159, 179–80
Dreyfus affair, 10
Drop of Milk Association of Cairo, 101

eastern Mediterranean, 10, 12, 46
ecumenism, 151
'edot ha-mizrah, 8, 66
education, 138, 143, 144, 147
Egypt, 1, 6, 9, 12, 123; exodus from, 139; Napoleonic expedition to, 1798, 10; pre-Nasserist, 33; Société d'Etudes Historiques Juives d'Egypte, 65
Egyptian Jews, 2–3, 5–6, 44–46, 47–49, 50–51, 148, 150; associational culture, 68–77; and belonging, 93; digital diaspora, 98–103; heritage associations, 65, 104
Eichmann trial, 134

Eliahou Hanabi Synagogue, 102
emancipation, 78, 80, 89
Emiliah u-melah ha-'aretz (Sucary), 129
'eseq ha-bish (Lavon affair), 69–70
ethnicity, 68, 71, 104
ethno-religious group, 3, 14, 24, 66, 149, 156; and Donne per la Pace, 157; and France and Europe, 126; and identity, 155; Jews of Algeria, 88
Europe, 2, 10, 53, 149–50; and antisemitism, 10; attitude of Tunisian Jews toward, 126, 127; and Egyptian Jews, 48
European antisemitic stereotypes, 10
European Day of Jewish Culture, 159
European Jews, 154–55. *See also* French Jews; Italian Jews
E venne la notte (Magiar), 34–35, 36–39, 54
everyday multiculturalism, 157
exile: expressed through writing, 24; and heritage, 105; memory of, 177; and migration, 33–34; trauma of, 30; from Tunisia, 32
exilic homecomings, 13, 178
Exit and Expulsion of Jews from Arab Lands and Iran Day, 136
exodus of the *français Juifs* of Algeria, 87–89, 88, 91
expulsion, 1492, Iberian Peninsula, 9, 14, 53, 81, 139

Facebook, 98, 99–101, 105
family, traditional structure, 11–12
farhud, 124, 141, 144
Fascism, 10, 34, 43, 52
Fedida, Yves, 101
Florence, 151–53
Florentine Jews, 151
France, 5–6, 27, 30–31, 126; Dreyfus affair, 10; and Egyptian Jews, 99; Jewish-Muslim interactions, 153–57; and Jews of Algeria, 66, 78, 79–80, 81–82, 83–92, 104, 140, 177; and religion, 158; and Tunisian Jews, 26, 52
Frenchification of Jewish society, 126, 177
French Jews, 26, 86, 153, 154, 155
French language, 81, 95
French nationality, 10

genizah, 65
Gerbi, David, 159
gerush Sefarad, 139
Giaddo, 123, 125
Goitein, Shlomo Dov, 6
Gormezano Goren, Yitzhaq, 51
Goshen, 72–73
grana Jews, 26
Greek Jews, 132
Greek-Orthodox communities, 10
Guardare negli occhi: Linguaggi e identità/identità e differenze, 159–60

Hakeillah, 153, 157
Halaqim 'enoshiyim (Castel-Bloom), 51
Halbwachs, Maurice, 13
Ha-panterim ha-shehorim, 133
Harat al-yahud, 181
Harissa Foundation, 94–95
Ha-roman ha-mitzri (Castel-Bloom), 45, 46–48, 49–52, 53–54, 181
Ha-shomer ha-tzair, 44
Hebrew language, 47
Hebrew postmodernism, 45
heritage, 64–67, 102, 104–5, 147, 161–62, 179; Algerian Jewish, 79, 80–91; difficult, 15, 77, 78; Egyptian Jews, 100; and the internet, 95–96, 99, 103; Jewish-Palestinian transcultural, 157; Libyan-Jewish, 131–32; and marginality, 92; Moroccan Jews, 94
heritage associations, 66, 68, 104. *See also* Association des Juifs Originaires d'Algérie (AJOA); Association Nationale Exode des Français Juifs d'Algérie (EFJA); *Goshen*; Hitahdut 'Oley Mitzrayim; 'Irgun nifga'ey ha-radifot ha-'anti-yehudiyot be-Mitzrayim; Morial
Herzl, Theodore, 10
Herzog, Haim, 73
history: and memory, 13; public, 67
Hitahdut 'Oley Mitzrayim, 73–74, 75, 76
Holocaust, 12, 15, 24, 85–87, 122–23, 128, 161; and *Benghazi Bergen-Belsen*, 129–30; how taught in schools, 143; and *Latzet mibli-lahazor*, 145; and Libyan Jews, 132, 133, 134, 162; *Mizrahi*, 124–25, 135–36; monetary compensation for Libyan and Tunisian Jews, 141

INDEX

homecomings, exilic, 13, 178
hoq yom le-tziyun ha-yetziah ve-ha-gerush shel ha-yehudim me-'artzot 'arav u-me-'Iran, 138–39, 140. *See also* Jews from Arab Lands and Iran Day

identity, 25, 53, 89, 104, 155, 179; collective, 9, 95, 146; and heritage, 64; and the Holocaust, 124; and the internet, 67, 95; and the Mediterranean, 24; postmigratory, 90; rediasporization of Moroccan Jewish, 93
IEMS—Institut européen du monde sépharade, 85
Institut du monde arabe, 84–85
Institut Montaigne, 153–54
intangible heritage, 65, 66, 68, 77, 103, 104
International Forum for Literature and Culture, 73
internet, 67, 92, 94, 95–96, 154; and heritage, 98, 99, 101, 103, 104–5, 179
internment camps, 123, 125
interreligious dialogue, 151
Iran, 5
Iranian Jews, 150
Iraq, 9, 41; *farhud*, 124, 141, 144
'Irgun nifga'ey ha-radifot ha-'anti-yehudiyot be-Mitzrayim, 68–70, 71, 72
'Irgun 'olami shel yehudei yotzei-Luv, 130
I rifugiati ebrei dai paesi arabi, 136–37, *137*
Islam, 23, 104, 149, 151, 153, 158. *See also* Muslims
Islamic community, Florence, 151
Islamic Cultural Centre of Florence, 151
Islamic movements, 11
Islamophobia, 154, 155, 168
Israel, 2–3, 5–6, 28–29, 30, 32, 159; birth of, 12, 54; and the Diaspora, 17; and Egyptian Jews, 46, 68–77, 99, 104; *hoq yom le-tziyun ha-yetziah ve-ha-gerush shel ha-yehudim me-'artzot 'arav u-me-'Iran*, 137–39, 140; and Jews of Algeria, 79; Law for the Preservation of the Rights to Compensation of Jewish Refugees from Arab Countries and Iran, 141; and Libyan Jews, 35, 36, 134; and *Mizrahim*, 8, 48, 66, 82, 132, 147; Western policies toward, 154–55

Israeli-Arab conflict, 3, 7, 12, 35, 76, 139, 154–55; Libya, 37, 42
Israeli Egyptians, 66
Istat, 151
Italian East Africa, 5
Italian Jews, 9, 42, 43
Italy, 5–6, 10, 34–36, 42–43, 52, 136–37; and antisemitism, 154; and Jewish-Muslim interactions, 156–57; and migrants, 150–53; and Syrian refugees, 159
Iya (Ballas), 41

Jerusalem, 27–28
Jewish-Arab relations, 7, 11, 53, 178–79, 182; in Libya, 35, 36; in Tunisia, 128
Jewish identity, 24, 28, 71, 122, 124, 147, 178; Egyptian Jewish, 48; French Algerian, 89; and the internet, 67; and migration, 5, 179; Moroccan, 93, 96
Jewish Museum of Rome, 136, *137*
Jewish-Muslim cohabitation, 103, 126, 127, 129
Jewish-Muslim interactions, 149, 154–57, 159, 161, 162, 180
Jewish refugees from the Arab lands exhibition, 136–37, *137*
Jews and Arabs (Goitein), 6
Jews from Arab Lands and Iran Day, 136, 137, 138, 142–43, 147, 161, 179; established in 2014, 16; and increased presence of *Mizrahim* in the public sphere, 146
Jews of Algeria, 5, 10, 25, 77–92, 140, 141, 181; heritage, 15, 65, 66; and identity, 104
Jews of Baghdad, 41
Jews of Djerba, 26
Jews of Libya. *See* Libyan Jews
Jews of Marrakech, 10
Jews of Morocco, 93–98
Jews of Rhodes, 123–24
Jews of the M'zab, 177
Jews of Tunis, 10, 125–29
Jews of Tunisia, 26, 32, 54, 86, 90, 134, 141
JIMENA, 144, 157
Joe 'Ish Qahir (Castel-Bloom), 45
Judaism: and Algerian Jews, 84, 90; central facet of European heritage, 149; French, 86, 91
judìo arabe, 8–9
Juifs d'Algérie exhibition, 83–84

Juifs d'Orient: Une histoire plurimillénaire exhibition, 84–85
Justice for Jews from Arab Countries (JJAC), 141

Kedem Forum for Israeli Public Diplomacy, 144
kibbutz, 44–45
kibbutz galuyiot, 69
Kohen-Sidon, Shlomo, 68–69, 70

labor camps, North African, 123, 125
Ladino, 11, 37, 38, 47, 132
Lagnado, Léon, 2
Lagnado, Lucette, 1, 2
laïcite, 156
La maison de mémoire (Bahloul), 126
La mémoire, l'histoire, l'oubli (Ricoeur), 13
La petite Jérusalem, 125
La Pira, Giorgio, 151
La présence juive en Algérie conference, 89–90
La statue de sel (Memmi), 126
Latzet mi-bli lahazor exhibition, 145, *145*
La valise de Mlle Lucie (Moati), 124–25
Lavon affair, 69–70
Law of Return, 140
Lebanese Jews, 150
Lebanon, 5, 9
Lebanon War, 1982, 30
Le chant des mariées, 125, 126–27, 128, 135
Lellouche, Jean-Luc, 27
Les enfants des Juifs d'Alexandrie et d'Egypte, 99–101, 105
Levi, Joseph, 157–58
Libya, 5, 9, 12, 34–44, 52, 123, 130; anti-Jewish riots, Tripolitania, 135; antisemitic legislation, 10
Libyan Jewish Heritage Centre, 130–31
Libyan Jews, 35, 42–43, 123, 125, 129–34, 135; and the Holocaust, 162; in Italy, 137, 150; seeking refuge from persecution, 141
Libyan Muslims, 148
lieux de mémoire, 24
Lieux saints partagés, 158
literature, 11, 13, 24, 25. *See also Benghazi Bergen-Belsen* (Sucary); *E venne la notte* (Magiar); *Ha-roman ha-mitzri* (Castel-Bloom); *Le chant des mariées*; *Pour l'amour du père* (Boukhobza); *Qual è la via del vento* (Dawan); *Tramonto libico: Storia di un ebreo arabo* (Luzon); *Un été à Jérusalem* (Boukhobza)
Lo' rahoq mi-merkaz ha-'ir (Castel-Bloom), 48
loss, feelings of, 90, 177, 182
Luzon, Raphael, 23, 35, 40, 41, 43, 44, 52, 54

Macìas, Enrico, 80
Maghrebine religious culture, 11, 127
Magiar, Victor, 23, 34–35, 36–39, 44, 52, 54
Malta, 32
Man in the White Sharkskin Suit, The (Lagnado), 2
March of Hope, 152
marginality, 11, 24, 99, 103, 120, 134; and heritage, 15, 92
Marrakech, 10
Matalon, Ronit, 44, 141
Me-Haifah le-Qahir ha-qrovah ha-rehoqah (Aharoni), 72
meldar, 11
Memmi, Albert, 6, 24–25, 42, 126, 127
Mémorial de la Shoah, 85–86, 179
Memorial of the exodus of the *français Juifs* of Algeria, 87–89, *88*
memory, 16, 17, 44, 93–94, 161, 181–82; and Confino, 54; and *Dafina*, 97; of the exile, 177; and heritage, 104; of Jews of Algeria, 77; of Libya, 39; and the Mediterranean, 24; and migration, 34; and nation-state, 64; and the past, 180; and rituals, 90–91; transmission of, 12–13; and Tunisia, 32
Merkaz le-shiluv moreshet yahadut ha-mizrah, 147
Middle East: literature, 11; migration from, 12. *See also* Egypt; Israel
Middle Eastern Jews: in Italy, 35, 150; migrants, 142; and refugee status, 140–41; teaching history and heritage of, 147
migrant associations, 67–68, 103
migrant heritage associations, 67–68, 76. *See also* heritage associations
migrants, 23, 147, 149, 153, 158–59, 161, 180; connected, 103; and Italy, 150–53. *See also* Egyptian Jews; Jews of Algeria; Libyan Jews; Moroccan Jews; Tunisian Jews

migration, 1–3, 4–5, 6, 7, 12, 157–58, 178–79; British Palestine, 11; and exile, 33–34; exilic homecomings, 13–14; to Israel, 147; Moroccan Jews, 93, 141–42
Milan, 150, 159
milieux de mémoire, 30
Mimouna, 90
minhagim, 9
Mi-ta'amei Mitzrayim (Zamir), 75
Mizrahi Holocaust, 124, 135
Mizrahim, 2–3, 47, 66, 68, 82, 132, 144; definition, 8; and *hoq yom le-tziyun ha-yetziah ve-ha-gerush shel ha-yehudim me-'artzot 'arav u-me-'Iran*, 147; identity, 25; Israel's attitude to, 48; and Jews from Arab Lands and Iran Day, 146; and *Nakba*, 142
mizug galuyiot, 146
Moati, Nine, 27, 125
modernization, 11, 12
Moked, 159
morashah, 64. See also heritage
Morial, 80, 82, 83, 85
Moroccan Jews, 90, 91, 104, 141–42, 148
Morocco, 9, 10, 12, 86, 93–98, 103, 150; in Second World War, 123
Mosseri family, 70–71
Musée d'art et d'histoire du Judaïsme of Paris, 83–84
Museum of Libyan Jews, 130–31, *131*
museums, in Israel, 68
Muslim Brotherhood, 11
Muslim-Jewish interaction, 149, 152–57, 161, 162, 178–79, 180
Muslims: Algerian, 79–80; anti-Jewish feelings, 79; antisemitism, 54; cohabitation with Jews, 103, 127, 129; in Florence, 151; in France, 153–54; in Italy, 150; Libyan, 148; relationship with Jews, 33, 128; Tunisian, 126
MUSSEF—Musée du monde sépharade, 85
mutual aid societies, 70, 75

Naggar, Jean, 49
Nakba, 142, 143
Napoleonic expedition to Egypt, 1798, 10
Nasser's Revolution, 46
national identity, 64, 104

nationalism, Arab, 126, 127, 140
nation-state, 11, 51, 64
Nazi concentration camps, 12, 123, 124, 132
Nazism, 127
Nebot, Didier, 77, 81
noeuds de mémoire, 24, 53
Non dite che col tempo si dimentica (Dawan), 39
North Africa, 6, 9, 10, 11; and Egypt, 46; exile from, 178; and France, 5, 27; and the Holocaust, 85, 86–87, 130; labor camps, 123; literature, 11; migration from, 12, 34
North African Jews, 2–3, 5–6, 54; in the Diaspora, 8; and France, 85; and Israel, 68; in Italy, 35, 150, 151; and Jews from Arab Lands and Iran Day, 138; and Muslims, 33, 161; and refugee status, 140–41; teaching history and heritage of, 147
nostalgia, 14, 54, 75, 83, 90
numerus clausus, 87
Nunes Vais, Roberto, 35

Ohayon, Shimon, 138
Operation Torch, 87
Oran, *crise anti-juive*, 10
Organisation des Originaires de Tunisie en Israël, 134
Or Yehudah, Libyan Jewish Heritage Center of, 130–31, *131*
other, the, in *Un été à Jérusalem*, 30
Ottoman Empire, 9, 11
Ottoman reformism, 11
Ottoman religious culture, 11
Out of Egypt (Aciman), 47
Oz, Kobi, 124

Palestine, British, 11
Palestine Week, 41
Palestinian-Israeli conflict, 33. See also Arab-Israeli conflict
Palestinian-Jewish transcultural heritage, 157
pan-Arabism, 12
Paris, 30–31, 33
Parler en paix, 156
Partition Plan for Palestine, 139–40
past, the: and Aharoni, 73; and Algerian Jews, 77, 78, 81, 83, 84; *E venne la notte*, 37; *Ha-roman ha-mitzri*, 50, 52; and heritage,

64–65, 161–62; and the internet, 92, 94, 98, 101; longing for, 182; and memory, 13, 16, 54, 177, 180; and migrant heritage associations, 67, 76; orienting present and future, 158; *Pour l'amour du père*, 32, 33; *Qol tze'adenu*, 44; transmitting through literature, 24, 25; *Un été à Jérusalem*, 29
patrimoine/patrimonio, 64–65. *See also* heritage
patrimonialization, 65
peace agreements: 2020, between Israel and Arab countries, 181; between Israel and Palestinians and compensation for refugees, 141
Pere' 'Atzil (Busi), 134
persecution, 91, 122, 134, 136, 139, 153, 180; Holocaust, 123, 124, 135; in Libya, 141; Spanish Inquisition, 81
Petit-Jean, massacre of, 97
pieds-noirs, 79, 80
polygamy, 11–12
Pour l'amour du père (Boukhobza), 26, 31–34, 54, 157
property rights, 73, 76, 99, 138, 143

Qol tze'adenu (Matalon), 44, 141
Qual è la via del vento (Dawan), 35, 39–40

radical Islam, 104, 153
rafle of Tunis, 127
refugees, 15, 136, 138, 140–41, 147, 159
Reminiscenze tripoline (Nunes Vais), 35
Resistance movement, Algerian, 87
Rhodes, 123–24
Romaniot Jews, 9
Rome, 150

Saharan Jews, 78
Saharan M'zab, 10
Salonika, 9, 11
Sayad, Abdelmalek, 142
schools: and Middle Eastern and North African Jewish history and heritage, 147; teaching about the Holocaust, 143
Second World War, 12, 86–87, 91, 122–23, 124–27, 135
Sefarad, 48, 49, 51
self-writing, 13

Sephardi ancestry, 53
Sephardi Diaspora, 8, 13, 25, 81
Sephardi Jews: definition, 8; identity, 25
Serfaty, Rabbi Michel, 155–56
Sfax, 123
She'elah shel zman, 129
Shenhav, Yehudah, 143
Si Khaddour Benghabrit, 128
Sippurim bilti-ratzoniyim (Castel-Bloom), 45
Sisi, President 'Abd-al-Fattah, al-, 101, 102
Six Days War, 36, 41
Smyrna, 9
social media, 98, 99–101, 105, 154
Société d'Etudes Historiques Juives d'Egypte, 65
southern Europe, 9, 10, 46, 150. *See also* Italy
Spain, expulsion from, 9, 14, 53, 81, 139
Stora, Benjamin, 84, 91
subalternity, 133
Sucary, Yossi, 125, 129, 132, 134
Suez War, 46
Sun at Midday, The (Alhadeff), 23
Svivah 'Oyenet (Castel-Bloom), 45
Synagogue de l'Union Nationale des Amis de Tlemcen, 90
Synagogue of Florence, 159–60, *160*
Syria, 10
Syrian Jews, 150
Syrian refugees, 159

Talmud Torah, 11
tangible heritage, 65, 68, 77, 103, 104
terrorism, 104, 154, 180
toshavim, Morocco, 93
Tramonto libico: Storia di un ebreo arabo (Luzon), 35, 40, 41, 42, 43
transcultural future, 149
transformation, and heritage, 66
Tripoli, 37, 41, 43, 130, 141
Tripolitania, 34
Tunis, 31
Tunisia, 5, 9, 27, 30, 31, 52, 123; exile from, 178; and *Pour l'amour du père*, 32, 33; in the Second World War, 12, 86, 125–29
Tunisian Jews, 26, 32, 54, 86, 90, 134, 141; of Tunis, 10, 125–29
Tunisie: Une mémoire juive, 178

Turkey, 9
twansa Jews, 26
tzaddiqim, 91, 96
tzedaqah, 11

Un été à Jérusalem (Boukhobza), 26, 27–30, 33–34
Ummi fi shughl (Castel-Bloom), 45, 124
UNESCO, 64

Va'adat Biton le-he'atzemet moreshet yahadut-Sfarad ve-ha-mizrah be-ma'arehet ha-hinukh, 147
Valensi, Lucette, 139, 177
Ventura, Moshe, 68
Vichy France, 10, 79, 86, 91, 123

welfare, nineteenth century, 11
Western Jews, 24–25

women, in the nineteenth century, 12
Women Wage Peace, 152
World Congresses of Jews from Egypt, 74, 76
World Organization of Jews from Arab Countries (WOJAC), 140
World Organization of Jews from Libya, 130

Yad Vashem, 143, 146
yehudei 'Afriqah ve-'Asiah, 8
Yemen, 9
Yerushalmi, Yosef Haim, 177
yetziat-Mitzrayim, 139
Yetziat-Mitzrayim shelanu (Hitahdut's bulletin), 74–75

Zamir, Levana, 75
Zemmour, Eric, 92
Zionism, 10–11, 46, 54, 69, 70–71, 139, 147

DARIO MICCOLI is Assistant Professor of Modern Hebrew and Jewish Studies at the Department of Asian and North African Studies of Ca' Foscari University, Venice. He is author of *Histories of the Jews of Egypt: An Imagined Bourgeoisie, 1880s–1950s* and editor of *Contemporary Sephardic and Mizrahi Literature: A Diaspora*.

www.ingramcontent.com/pod-product-compliance
Lightning Source LLC
Chambersburg PA
CBHW030648230426
43665CB00011B/1007